To

Welikandage Nandawathie

Anna, Ceri and Ralph

Ben, Caspar, Jacob and Maisie

SOCIAL WORK AND GLOBAL HEALTH INEQUALITIES

HEALTH INEQUALITIES

Practice and policy developments

Edited by Paul Bywaters, Eileen McLeod and
Lindsey Napier

This edition published in Great Britain in 2009 by

The Policy Press
University of Bristol
Fourth Floor
Beacon House
Queen's Road
Bristol BS8 1QU
UK

Tel +44 (0)117 331 4054
Fax +44 (0)117 331 4093
e-mail tpp-info@bristol.ac.uk
www.policypress.co.uk

North American office:
The Policy Press
c/o International Specialized Books Services
920 NE 58th Avenue, Suite 300
Portland, OR 97213-3786, USA
Tel +1 503 287 3093
Fax +1 503 280 8832
e-mail info@isbs.com

British Library Cataloguing in Publication Data
A catalogue record for this book is available from the British Library.

Library of Congress Cataloging-in-Publication Data
A catalog record for this book has been requested.

ISBN 978 1 84742 195 1 paperback
ISBN 978 1 84742 196 8 hardcover

Cover design by Jana Broadfoot
Front cover: image kindly supplied by Paul Green
Printed and bound in Great Britain by MPG Books Group

Contents

Part Four: Global health inequalities: social work policy and practice development

List of tables and figures

Tables

Figures

Notes on contributors

Margaret Alston is Professor of Social Work and Head of Department at Monash University. She has published widely in the field of rural social issues, rural social work and gender. She is currently working on an international UN study on gender and climate change and has been researching the social impacts of drought and climate change in Australia.

Norma Baldwin is Emeritus Professor in the Social Dimensions of Health Institute (Universities of Dundee and St Andrews, Scotland). She has published widely on links between disadvantage and harm to children and on population-wide and individualised assessments of need and risk, including Spencer, N. and Baldwin, N.,'Economic, social and cultural contexts of neglect', in J. Taylor and B. Daniel (eds) *Child Neglect* (2004, Jessica Kingsley Publishers); and J. Taylor and N. Baldwin (2008) 'Predicting child abuse and neglect: ethical, theoretical and methodological challenges', *Journal of Clinical Nursing*, pp 1193-2000.

Eric Blyth is Professor of Social Work at the University of Huddersfield, England, and has also held honorary and visiting professorships at universities in Canada and Hong Kong. He is co-chair of the British Association of Social Workers' Project Group on Assisted Reproduction and has written and researched extensively on infertility and assisted reproduction. He is co-editor, with Ruth Landau, of *Third Party Assisted Conception across Cultures: Social, Legal and Ethical Perspectives* (2004, Jessica Kingsley Publishers).

Paul Bywaters is Emeritus Professor of Social Work at Coventry University and Honorary Professor at the University of Warwick, England. He was the first convener of the Social Work and Health Inequalities Network and joint author with Lindsey Napier of the International Federation of Social Workers' *International Policy on Health*. He has been writing about social work and health for over 20 years.

Yvonne Cadet-James is Professor and Chair of Indigenous Australian Studies and Head of School of Indigenous Australian Studies at James Cook University. She has been a chief investigator on the Empowerment Research Program, working with individuals and communities to assist them to identify their issues and bring about positive change in their lives. Yvonne is particularly interested in the sustainability of Indigenous health programmes. As an Aboriginal person, her other research interests include recording the history and language of her language group, the Gugu Badhun people.

Charlene Laurence Carbonatto is a senior lecturer and programme manager of the MSW (Health Care) programme, Department of Social Work and Criminology, Faculty of Humanities, University of Pretoria, South Africa. She is a Fulbright Alumni with an MSW degree from George Warren Brown School of Social Work, Washington University, St. Louis, USA. Her fields of specialisation are social work in health care, health policy, primary health care, women's health, reproductive health, infertility, third-party-assisted conception, trauma, HIV/AIDS and palliative care.

Maria Cheung is Associate Professor at the Faculty of Social Work, University of Manitoba, Canada. Her area of research is in cross-cultural studies of gender issues and marital relationships in Chinese and Canadian families. She is active in the development of the publication of social work research in China. She has several publications herself in *China Social Work Research* and one in the *Social Sciences Review of China*. Her research interests include narrative approaches in clinical social work practice and indigenisation of social work practice in China.

Angela Clarke is a Gunditjmara woman, whose traditional homeland is the Western District of Victoria, Australia. Angela is Deputy Director at Onemda Vic Health Koori Health Unit at the University of Melbourne. Angela brings to the Unit considerable experience in Aboriginal health programme development, research and community development. Angela has co-authored two books, *Nyernila Koories Kila Degaia: Listen up to Koories Speak about Health* (2005, Koorie Heritage Trust Incorporated with Karen Adams and Joan Vickery) and *Supporting Aboriginal Families through the Hospital Experience* (1999, Royal Children's Hospital, Melbourne, with Shawana Andrews and Neville Austin), both documenting Aboriginal people's experiences of health.

Jean Clarke is a senior lecturer in the School of Nursing, Dublin City University. Her research interests include nursing care with special emphasis on oppression, and caring and paediatric palliative care. She is a former member of the editorial board of the *Journal of Community Nursing*. She was a public health nurse and has published in the areas of public health nursing and the gendered role of nursing within health care organisations.

Ann Davis is Professor of Social Work and Director of the Centre of Excellence in Interdisciplinary Mental Health at the University of Birmingham, England. Ann trained as a psychiatric social worker. Her research and teaching interests are in the experiences that service users have of poverty, social exclusion and the receipt of social welfare services. Her most recent book, co-authored with Viv Cree, is *Social Work: Voices from the Inside* (2006, Routledge).

Lawrence Deane is Associate Professor at the Faculty of Social Work, University of Manitoba. His areas of focus are community economic development, social policy, cross-cultural social work and international social work. He has practised community development and community economic development in India and with Canadian Aboriginal groups in inner-city Winnipeg. Most recently he has been teaching and undertaking research in China.

Imelda Dodds is Protective Commissioner and Public Guardian of New South Wales and formerly Public Guardian of Western Australia. For four years until 1997 she was National President of the Australian Association of Social Workers and for six years until mid-2006 President of the International Federation of Social Workers. She has extensive knowledge and expertise in the fields of law and disability, substitute decision making and advocacy, social policy and organisational development and change.

Barbara Fawcett is Professor of Social Work and Policy Studies in the Faculty of Education and Social Work at the University of Sydney. Previously she was Head of the Department of Applied Social Science and Humanities at the University of Bradford (England). Prior to joining the University of Bradford, she spent 13 years in the field. Her research interests focus on disability, mental health, women and violence, participative action research and postmodern feminism. Her most recent book, co-authored with Fran Waugh, is *Addressing Violence, Abuse and Oppression: Debates and Challenges* (2007, Routledge).

Julie Fish is Senior Lecturer and Research Fellow in Social Work at De Montfort University, Leicester, England. She wrote *Reducing Health Inequalities for LGBT People* (2007), for the Department of Health. In addition to a number of peer-reviewed articles, she authored *Heterosexism in Health and Social Care* (2006, Palgrave). She is a member of the National Cancer Equality Initiative and recently collaborated with Stonewall on a lesbian and bisexual women's health survey.

Lou Harms is Associate Head (Teaching and Learning) and a senior lecturer in social work in the School of Nursing and Social Work, University of Melbourne, Australia. She teaches in the areas of human risk and resilience, and communication skills. Her research interests relate to health and experiences of stress, trauma and grief, and social work with Indigenous communities. She is the author of three books published by Oxford University Press: *Understanding Human Development: A Multidimensional Approach* (2004), *Working with People: Communication Skills for Reflective Practice* (2007) and (with Marie Connolly) *Social Work: Contexts and Practice* (2009).

Tuula Heinonen is Associate Professor at the Faculty of Social Work, University of Manitoba, Canada. She currently teaches qualitative research and health in social work and supervises graduate students. Her research interests are in social work and social policy in health, gender and social development with particular reference to China, immigration and integration among newcomers, and the socio-cultural context of ageing in rural areas.

Amy Po Ying Ho is a senior lecturer in the Department of Applied Social Sciences at the Hong Kong Polytechnic University. Her primary research interests are health policy and health promotion, especially for vulnerable groups in the community. She is also engaged in third sector studies, such as the development of civil society and social enterprise in Hong Kong.

Yang Jiao, Associate Professor and Vice-Director of the Social Work Department at the China Women's University, is an educator and trainer who makes use of participatory social work approaches in her university teaching and with Women's Federation trainees providing services in rural China. Professor Jiao's research interests are primarily in social work and ageing.

Lee Knifton has roles combining research, policy and practice. He is Associate Head of the Mental Health Foundation in Scotland, NHS Mental Health Improvement Lead and a visiting lecturer at the Glasgow School of Social Work, University of Strathclyde. His research interests focus on stigma and discrimination and he organises the Scottish Mental Health Arts and Film Festival.

Lesley Laing is a senior lecturer in social work and policy studies at the University of Sydney, Australia. Prior to this she was the founding Director of the Australian Domestic and Family Violence Clearinghouse, and Director of the New South Wales Health Education Centre Against Violence. Current areas of research include coordinated responses to domestic violence, post-separation violence against women and children, domestic violence and women's mental health, and treatment of young people who have sexually abused.

Agnes Koon-chui Law, is Professor and founding Director of the Centre for Social Work Education and Research, Sun Yat-sen University, Guangzhou, China. Prior to joining Sun Yat-sen University in 2003, she had extensive working experience in Hong Kong, in both non-governmental and university settings, in direct practice and training, as well as in curriculum planning and administration. Her research interests include gender issues, social policy and community service development for disadvantaged groups.

Carrie Lethborg has worked with people living with cancer and HIV/AIDS for 20 years. She currently holds the position of Grade 4 Clinical Educator and Cancer Social Work Research Coordinator at St Vincent's Melbourne, Australia. She is the deputy chair of the Victorian Cooperative Oncology Group Psycho-oncology Committee, and an executive member (past Director) of the Victorian Oncology Social Work Group. She received her PhD in psycho-social oncology from the University of Melbourne in 2006.

Eileen McLeod is Associate Professor in Social Work at the School of Health and Social Studies, University of Warwick, England. Her current research interests centre on social work's contribution to tackling health inequalities and she has published extensively in this area. A co-founder of the Social Work and Health Inequalities Network, her publications include McLeod, E. and Bywaters, P., *Social Work, Health and Equality* (2000, Routledge).

David Moxley is the Oklahoma Health Care Authority Professor, and Professor of Social Work in the University of Oklahoma School of Social Work, USA, and chairs the School's Graduate Concentration in Social Administration and Community Practice.

Vimla Nadkarni is Professor at the Centre of Health and Mental Health at the Tata Institute of Social Sciences in Mumbai, India. She has specialised in medical and psychiatric social work and has expertise in community health, integrated social work practice, social work education, and HIV/AIDS. She was the second annual Hokenstad lecturer at the Council on Social Work Education Congress 2008 in Philadelphia. She is Member at Large for the International Association of Schools of Social Work.

Lindsey Napier is Pro-Dean in the Faculty of Education and Social Work, University of Sydney. Her current research and teaching interests centre on the social dimensions of ageing, dying and death, where health and social inequalities are writ large. She is the current convenor of the Social Work and Health Inequalities Network.

Grace Fung-Mo Ng served as the Project Management Officer of the Community Investment and Inclusion Fund, under the policy purview of the Labour and Welfare Bureau, Hong Kong Special Administrative District from June 2002 to June 2009. Grace has worked both as a health services analyst and policy and planning manager in various New Zealand public bodies during two decades of public sector reforms (1980s to 2000). She has published on deinstitutionalisation, outcome measurement and social capital development. Email: ng5566@ netvigator.com

Rosalie Pockett is a lecturer in social work and policy studies at the University of Sydney. Prior to this she worked in the health field as a social worker and health service manager. Her research interests include health and hospital practice, interprofessional practice and practice-based research. Her most recent publication is 'Human service professionals, violence and the workplace', in B. Fawcett and F. Waugh (eds) *Addressing Violence, Abuse and Oppression: Debates and Challenges* (2008, Routledge).

Raymond W. Pong is the Research Director of the Centre for Rural and Northern Health Research and a professor at the School of Rural and Northern Health, Laurentian University, Ontario, Canada. A sociologist by training, Professor Pong has considerable public service and academic experience in health services research, policy and planning, and has published extensively on issues pertaining to rural health, health services, the health workforce and population health.

Sonia Posenelli is the Chief Social Worker and Supervisor of the Aboriginal Hospital Liaison Program at St Vincent's Melbourne, Australia. She has been in this role since 1991. St Vincent's is part of the Sisters of Charity Health Service which is the largest not-for-profit health care provider in Australia.

Suzanne Quin is Professor and Head of the School of Applied Social Science in University College Dublin. Her areas of teaching are social work and health care, disability and groupwork. She has undertaken a number of funded research studies in psycho-social aspects of illness and service responses. She has published articles, a book and has co-edited two books on children in contemporary Ireland as well as a series of books on different aspects of Irish social policy.

Neil Quinn combines a practice and academic role in relation to mental health inequalities. He is a lecturer in social work at the Glasgow School of Social Work, University of Strathclyde, Scotland, and has published on stigma and discrimination, community development and cross-cultural mental health. His background is as a mental health social worker and a community development worker, leading a successful programme to address stigma, discrimination and mental health inequalities in east Glasgow.

Shulamit Ramon is Professor of Interprofessional Health and Social Studies at Anglia Ruskin University, England. A social worker and clinical psychologist by training she has researched political conflict in Israel, set up a website on social work and political conflict with Jane Lindsay (www.isw4peace.org), and in 2008 published an edited book: *Social Work in the Context of Political Conflict* (Venture Press) sponsored by both the International Association of Schools of Social Work and the British Association of Social Workers.

Stephen M. Rose is Professor of Social Work at the University of New England/Portland, Maine, USA. His current research interests include using social epidemiology to study population health; seeing chronic illness as embodied class position; integrating exposure to childhood poverty and family violence with adult chronic illness; and using social epidemiology theory to develop social work roles in primary care and in the design and implementation of empowering practice in primary health care settings.

Gracious Thomas is Professor and one of the Directors at the Indira Gandhi National Open University (IGNOU), New Delhi. He is the Coordinator of the IGNOU Chair, founder Vice-President of the National Association of Professional Social Workers in India, founder Chairman of the Annual National Seminar on social work response to HIV/AIDS, Adviser to the Indian Parliamentary Forum on HIV/AIDS, and Consultor to the Pontifical Council for Health Pastoral Care, the

Vatican. He is the author of over 200 publications, including 17 books, and a pioneer in introducing programmes of study on HIV/AIDS and Social Work into the Indian Higher Education System through Open Distance Learning.

Komla Tsey is Associate Professor in the School of Indigenous Australian Studies and School of Public Health and Tropical Medicine at James Cook University and is programme leader of a 10-year collaborative Empowerment Research Program, which examines the role and contribution of empowerment and control in addressing the social determinants of health. Komla has published on a wide range of health social science topics including traditional healers and mental health care in Ghana and Australian Indigenous education and health.

Kriti Vikram is a doctoral student of sociology at the University of Maryland, College Park, USA. She has a Master's degree from the Tata Institute of Social Sciences and is primarily interested in issues of population, health and education in developing countries.

Olivia Washington is Associate Professor of Gerontology and Nursing in the Wayne State University College of Nursing, Detroit, USA, and co-Director of the Healthier Black Elders Center in the University's Institute of Gerontology.

Mary Whiteside is a social worker with interests in Indigenous health and well-being and the contribution of social work to public health interventions. She is currently a PhD student within the Empowerment Research Program, School of Indigenous Australian Studies, James Cook University. Her research is exploring the manifestation and meaning of empowerment in Australian Indigenous contexts in order to contribute to the evidence base for empowerment-based interventions in Indigenous settings.

John Douglass Whyte is a lecturer in the School of Global Studies, Social Science and Planning at RMIT University, Melbourne, Australia. He teaches in the areas of Indigenous studies, self and society, social work research and programme management. His research interests are in the areas of cross-worldview social work practice and the development of chaos and complexity approaches in social work practice. He has published articles related to Indigenous health, Indigenous social work practices and spirituality in cross-worldview contexts.

Part One

Introduction

Social work and global health inequalities

Paul Bywaters, Eileen McLeod and Lindsey Napier

Introduction

This book explores health inequalities as a central global issue for social work. Authors drawn from many countries analyse key questions and practice and policy initiatives, to develop understanding of social work's contribution to addressing this profound and pervasive social problem. In doing so, social work practice is treated as multifaceted. Direct interventions with individuals, families, groups, communities and populations are considered, together with policy formulation, service design, and development, research and education. Throughout, we also take a holistic view of health, emphasising the interconnectedness of psychological or emotional well-being and physical dimensions to health.

Socially constructed health inequalities profoundly influence the quality and length of life of everyone on the planet. They result in avoidable physical and emotional human suffering, damaged relationships, lost opportunities, pain and grief. Tackling health inequalities, defined as 'disparities in health (and in its key social determinants) that are systematically associated with social advantage/disadvantage' (Braveman and Gruskin, 2003, p 256), needs to become a central focus of social work action, worldwide and in all settings (IFSW, 2008).

There are three basic arguments which underpin this position. First, inequalities in health are unjust and a breach of the fundamental human right to health (see Chapter 2).[1] 'Social justice is a matter of life and death', as the opening words of the final report of the World Health Organization's Commission on the Social Determinants of Health expresses it (CSDH, 2008, p 1, Preface). Social workers are therefore bound by the international statement of ethics to work to prevent and reduce avoidable inequalities in health (IFSW/IASSW, 2004).

Second, inequalities in health are socially determined (CSDH, 2008). 'Inequalities in people's health are intimately and inextricably connected to inequalities in their material and social circumstances' (Graham, 2007, p xi). Consequently social workers cannot choose whether or not to involve themselves with health inequalities, the social context of their practice means they are involved. It is unavoidable.

Because social workers deal on a daily basis with the social determinants of health inequalities, it is hard to think of a social work contact in which damaged health is not already a factor or in which the issues under discussion will not influence future health (McLeod and Bywaters, 2000). Whenever a social worker intervenes in a young person's life, to protect him or promote his development, that young person's physical and emotional health is affected not only then but in the future. Whenever a social worker advocates someone's need for land, housing or money to pay for essentials such as food, water, clothing or fuel, she is engaging in the struggle to secure the conditions for health. Whenever a social worker encourages someone to enter a programme to address addiction, that individual's present and future health (and the health of those close to him) is at stake. Whenever a social worker supports someone to oppose stigma or discrimination in the workplace or the criminal justice system she is influencing that person's emotional and physical health. Whenever a social worker deals with someone who is the victim or the perpetrator of violence she is dealing with physical and emotional health issues. Whenever a social worker helps an older person to resolve a family dispute about personal care, physical and emotional health is a live issue.

Sometimes, social workers fail to recognise the potential of their work for influencing people's health. They may simply take for granted the illness which has been a precipitating factor in a social work contact or referral. Alternatively, social workers can think that dealing with health and illness is a specialist sphere of social work, for those who work in health settings. But because both the causes and consequences of ill-health are as much social as biological in nature, all social work necessarily affects people's health chances and health experience (McLeod and Bywaters, 2000) and this needs to be an explicit focus of social work theory and practice.

Third, we argue, as have others (People's Health Movement, 2000; GHW, 2005; CSHD, 2008), that health inequalities cannot be adequately understood or addressed except in their global context, including the processes of globalisation. Globalisation is a contested concept (Labonte and Schrecker, 2007a) and one which is only beginning to exercise much purchase on social work practice and thought (Lyons, 2006).

But, increasingly, it is global forces which shape the social conditions that underpin health in everyday life. As the UK government recently put it:

> Global health is determined by factors which themselves often show scant respect for national boundaries – such as international trade, climate change, pollution, conflict, environmental degradation and poverty.... Because so many sectors affect health, and so many countries and agencies are involved in healthcare, improving health around the world requires co-operative actions and solutions. (HM Government, 2008, p 7)

The CSDH final report also makes the point that health inequalities are a global issue because patterns of ill-health are 'converging'. In all but the poorest parts of the world, the predominant burden of disease comes increasingly from non-communicable diseases such as heart disease, cancer and diabetes and from chronic illness (see Chapter 9). 'The global picture of non-communicable and communicable disease dictates the need for a coherent framework for global health action' (CSDH, 2008, p 32).

So our aim here is to locate social work action to combat health inequalities, necessarily primarily local or national in focus, not simply in a comparative framework – comparing country with country – but in the context of globalisation. In doing so, we try to balance the necessity of reading and responding to health inequalities in their particular local contexts with the clear evidence of global patterns in the social causes and consequences of inequalities in health (Bonnefoy et al, 2007).

This opening chapter prepares the ground for the work that follows. First, we briefly analyse and exemplify the nature and extent of global health inequalities as a product of social inequalities; second, we outline how social work is engaged in producing and combating health inequalities across the life course; and, third, we show why social work action to tackle health inequalities has to be understood in the context of neoliberal globalisation. Finally, we present the structure of the remainder of the book and highlight how constituent chapters engage with these key issues.

Unequal global health: embodied social inequalities

The basic evidence about the nature and extent of health chances has become all too familiar but remains shocking. Unequal health outcomes are the physical embodiment of social inequalities. Five important elements of the evidence link health inequalities to their social determinants. First, although the data from individual countries is not always fully comparable or accurate (Bonnefoy et al, 2007), there is no doubt that inequalities in health between countries are profound, reflecting differences in patterns of national wealth per person. For example, one child in four born in Sierra Leone in 2006 would die before their fifth birthday compared to one child in 40 in China and only one in 250 in Japan (Table 1.1). Correspondingly, average life expectancy, around 40 years in Sierra Leone and 50 in Malawi, is over 80 in Japan, Australia and other developed countries. No human right is more fundamental than the right to life.

Table 1.1: Under-5 mortality and life expectancy by country, 2006

	Sierra Leone	Malawi	China	Australia	Japan
Under-5 mortality (per 1,000 live births)	269	120	24	6	4
Average life expectancy at birth	40	50	73	82	83

Source: Adapted from World Health Organization Core Health Data (2008)

Second, socially structured inequalities in health chances *within* countries are also substantial, understood in terms of individual or geographical socio-economic position (see Chapter 3). Social position is measured in a variety of ways – sometimes as occupational status, sometimes by education, income or other signals of economic standing. For example, a headline CSDH (2008) statistic compares the life expectancy of 54 years for men in an inner-city area of Glasgow in the UK with the 82 years in a nearby affluent suburb. In Bolivia, babies born to women with no education have an infant mortality rate greater than 100 per 1,000 live births; the infant mortality rate of babies born to mothers with at least secondary education is under 40 per 1,000.

Third, patterns of relatively poor health are found among members of socially disadvantaged minority groups as social identities are reflected in health chances and experience. For example:

- Australian Indigenous peoples have a life expectancy around 17 years less than those of the majority population (Aboriginal and Torres Strait Islander Social Justice Commissioner, 2005).
- Black male life expectancy in Washington DC averages 12 years less than for men in the US as a whole (CSDH, 2008).
- There is increasing evidence of the impact of discrimination on the health and life expectancy of people with learning disabilities (Hollins et al, 1998).

In part, these dimensions of inequality reflect patterns of income and wealth, but additional factors are also at work. One characteristic of our authors' discussion, not always found in writing about health inequalities, is their emphasis on a variety of aspects of difference and discrimination including gender, ethnicity, disability and sexual orientation.

Fourth, notwithstanding the position of particular minorities, it has also become clear that there is a social gradient of unequal health chances which runs right across societies, each incremental step up in status improving life expectancy and reducing the chances of debilitating illness (Acheson, 1998; Marmot, 2004). Health inequalities cannot be dealt with by targeting only the poorest people in societies and the 'social gradient in health ... affects people in rich and poor countries alike' (CSDH, 2008, p 31).

Finally, it is clear that unequal health outcomes primarily reflect social position rather than individual lifestyle choices. As Blaxter's (1990) research has powerfully demonstrated, the capacity as well as the opportunity to make healthy choices and decisions is constrained by socio-economic status. Unequal social structures are reflected in people's access to social and cultural capital and reproduced through everyday processes of thought and action (see Chapter 3). It is not that people are just passive products of broader social structures but that both the capacity to exercise control and the sense of being active agents are influenced by the social position people hold.

The all-pervasive nature of the impact of social conditions on health is vividly conveyed by the following CSDH summary, reflecting the processes we have highlighted:

> The poor health of the poor, the social gradient in health within countries, and the marked health inequities between countries are caused by the unequal distribution of power, income, goods, and services, globally and nationally, the consequent unfairness in the immediate, visible

circumstances of peoples [sic] lives – their access to health care, schools, and education, their conditions of work and leisure, their homes, communities, towns, or cities – and their chances of leading a flourishing life. This unequal distribution of health-damaging experiences is not in any sense a 'natural' phenomenon but is the result of a toxic combination of poor social policies and programmes, unfair economic arrangements, and bad politics. Together, the structural determinants and conditions of daily life constitute the social determinants of health and are responsible for a major part of health inequities between and within countries. (CSDH, 2008, p 1)

The social construction of health inequalities is also a dynamic process, as social conditions change over time. Fundamentally, there is a strong correlation between the per capita wealth of a nation and measures of population health (World Bank, 2003), but patterns of inequalities in health change within and between countries. Substantial differences can be seen between countries with similar income levels at a given moment and over time, as Table 1.2 shows.

Table 1.2: Infant mortality and life expectancy by country, 1990 and 2006

Location	Life expectancy at birth (years) both sexes, 1990	Life expectancy at birth (years) both sexes, 2006	Infant mortality rate (per 1,000 live births) both sexes, 1990	Infant mortality rate (per 1,000 live births) both sexes, 2006
Niger	34	42	191	148
Sierra Leone	38	40	169	159
Bangladesh	55	63	100	52
Bolivia	58	66	89	50
Zimbabwe	62	43	52	55
South Africa	63	51	45	56
Brazil	67	72	48	19
Sri Lanka	67	72	26	11
Norway	77	80	7	3

Source: Adapted from World Health Organization Core Health Data (2008)

Against a general background of rising life expectancy, for many countries in Africa, particularly sub-Saharan Africa, measures of infant mortality and life expectancy showed little improvement or even declined between 1990 and 2006. Both Zimbabwe and South Africa exemplify this, with life expectancy plummeting by 20 and 10 years, respectively. It is common to attribute this solely to HIV/AIDS but there are many social factors, global, national and local, which have made AIDS so damaging in sub-Saharan Africa, including poverty, debt repayments, unfair trade structures, conflict, gender inequalities, the policies of pharmaceutical companies, a lack of public health infrastructure and poor governance (see, for example, Pharaoh and Schönteich, 2003).

In other developing countries, such as Brazil, Bangladesh and Bolivia, the same period saw a substantial fall in infant mortality and rise in life expectancy, while Sri Lanka continued to outperform expectations. Even countries with already low infant mortality and high life expectancy, such as Norway, showed marked improvements. However, within countries as well as between countries, growth in average life expectancy can go hand in hand with widening inequalities. In the UK, a three-and-a-half-year gain in overall average life expectancy at birth between 1991–93 and 2004–06 has been accompanied by a widening gap between the most advantaged (Kensington and Chelsea) and the least advantaged (Glasgow) local council areas from around nine years to over 12.5 years for boys, mirroring growing income inequality (National Statistics, 2007).

Graham (2007) argues that these radically different patterns and levels of health chances demonstrate that national and local as well as global policies can have an impact. For example, Sri Lanka's gross national income per capita is less than half that of Brazil or South Africa but it achieves equal or better health outcomes (Table 1.2). Sri Lanka has 'linked economic growth to income redistribution by devoting a relatively high proportion of its national wealth to poverty alleviation … [and] invested, too, in primary education and public health provision from the early decades of the twentieth century, and … free or heavily subsidised rice' (Graham, 2007, p 69). Kerala, in India, provides similar evidence of the impact that regional policy making can have on health (Thankappan and Valiathan, 1998). The CSDH final report (2008, p 33) identifies five shared political factors which link Sri Lanka and Kerala with other 'overachieving' countries (Costa Rica, Cuba and China):

- historical commitment to health as a social goal
- social welfare orientation to development
- community participation in decision-making processes relevant to health

- universal coverage of health services for all social groups
- intersectoral linkages for health.

Social work action: across the life course

Social workers observe at first hand every day how these structural determinants and conditions of daily life act across the life course to affect life chances, but do not always recognise the health dimensions of these scenarios (Bywaters, 2007). The precise pathways by which the social becomes biological may not be sufficiently understood (Bonnefoy et al, 2007), but life course research has produced substantial evidence that the body accumulates socially-created benefits and insults from the moment of conception to death (Kuh et al, 2003). Some of these are hereditary but many others reflect the environment of the growing child and adult, progressively conferring not only immediate advantages or disadvantages with implications for health but also influencing future potential and opportunities (see Chapter 7).

This research also suggests that critical moments in life course development, like points on a train track, can have an enduring influence on health chances and experience. These include events and opportunities, such as transitions from education to work or parenthood, which are highly socially patterned and, sometimes, self-reinforcing. Social workers will often be involved in these critical moments with people who are at risk of avoidable ill-health and premature death, such as young children living in multidimensional poverty (see Chapter 7) or entering public care, adolescents caught up in the criminal justice or mental health systems, couples seeking fertility treatment (Chapter 6), women fleeing violence and rape (Chapter 8), trafficked migrants and older people entering residential care. Significant health consequences follow from how these and other threats and opportunities are managed and resourced.

In these critical moments and across the life course, people's social position 'marks the point at which the resources distributed through major social institutions ... enter and shape people's lives' (Graham, 2007, p 111). It is not just that social workers work with individuals who are ill and people whose future health is at risk from cumulative insults but also that most health work is carried out by lay people, informally, and not by health or social work professionals (Stacey, 1988; McLeod and Bywaters, 2000, Ch 4). People work for their own health and for the health of others, as workers, friends, parents and children. Lay health workers are mothers-to-be revising their alcohol, drugs or tobacco intake during pregnancy; foster parents providing a safe and emotionally supportive home; adults managing their medication for a chronic condition or campaigning for a living wage; and informal carers providing food, domestic support or personal care. Again, social workers commonly encounter people as they struggle to carry out these critical tasks, often poorly equipped by their previous life experiences (see Chapter 3) and by the resources they can command.

In order for this lay health work to lead to socially just outcomes, people need access to the basic social, economic and environmental resources that are essential to the tasks of promoting health, preventing illness or managing ill-health. Crucially, this means the material resources which underpin health, such as income, food, shelter, warmth, clean water; social resources, such as safety, access to information and education, and opportunities for meaningful work; personal resources, such as resilience, clarity of thought and social skills; informal resources, such as personal and social supports; and professional resources in the form of health, social and other services (Wilkinson, 2005). Locally, overt and covert forms of discrimination prevent or distort access to these resources, within a societal framework permeated by globalisation. For example, the privatisation of health services often means that universal access is no longer a goal of service provision, that services cannot be afforded and that the human cost of affording them is health-damaging poverty (GHW, 2005).

As social workers engage with lay health workers, struggling against 'the social odds', to secure their own health and the health of those close to them, they are involved in the production, maintenance, mitigation and transformation of social inequalities and their health consequences. Social work in all settings is concerned with the impact on people's lives of the social forces which determine health chances and health experience. Social workers, in all settings, are involved in processes which affect the health resources available to people – money, work, education and information, social and health services, networks and relationships, and emotional support – and their capacities to access and make use of them. Social workers in all settings need to integrate into their practice awareness of the impact of poor health on people's everyday lives, their choices and their opportunities. Those working in health settings play particular roles, for example, in helping people access health care, negotiate treatment decisions or secure the services to manage illness at home. But all social work has health impacts. As the examples presented in later chapters confirm, social work can act against inequalities in health through direct front-line intervention and service provision (see Chapters 10–12) and also through policy making, research and education (see Chapters 13 and 14). And as all these chapters demonstrate, understanding how global health inequalities are produced and maintained calls for an extended repertoire of social work interventions.

Social work action: the global context

The context for understanding the social determinants of health is global as well as national and local. Indeed, the global context of people's everyday lives has never been more immediately apparent. We are writing at the height of the credit crunch (Stanton, 2008) and shortly after the High-Level Conference on World Food Security: the Challenges of Climate Change and Bioenergy orchestrated by the Food and Agriculture Organization of the United Nations in June 2008. Intrinsic to the global context of health is the phenomenon of globalisation.

The definition of globalisation, how it affects health and the consequences for health inequalities are all contested. Our position as editors is closest to that of Labonte and Schrecker (2007a) who emphasise the economic drivers behind the emergence of a global marketplace and the specific, neoliberal policies which have been dominant in the past 35 years. By neoliberal policies they mean 'trade liberalization, the global reorganization of production and labour markets, debt crises and economic restructuring; financial liberalization …; influences that operate by way of the physical environment; and health systems changed by the global marketplace' (Labonte and Schrecker, 2007b, p 2). In other words, we are critical of the impact on health of the profit-driven, free market mode of globalisation that has been dominant in the past three decades with scant regard for the impact on populations, on welfare systems or on the physical environment. It is this ideology and practice that has led to exacerbated health inequalities rather than changes in global governance, global markets, global communications, global mobility, cross-cultural interaction and the global environment per se (Huynen et al, 2005).

In this introduction we only sketch out some of the key mechanisms through which globalisation has an impact on health inequalities. For more detailed analyses see GHW (2005), Labonte and Schrecker (2007a, 2007b, 2007c), CSDH (2008) and the International Federation of Social Workers (IFSW, 2008) policy statement on health.

Structural adjustment and trade conditions

From the 1980s onwards the World Bank required 'structural adjustments' to be made by many national governments as a condition of economic support, later modified to require governments seeking support also to present 'Poverty Reduction Strategy Papers'. Despite this addition of a focus on poverty reduction, the central driver has remained the neoliberal economic assumptions which have required reduced public expenditure and state intervention in industry; cuts in taxation and social protection; and limits to the regulatory powers of governments (Verheul and Rowson, 2001). A number of health-damaging consequences have usually followed. Income inequality and unemployment has increased, accompanied by reduced social protection; conditions of work and access to compensation for industrial injury have worsened; land rights have been lost; and education, health and other social welfare services have been cut and privatised (Deacon, 2000; Whitehead et al, 2001).

International policies and treaties covering world trade have also often damaged local economies or transferred economic benefits from small local producers to large, often multinational, companies and from developing to developed countries (Labonte et al, 2005). These factors have been disruptive of established livelihoods and ways of life, leading to large-scale population movements both from rural to urban living and from developing to developed countries (see Chapters 10 and 11). Human trafficking has thrived in these conditions with often degrading and sometimes fatal consequences (Zierer, 2007).

Privatisation and commodification

Privatising health (and other human) services and their assets has changed their purpose from service provision to profit generation while removing responsibility for ensuring universal access (see Chapter 6). For hundreds of millions of people in both developing and developed countries, newly introduced or increased health care costs mean that either health services are not accessed or that families enter into a vicious circle of payments leading to poverty, resulting in worse health and the need for further costly treatment.

Privatisation and managerialism have frequently meant the erosion of services as well as charges. One example is the drive to reduce lengths of hospital stay or to close psychiatric and convalescent facilities, often without sufficient investment in community services. The opportunity to pass costs between service providers as a consequence of fragmented privatised service design leads to poor–quality experiences for patients and their families, with costs being transferred from the state and from private companies to individuals and families: the domestication of suffering (Cartier, 2003).

Implicit in privatisation is the idea that health and health care are products which can be bought and sold rather than services or rights, replacing allocation on the basis of need with the ability to pay. This process of commodification also involves the creation of new markets in health–related products such as cosmetic treatments, reproductive technologies and organs for transplant as well as claims of commercial ownership over genetics (see Chapter 6). Failures of regulation have resulted in avoidable suffering and created unrealisable expectations of the perfect body (Filc, 2005).

There is widespread evidence that treating health as a commodity cannot deliver socially just or efficient health systems. For example, pharmaceutical research is heavily skewed towards the treatment of conditions which are prevalent in developed countries where there is greater potential for a large financial return on investment (Global Forum for Health Research, 2004). Where new treatments become available, as with the combination drugs used to manage HIV/AIDS, the market has failed to meet the standard of access according to need with lethal consequences for individuals and devastating effects on economies and on families. International attempts to solve the problem of intellectual property rights and to ensure that treatment development includes effective safeguards have not yet been successful (Forman, 2006).

Popular and professional campaigns against privatisation and commodification are currently active in many countries, including in Egypt, where the Egyptian National Committee on the Right to Health (2008) is resisting the wholesale privatisation of not-for-profit health service assets, and internationally, such as the campaign over the price of drug treatments for HIV/AIDS (Knowledge Ecology International, 2003).

Environmental destruction and climate change

The CSDH (2008) urged the coming together of agendas around health inequalities and climate change, seeing climate change as one of the greatest threats to human health. Climate change and environmental change more broadly are driven primarily by economic factors and underlying geopolitical imbalances. The drive for growth and profit, often neglectful of environmental impact, taking advantage of inadequate regulatory systems and backed by the unfair trade conditions mentioned above, is damaging health and storing up future problems (GHW, 2005). Two examples are the use of toxic chemicals and pesticides leading to water and air pollution, and the replacement of food production with biofuels pushing millions into under-nutrition. The privatisation of essential resources for health, such as water, is a further example of neoliberal economic policies producing unequal outcomes. Despite its caution about identifying the causes of climate change, the WHO (2008, p 2) is in no doubt that the consequences will be unequally distributed: 'Health effects are expected to be more severe for elderly people and people with infirmities or pre-existing medical conditions. The groups who are likely to bear most of the resulting disease burden are children and the poor, especially women.' Effects on health are both direct and indirect. For example, rural populations face disproportionate risks from drought (see Chapter 4), deforestation and flooding and the resulting intra- and international migration brings further health consequences for urban dwellers (see Chapter 10).

Political conflict and violence

The Alma Ata Declaration (International Conference on Primary Health Care, 1978) rightly referred to military expenditure as a wasted opportunity to fund improved health. Political conflict and violence of all kinds directly damages health. It forces people to leave their homes and destroys their livelihoods, supportive relationships, opportunities for personal development, and their sense of identity and personal security, causing both physical and emotional difficulties (see Chapters 5 and 8). Again, it is the poorest and least powerful members of societies who are least able to protect themselves from such violence or to take remedial action.

Social work and global health inequalities

Our book demonstrates that global processes, institutions and agreements provide the backdrop for social work policies and practices tackling health inequalities. Social workers cannot fully understand people's health-undermining circumstances – their reasons for migration, their lack of access to services, their poverty – without referring to globalisation. A global perspective also enables social workers to decentre their own practice, to learn lessons from others' divergent or convergent forms of practice. Finally, social work can contribute to a richer understanding of the relationship of globalisation to health inequalities through its emphasis on the need to engage with multiple aspects of difference, in addition to the impact of relative poverty.

Our authors are drawn from 10 countries and five continents. However, their work should be thought of as exemplary rather than representative. First, there is a relative excess of authors from developed countries. Second, there are no examples from important regions of the world – South America, Eastern Europe, the Middle East. To some extent this reflects what has been described as the 'eurocentric approach to the question of inequity' (Bonnefoy et al, 2007, p 211), but also the current state of international social work, and inequalities in the resources, opportunities and capacities for communication available to social workers across the world. The current limited exchange between social workers in South and Central America and the English-speaking world is a major loss for social work as a whole. Social work is also not uniformly well established. At present, for example, social work in mainland China is an emergent discipline and profession (see Chapter 10).

The remainder of the book is divided into three parts. Following this introduction, in Part Two eight succeeding chapters provide an in-depth rationale for social work's engagement in tackling global health inequalities through a selective examination of key topics, for example, health as a human right (Chapter 2) and as an issue of social justice (Chapter 3). In differing ways, these chapters also address the relationship of health inequalities to globalisation, for example, analysing the impact of climate change (Chapter 4), political conflict (Chapter 5) and the commodification of reproduction (Chapter 6). All chapters also address the ways in which policy and practice development are intertwined, for example, focusing on greater equity in childhood (Chapter 7), the consequences of violence for women's health (Chapter 8) and the relationship between illness and disability (Chapter 9). As all eight chapters analyse global issues for inequalities in health through a social work lens, part of what emerges is a fine-grained account of the ways in which global health inequalities impact on people's daily lives.

In Part Three, five chapters provide multiple case examples, from 10 developing and developed countries, of social work interventions which address inequalities in health. The chapters cover, respectively, the following dimensions of social work practice:

- identifying specific aspects of health inequalities as targets for social work;
- employing preventive interventions addressing whole populations;

- developing new forms of service design and delivery;
- using research as the vehicle for change;
- generating change through educational programmes.

The case examples are not presented as ideal types or as exhausting the full range of practice possibilities. The authors reflect on the strengths and weaknesses of their practice, consider these essentially local initiatives in the context of globalisation and draw lessons about their wider relevance.

Part Four focuses on wider policy issues: reflecting on the possibilities for social work to act in alliance with experts by experience and with social movements in combating health inequalities (Chapter 15) and the experience of social work's major international organisation, the International Federation of Social Workers, in acting on health inequalities on the global stage (Chapter 16). We conclude by drawing together the themes which emerge from the book as a whole, exploring the insights which social work can offer in analysing global health inequalities and the implications for future directions for social work interventions in tackling health inequalities.

Our work breaks new ground by providing analysis and evidence on social work and health inequalities in a global and globalised context. In doing so it also pioneers examination of social work as a constituent element in the social processes constructing and contesting health inequalities around the world. Through the combination of a common focus, and the diverse ideas, views and experience represented in this book, we aim to provide a better understanding of what social work can contribute to tackling health inequalities globally, and encourage our readers to take action on this key issue.

Notes

[1] The Constitution of the World Health Organization (WHO, 1948, p 1) states that, 'The enjoyment of the highest attainable standard of health is one of the fundamental rights of every human being without distinction of race, religion, political belief, economic or social condition.'

References

Aboriginal and Torres Strait Islander Social Justice Commissioner (2005) *Social Justice Report*, Sydney: Human Rights and Equal Opportunity Commission.

Acheson, D. (1998) *Independent Inquiry into Inequalities in Health*, London: The Stationery Office.

Blaxter, M. (1990) *Health and Lifestyles*, London: Routledge.

Bonnefoy, J., Morgan, A., Kelly, M., Butt, J. and Bergman, V. (2007) *Constructing the Evidence Base on the Social Determinants of Health: A Guide*, Geneva: World Health Organization.

Braveman, P. and Gruskin, S. (2003) 'Defining equity in health', *Journal of Epidemiology and Community Health*, vol 57, no 4, pp 254–8.

Bywaters, P. (2007) 'Understanding the life course', in M. Lymbery and K. Postle (eds) *Social Work: A Companion to Learning*, London: Sage.

Cartier, C. (2003) 'From home to hospital and back again: Economic restructuring, end of life, and the gendered problems of place-switching health services', *Social Science and Medicine*, vol 56, no 11, pp 2289–301.

CSDH (Commission on the Social Determinants of Health) (2008) *Closing the Gap in a Generation: Health Equity through Action on the Social Determinants of Health*, Final Report of the Commission on Social Determinants of Health, Geneva: World Health Organization.

Deacon, B. (2000) 'Eastern European welfare states: The impact of the politics of globalization', *Journal of European Social Policy*, vol 10, no 2, pp 146–61.

Egyptian National Committee on the Right to Health (2008) Declaration from the National Egyptian Committee on the Right to Health, www.phmovement.org/cms/en/node/806

Filc, D. (2005) 'The health business under neo-liberalism: The Israeli case', *Critical Social Policy*, vol 25, no 2, pp 180–97.

Forman, L. (2006) 'Incentivizing justice: Linking human rights, trade and access to medicines', Munk Centre for International Studies, Comparative Program on Health and Society Lupina Foundation Working Papers Series 2005–2006, pp 129–53.

Global Forum for Health Research (2004) *10/90 Report on Health Research 2003–2004*, Geneva: Global Forum for Health Research.

GHW (Global Health Watch) (2005) *Global Health Watch 2005–2006. An Alternative World Health Report*, London/New York: Zed Books.

Graham, H. (2007) *Unequal Lives*, Maidenhead: Open University Press.

Hollins, S., Attard, M., von Fraunhofer, N. and Sedgwick, P. (1998) 'Mortality in people with learning disability: Risks, causes and death certification findings in London', *Developmental Medicine and Child Neurology*, vol 40, pp 50–6.

HM Government (2008) *Health is Global*, London: Department of Health.

Huynen, M., Martens, P. and Hilderink, H. (2005) 'The health impacts of globalisation: A conceptual framework', *Globalization and Health*, vol 1, article number 14, www.globalizationandhealth.com/content/1/1/14

International Conference on Primary Health Care (1978) Declaration of Alma Ata, www.searo.who.int/LinkFiles/Health_Systems_declaration_almaata.pdf

IFSW (International Federation of Social Workers) (2008) *International Policy on Health*, Berne: IFSW, www.ifsw.org/en/p38000081.html

IFSW/IASSW (International Association of Schools of Social Work) (2004) *Ethics in Social Work: Statement of Principles*, Bern: IFSW and IASSW, www.ifsw.org/en/p38000324.html

Knowledge Ecology International (2003) 'Letter from 65 NGOs to leaders of the branded pharmaceutical industry on the pricing of antiretrovirals in non-OECD countries', www.cptech.org/ip/health/ngos06302003.html

Kuh, D., Ben-Shlomo, Y., Lynch, J., Hallqvist, J. and Power, C. (2003) 'Life course epidemiology', *Journal of Epidemiology and Community Health*, vol 57, pp 778–83.

Labonte, R. and Schrecker, T. (2007a) 'Globalization and social determinants of health: Introduction and methodological background (part 1 of 3)', *Globalization and Health*, vol 3, article no 5, www.globalizationandhealth.com/content/3/1/5

Labonte, R. and Schrecker, T. (2007b) 'Globalization and social determinants of health: The role of the global marketplace (part 2 of 3)', *Globalization and Health*, vol 3, article no 6, www.globalizationandhealth.com/content/3/1/6

Labonte, R. and Schrecker, T. (2007c) 'Globalization and social determinants of health: Promoting health equity in global governance (part 3 of 3)', *Globalization and Health*, vol 3, article no 7, www.globalizationandhealth.com/content/3/1/7

Labonte, R., Schrecker, T. and Sen Gupta, A. (2005) 'A global health equity agenda for the G8 summit', *British Medical Journal*, vol 330, pp 533–6.

Lyons, K. (2006) 'Globalization and social work: International and local implications', *British Journal of Social Work*, vol 36, pp 365–80.

Marmot, M. (2004) *The Status Syndrome: How Your Social Standing Affects Your Health and Life Expectancy*, London: Bloomsbury.

McLeod, E. and Bywaters, P. (2000) *Social Work, Health and Equality*, London: Routledge.

National Statistics (2007) 'Life expectancy at birth (years), United Kingdom, males and females, 1991–1993 to 2004–2006', www.statistics.gov.uk/statbase/Product.asp?vlnk=8841

People's Health Movement (2000) *People's Charter For Health*, www.phmovement.org/cms/en/resources/charters/peopleshealth

Pharaoh, R. and Schönteich, M. (2003) *AIDS, Security and Governance in Southern Africa Exploring the impact*, ISS Paper 65, Pretoria: Institute for Security Studies.

Stacey, M. (1988) *The Sociology of Health and Healing*, London: Unwin Hyman.

Stanton, E. (2008) 'US stocks decline, Dow average has biggest drop since 1987', Bloomberg.com, www.bloomberg.com/apps/news?pid=20601103&sid=aAZihoYr_JsA&refer=news

Thankappan, K. and Valiathan, M. (1998) 'Health at low cost, the Kerala model', *The Lancet*, vol 351, pp 1274–5.

Verheul, E. and Rowson, M. (2001) 'Poverty Reduction Strategy Papers', *British Medical Journal*, vol 323, pp 120–1.

Whitehead, M., Dahlgren, G. and Evans, T. (2001) 'Equity and health sector reforms: Can low-income countries escape the medical poverty trap?', *The Lancet*, vol 358, no 9284, pp 833–6.

Wilkinson, R. (2005) *The Impact of Inequality: How to Make Sick Societies Healthier*, New York, NY: The New Press.

World Bank (2003) World Development Indicators CD-ROM, Washington, DC: World Bank.

WHO (World Health Organization) (1948) *Constitution*, Geneva: World Health Organization.

WHO (2008) *Protecting Health from Climate Change – World Health Day 2008*, Geneva: World Health Organization.

Zierer, B. (2007) 'Comparative social work and trafficking in women', *Social Work & Society Newsmagazine Newsletter*, 30 July, www.socmag.net/?p=175

Part Two

Global health inequalities: issues for social work

The right to health: illusion or possibility?

Vimla Nadkarni and Kriti Vikram

Introduction

The World Health Organization's (WHO's) constitution defines health as 'a state of complete physical, mental and social well being and not merely the absence of disease or infirmity' (WHO, 1948, p 1). This may be widely accepted as an ideal, but in practice health continues to be perceived differentially by policy makers, health care providers, civil society groups and the general populace. One thing is certain: the evidence that health cannot be achieved through only biological and technological interventions is overwhelming.

Thirty years ago, there was a 'revolution in thinking' about health and health care at the International Conference on Primary Health Care at Alma Ata (WHO, 2008, p 747). The conference asserted that primary health care was the preferred strategy for global health policy, underpinned by core values. The Alma Ata Declaration (WHO, 1978) reaffirmed that health is a fundamental human right and proclaimed that the gross inequalities in health status between and within developed and developing countries were politically, socially and economically unacceptable. Governments who signed the Declaration committed themselves to making appropriate investments in economic and social development, and in health systems, to ensure 'Health for All' their citizens, including the poor; to provide access to affordable health care; and to community ownership of the organisation of health services. The resultant 'Global Strategy of Health for All by the Year 2000' determined that 'all people in all countries should have at least such a level of health that they are capable of working productively and of participating actively in the social life of the community in which they live' (WHO, 1981, p 15).

However, this vision was rapidly undermined by the International Monetary Fund's promotion of its 'structural adjustment' approach to economic development, supported by the World Bank, and was replaced with a 'selective primary health care' approach (Walsh and Warren, 1979) which focused on vertical single issue interventions (WHO, 2008). It has been argued that 'Health for All', based in primary health care, was not really given a chance, although countries like Mozambique, Cuba and Nicaragua demonstrated that the principles of equity and justice on which 'Health for All' was based could work (Magnussen et al, 2004). Recently the holistic, rights-based philosophy of Alma Ata has again been recognised in the work of the WHO Commission on Social Determinants of Health (CSDH) (CSDH, 2008), and been endorsed by the current WHO Director-General (Chan, 2008).

Principles of human rights and social justice are fundamental to social work. Building on the United Nations Universal Declaration of Human Rights (UDHR) and International Covenants, the International Federation of Social Workers' (IFSW's) policy statement on human rights states that: 'The social work profession is convinced that the achievement of human rights for all people is a fundamental prerequisite for a caring world and the survival of the human race' (IFSW, 1996). In this chapter, we argue that while over more than 60 years diverse international instruments have asserted that health is a human right, for this to become a reality much has to be done to ensure that all citizens have access to the social, political, economic and cultural determinants of health beyond the proximate medical determinants. Examples of the barriers to achieving the right to health and of campaigns to secure rights are drawn mainly from our own country, India, and focus particularly on women and children. We conclude with a consideration of the place of social work in this struggle.

Health and human rights

Human rights can assume a powerful role in defining and advancing human development especially in a milieu of weak or inadequate public health systems, unregulated growth of the private sector and restricted access to health care for the poor. Adopting a human rights perspective can assist policy makers, practitioners and advocates to achieve practical benefits as it reorients thinking on global health challenges (Mann et al, 1999). Mann et al have proposed a tripartite framework for connecting health and human rights:

- the impact of health policies, programmes and practices on human rights;

- the impact of gross as well as subtle human rights violations on people's health; and
- the fundamental connections between the protection and promotion of human rights and health rights.

Human rights instruments and health

The extreme human and economic losses caused by the Second World War led to an international focus on rights. The Universal Declaration of Human Rights recognised that freedom, justice and peace in the world are founded on the inherent dignity and the equal and inalienable rights of all members of the human family (UN, 1948). Two years earlier, the Constitution of the World Health Organization (WHO, 1948, p 1) had adopted the principle that 'the enjoyment of the highest attainable standard of health' was 'a fundamental right of every human being without distinction of race, religion, political belief, economic or social condition'. It is now recognised that this right can only be realised when particular social arrangements – norms, institutions, laws, and an enabling environment – are in place (Sama, 2005).

The right to health is a broad canvas of issues and concepts which has been elaborated through many human rights instruments which address health and highlight the importance of addressing the broader social determinants. For example, General Comment No. 14 (2000) (UN Economic and Social Council, 2000) on Article 12 of the International Covenant on Economic, Social and Cultural Rights (1976) asserts that for the highest standard of health to be attained, people must have access to basic resources like food, housing, work, education and human dignity. These underpinnings of health are closely related to the realisation of other rights, including the rights to participation, to the enjoyment of the benefits of scientific progress, to life, non-discrimination and equality (WHO, 2002). Health services must be available and accessible, especially to the most vulnerable and marginalised. They must be acceptable to people of diverse ethnicities and cultures and of good quality.

The International Convention on the Elimination of All Forms of Racial Discrimination (OHCHR, 1965) provides a second example. It mandates the prohibition and elimination of racial discrimination in all its forms, and articulates the universal right to public health, medical care, social security and social services.

Third, the Convention on the Elimination of All Forms of Discrimination against Women (CEDAW) affirms the right to health in pursuit of equality of rights (OHCHR, 1979). Article 12 identifies the importance of access to family planning services and to 'appropriate services in connection with pregnancy, confinement and the post natal period', including nutrition and lactation.

Fourth, Article 24 (2) of the Convention on the Rights of the Child (OHCHR, 1989) elaborates the appropriate measures necessary to diminish infant and child mortality, to provide essential medical assistance to all children, to prevent child abuse and to provide pre-natal care.

From philosophy to practice: social determinants as human rights

The WHO performs an important role in advocating for universal rights to health. In 2005, it established the Commission on Social Determinants of Health (CSDH). The Commission's vision is of a socially just world, where health and its key determinants are inseparable from human rights and a society's success is judged by the quality and fair distribution of its population's health. The CSDH argues for a concentration on 'the causes of the causes' of health inequalities, which it describes as, 'the social conditions in which people live and work, reflecting their different positions in hierarchies of power, prestige and resources' (Irwin, 2005, 3).

The CSDH (2008, p 18) recognises the importance of health-related political rights which it says are threatened by 'entrenched structural inequities'. It views 'fair representation in decision making' and the engagement of civil society as vital to the achievement of such rights. Among other strategies, it seeks to provide a global platform for civil society voice, broaden the political uptake of its findings and improve the chances of sustainable impact by incorporating specificities of global regions via local facilitators. Community participation helps to ensure that the health system is responsive to the particular health needs of disadvantaged groups.

Barriers to health rights

However, the barriers against securing rights to 'Health for All' are substantial. Globalisation, privatisation and liberalisation processes have affected political and social systems. Neoliberal globalisation has not only increased health and other disparities within countries but also between countries and has influenced patterns of morbidity and mortality (see Chapter 1). Ten years ago, Ress (1997) warned that, although it is recognised that countries cannot progress economically without a healthy population, governments have continued to direct their efforts towards developing and providing technological solutions catering to the rich while leaving the poor far behind.

Health has come to be seen as a commodity within a market that can be traded like other goods. This negatively affects access to health care (Collins, 2003). Since the early 1990s, the structural adjustment model of development has promoted privatised health care over public provision. In India we have seen an unprecedented rise of a poorly regulated private sector, almost entirely based on user fees and thus less accessible to the poor. Income inequalities mean unequal access to good-quality care. Out of pocket expenses on health care by the poor have accounted for over 4% of GDP as against only 0.9% of GDP spent by the state (Ministry of Health and Family Welfare, 2005). The poor contribute disproportionately greater shares of their income than the rich to obtain basic health services – public or private – while health costs drive many into poverty (Duggal, 2000; Ellis et al, 2000; JSA, 2006).

In many countries, the right of access to essential cost-controlled medicines is being flouted under the WTO's Trade Related Intellectual Property Rights scheme which has mandated a patent protection regime in which multinational pharmaceutical companies can claim intellectual property rights over (and therefore exclusive rights to manufacture and market) medicines (JSA, 2006). This creates significant barriers to access when cheaper alternatives may already have been developed by companies in countries like India. In such a scenario, it is likely that competing pharmaceutical companies will invest in the research and development of drugs for those that can afford them (Burke and Matlin, 2008).

In India, the stimulation of private sector growth, downsizing the public sector, contracting out of services and the introduction of user charges have had a negative impact on the four essential standards of health care services: availability, accessibility, acceptability and quality (OHCHR, 1976). But the negative effects of privatised health care are also seen in developed countries. The US health care model of private insurance-led service delivery results in a 44% higher expenditure on health care per person than in Switzerland, the country with the next highest per capita expenditure (Anderson et al, 2003). Yet, the US has a lower than average physician to patient ratio, one of the lowest rates of acute care beds per capita among industrialised countries and is the only country that does not provide universal access to medical services (OECD, 2004). The lack of available care is even more acute for minority patients, and in particular for patients who are black or Hispanic (Agency for Healthcare Research and Quality, 2005). This directly violates the Centre for Economic and Social Rights' guideline that 'poorer households should not be disproportionately burdened with health expenses as compared to richer households' (http://cesr. org/index.php).

These recent trends create new or renewed health inequalities in contravention of the commitment made by governments at Alma Ata to protect the health rights of the poor. The health rights of women and children, to which we now turn, are central to this (CSDH, 2008).

Health and human rights violations: women and children

The status of women in most developing regions is linked to the historical, cultural, social and economic disadvantage that is meted out to women in patriarchal societies. Sociocultural forces marginalise women and children, systematically deny their human rights and, in turn, reduce their chances of achieving health (CSDH, 2008). Here we illustrate three of the many ways in which, despite human rights instruments like CEDAW, human rights violations continue to occur throughout women's lifespans.

Female feticide

Female feticide continues to be practised in a context of son preference. The 1994 International Symposium on Son Preference (Banister, 1999) noted that, despite development, Taiwan and South Korea faced widespread sex-selective abortions. It was argued that economic development alone could not solve the problem unless cultural norms changed. In South Korea, for instance, it was shown that parents wanted boys primarily not for economic reasons but for prestige, family harmony and family lineage reasons. Two countries in the Indian subcontinent continue to display highly biased overall sex ratios. In 1998, Pakistan reported 925 females per 1,000 males; likewise India reported 933 females per 1,000 males. The 2001 Census of India revealed 3.34 million 'missing girls' in the 0–19 age group (UNICEF and Bernard van Leer Foundation, 2006). Dowry and other economic reasons are often cited as the main causes for son preference. The predominance of a poor sex ratio in the relatively better economically developed regions of the country reveals other motives. The lowest female to male sex ratio for children aged 0–6 years old in India (793:1,000) is in the rich state of Punjab (UNICEF and Bernard van Leer Foundation, 2006).

Girl child mortality

Gender discrimination adds to the likelihood of poor girl children dying in infancy and childhood. As UNICEF points out: 'Gender discrimination, leading to continuing inequities in the care and feeding of girls in various parts of the world, including female infanticide, contributes to higher rates of infant and child mortality (UNICEF and Bernard van Leer Foundation, 2006, p 18).

In India, 2006 official statistics show that girls have higher mortality rates compared with boys. In rural Rajasthan, a relatively underdeveloped state, 49.4% of all female deaths are of girls below the age of 20. Of these, 42% of deaths are of girls under five. Girls are married off early, deprived of education and exposed to a life for which they are physically and psychologically unprepared. A deep gender bias leads to female infants and girl children being killed and/or neglected. Such violations of basic rights are not manifestations of a particular region or religion but of deeply entrenched, institutionalised patriarchal norms. As the UNICEF report says:

> Early childhood care and education rights and all the underlying protections and entitlements needed for the first five years of life begin with the assurance of three simple essentials: the right to be born, the right to survive birth and the right to stay alive through infancy and to the fifth birthday. For half of India's children, this assurance is at grave risk simply because they are girls, and daughters are not wanted. (UNICEF and Bernard van Leer Foundation, 2006, p 101)

In Iran, the Nobel Peace Prize Laureate and lawyer, Shirin Ebadi, has written about how a woman's right to health, including reproductive health, is violated due to the violation of other human rights provisions there. The early legal age of marriage, 13 years for girls and 15 for boys, demonstrates the limited choices available to children, particularly to girls (Loveland, 2006). In India, though the legal age of marriage for girls is 18 years, more than 50% of girls in rural areas get married before 18 (Institute for Population Sciences, 2007).

Reproductive health

The UN International Conference on Population and Development in Cairo (1994, para 7.2) asserted that 'the capability to reproduce and the freedom to decide if, when and how often to do so' was basic to reproductive health. The Conference declared that men and women have the right 'to be informed and to have access to safe, effective, affordable and acceptable methods of family planning of their choice'. However deprivation of these rights continues.

The two-child norm in India and one-child norm in China, for instance, are among official methods employed to reduce population growth. In China, heavy fines are imposed on couples for bearing more than one child (Doherty et al, 2001). In India, the most worrying aspect of the two-child norm is the way it has reinforced son preference and legitimated the practice of sex-selective abortion and infanticide, much as the one-child policy has done in China (UNICEF and Bernard van Leer Foundation, 2006). As the UNICEF report says, 'The small family norm is disposing of daughters' (p 101).

Access to safe abortion assists women to exercise health rights. But this is threatened by US government policy, making receipt of federal funding by non-governmental organisations conditional on their agreeing not to provide clinical abortion services or, indeed, information on them. Non-governmental organisations which have failed to comply, risk suffering funding cuts; in turn access to public health services like pre-natal care is reduced (Motluk, 2004).

Lack of access to safe abortion contributes to maternal morbidity and mortality. According to WHO estimates (2007), the proportion of maternal mortality due to abortion complications worldwide is 13%. It ranges drastically from 8% in Western Asia to as high as 26% in South America. A recent report (Human Rights Watch, 2005) elaborates women's severely limited access to reproductive health choices and services in Argentina where the woman and the service provider are punishable by law. Illegal abortions cause an estimated 30% of maternal mortality in Argentina and an estimated 40% of all pregnancies are illegally terminated.

Globally, reproductive rights are flouted frequently when women are the most vulnerable. Lakshmi (2001) emphasises that most technological options in the area of reproduction, such as contraceptives and sex determination tests, are declared as adding to the range of 'choices' available for women. But women do not have an unfettered choice except in the context of material, social and gender equity (see Chapter 6).

Working for the right to health equity

'Health for All' continues to be an objective for both inter-professional and popular activist groups. Physicians for Human Rights (PHR) mobilises a range of health professionals to advance the right to Health for All through undertaking research on issues like violence in Darfur, unequal access to treatment for HIV/AIDS, torture and landmines (http://physiciansforhumanrights.org/#). PHR advocates for health rights, dignity and justice on the basis of its research and aims at policy change.

The People's Health Movement (PHM) (http://phmovement. org/cms/) has its roots deep in the grassroots people's movement and owes its genesis to many health networks and activists concerned about the violation of health rights. They have demonstrated how national priorities designed in the form of narrow vertical programmes have failed to create comprehensive and sustainable health systems; how globalisation has brought unfair trade practices that have undermined nations' abilities to support their health systems; and how people are routinely viewed as passive recipients of care (Narayan, 2006).

The PHM (2008) has called for a revitalisation of the principles of the Alma Ata and advocates for a health system which goes beyond the minimal package approach for the poor, addresses the social, political and economic determinants of health, empowers communities, fosters 'bottom-up' planning and aims to create global partnerships to build horizontal programmes.

In India, the Jan Swasthya Abhiyan (http://phm-india.org/) is the counterpart of the PHM. It advocates for equitable development and Health for All through comprehensive primary health care and action on the social determinants of health. Professional social workers in India have been critical actors in presenting evidence of health rights abuses in the *jan sunwais* or people's (public) hearings. These are a unique strategy of the JSA. These hearings occur before government and non-government stakeholders, who together take corrective action, which social workers and the communities jointly monitor.

Tactics to build a larger public campaign include public hearings, rallies, *dharnas* (sit outs), conventions, action-oriented research, media advocacy and lobbying members of parliament. This has resulted in significant legislation like the 2005 National Rural Employment Guarantee Act. This ensures periods of employment on public works at the minimum wage. Similar action by the Indian 'Right to Food' group has also led to the introduction of cooked midday meals in all primary schools run by the municipal bodies (www.righttofoodindia.org/).

Again in India, civil society organisations are also taking a human rights perspective to health in a variety of ways. The Self Employed Women's Association (SEWA), Ahmedabad, works towards women's empowerment and economic independence through interventions including micro-finance and financial assistance schemes. When they found that ill-health, including post-natal complications and maternal death, was the reason women were defaulting on loans, they designed a Maternal Protection Scheme. The Scheme provided packages of services, including registration of women and provision of health and financial assistance on nominal fees. It has also proved to be an effective entry point into poor women's lives, one that encourages women to look after their health (SEWA, undated).

Conclusion: social work and health rights

Ife (2001, viii) argues that 'human rights can provide social workers with a moral basis for their practice, both at the level of day to day work with "clients", and also in community development and in policy advocacy and activism'. A human rights approach to tackling health inequalities provides a moral and a legal basis for understanding, analysis and action, to support people whose rights are threatened or have been violated and to promote rights which are not being realised. This is recognised in the IFSW (2008) *International Policy on Health*:

> All people have an equal right to enjoy the basic conditions which underpin human health. These conditions include a minimum standard of living to support health and a sustainable and health promoting environment. All people have an equal right to access resources and services that promote health and address illness, injury and impairment, including social services.

Healy (2008, p 745) concludes that 'social workers have usually paid more attention to human needs than human rights'. At the same time she suggests that it is unhelpful to set a focus on rights against one on needs. Rather, as an 'action profession', social work efforts to assist people to meet their basic human needs are consistent with efforts to assist people to assert their rights. A human rights perspective should inform a wide range of social work activity to address health inequalities, including individual case advocacy in clinical and non-clinical settings; policy advocacy, lobbying and campaigning; community development, directly and in alliance with civil society organisations; and through research, publication, education and training. As we have demonstrated, health rights have to be fought for in their local *and* global context.

Acknowledgements

We thank Ms Aasia Qayium, Research Assistant, for helping to develop the first draft of this chapter. We are also grateful to Dr Yesudian, Dean, Research and Development, for providing support to hire the research assistant for one month to work on the first draft. We thank Mr Naveen Thomas, doctoral student, Tata Institute of Social Sciences, for reviewing the chapter in great detail and making valuable suggestions.

References

Agency for Healthcare Research and Quality (2005) 'National healthcare disparities report', www.ahrq.gov/qual/nhdr05/fullreport/Dispar.htm

Anderson, G.F., Reinhardt, U.E., Hussey, P.S. and Petrosyan, V. (2003) 'It's the prices, stupid: Why the United States is so different from other countries', *Health Affairs*, vol 22, no 3, pp 89–105.

Banister, J. (1999) 'Son preference in Asia – Report of a symposium', US Census Bureau, www.census.gov/ipc/www/ebspr96a.html

Burke, M.A. and Matlin, S.A. (eds) (2008) *Monitoring Financial Flows for Health Research 2008. Prioritizing Research for Health Equity*, Geneva: Global Forum for Health Research.

Chan, M. (2008) 'Return to Alma Ata', *The Lancet*, vol 372, no 9642, pp 865–6.

Collins, T. (2003) 'Globalization, global health, and access to healthcare', *International Journal of Health Planning and Management*, vol 18, no 2, pp 97–104.

CSDH (Commission on the Social Determinants of Health) (2008) *Closing the Gap in a Generation: Health Equity through Action on the Social Determinants of Health*, Geneva: World Health Organization.

Doherty, J.P., Norton, E.C. and Veney, J.E. (2001) 'China's one-child policy: The economic choices and consequences faced by pregnant women', *Social Science and Medicine*, vol 52, no 5, pp 745–61.

Duggal, R. (2000) *The Private Sector in India – Nature, Trends and a Critique*, New Delhi: VHAI.

Ellis, R., Ellis, P., Alam, M. and Gupta, I. (2000) 'Health insurance in India: Prognosis and prospectus', *Economic and Political Weekly*, vol 35, no 4, pp 207–17.

Healy, L.M. (2008) 'Exploring the history of social work as a human rights profession', *International Social Work*, vol 51, no 6, pp 735–48.

Human Rights Watch (2005) 'Decisions denied: Women's access to contraceptives and abortion in Argentina', www.hrw.org/en/reports/2005/06/14/decisions-denied

Ife, J. (2001) *Human Rights and Social Work*, Cambridge: Cambridge University Press.

IFSW (International Federation of Social Workers) (1996) *International Policy on Human Rights*, Berne: IFSW, www.ifsw.org/en/p38000212.html

IFSW (2008) *International Policy on Health*, Berne: IFSW, www.ifsw.org/en/p38000081.html

Institute for Population Sciences (2007) *National Family Health Survey (NFHS-3) 2005–06: India. Volume I*, Mumbai: International Institute for Population Sciences.

Irwin, A. (2005) 'Tackling the "causes of the causes" of disease and health inequities', www.who.int.intellectualpropertyeventsThemeAAlecIrwin.pdf

JSA (Jan Swasthya Abhiyan) (2006) *Health System in India: Crisis & Alternatives Towards the National Health Assembly II Booklet 2*, New Dehli: Jan Swasthya Abhiyan.

Lakshmi, L. (2001) 'Sex determination tests and female foeticide: Discrimination before birth, abortions in India', *Health Panorama*, no 2, June, CEHAT.

Loveland, E. (2006) 'Towards equality for all: Interview with Nobel Peace Prize Laureate Shirin Ebadi', *International Educator*, July–August, pp 20–33.

Magnussen, L., Ehiri, J. and Jolly, P. (2004) 'Comprehensive versus selective primary health care: Lessons for global health policy', *Health Affairs*, vol 23, no 3, pp 167–76.

Mann, J.M., Gostin, L., Gruskin, S., Brennan, T., Lazzarini, Z. and Fineberg, H. (1999) 'Health and human rights', in J. Mann, S. Gruskin, M.A. Grodin and G.J. Annas (eds), *Health and Human Rights: A Reader*, New York and London: Routledge.

Ministry of Health and Family Welfare (2005) *National Commission on Macroeconomics and Health*, New Dehli: Ministry of Health and Family Welfare.

Motluk, A. (2004) 'US abortion policy: A healthy strategy for whom?', *New Scientist*, 6 October, www.newscientist.com/article.ns?id=dn6485

Narayan, R. (2006) 'The role of the People's Health Movement in putting the social determinants of health on the global agenda', *Health Promotion Journal of Australia*, vol 17, no 3, pp 186–8.

OECD (Organisation for Economic Co-operation and Development) (2004) *Private Health Insurance in OECD Countries*, Paris: OECD.

OHCHR (Office of the High Commissioner for Human Rights) (1965) 'International Convention on the Elimination of all Forms of Racial Discrimination', www.unhchr.ch/html/menu3/b/d_icerd.htm

OHCHR (1976) 'International Covenant on Economic, Social and Cultural Rights', www.unhchr.ch/html/menu3/b/a_cescr.htm

OHCHR (1979) 'Convention on the Elimination of all Forms of Discrimination Against Women', www.unhchr.ch/html/menu3/b/e1cedaw.htm

OHCHR (1989) 'Convention on the Rights of the Child', www2.ohchr.org/english/law/crc.htm

PHM (People's Health Movement) (2008) 'Primary health care remains the best tool to achieve "Health for All" – Interim position by the People's Health Movement', www.phmovement.org/cms/en/node/588

Ress, P. (1997) 'Health care systems for the 21st century', *British Medical Journal*, vol 314, p 1407.

Sama – Resource Group for Women and Health (2005) *Beyond Numbers: Implications of the Two-Child Norm*, New Delhi: Sama.

SEWA (Self Employed Women's Association) (undated) 'SEWA social security', www.sewainsurance.org/childcare.htm#Healthcare

UN (United Nations) (1948) Universal Declaration of Human Rights, www.un.org/Overview/rights.html

UN (1994) 'Programme of action of the United Nations International Conference on Population and Development', para 7.2, www.iisd.ca/Cairo/program/p07002.html

UN (2000) The right to the highest attainable standard of health: 11/08/2000. E/C. 12/2000/4. (General Comments) www.unhchr.ch/tbs/doc.nsf/(symbol)/E.C.12.2000.4.En?OpenDocument

UNICEF and Bernard van Leer Foundation (2006) *A Guide to General Comment 7: Implementing Child Rights in Early Childhood*, The Hague: Bernard van Leer Foundation.

Walsh, J. and Warren, K. (1979) 'Selective primary health care: An interim strategy for disease control in developing countries', *New England Journal of Medicine*, vol 301, no 18, pp 967–74.

WHO (World Health Organization) (1948) *Constitution*, Geneva: WHO.

WHO (1978) Declaration of Alma Ata, www.who.int/hpr/NPH/docs/declaration_almaata.pdf

WHO (1981) *Global Strategy of Health for All by the Year 2000*, Geneva: WHO.

WHO (2002) *25 Questions and Answers on Health and Human Rights: Health and Human Rights Publication Series Issue 1*, Geneva: WHO.

WHO (2007) *Unsafe Abortion: Global and Regional Estimates of Incidence of Unsafe Abortion and Associated Mortality in 2003*, Geneva: WHO.

WHO (2008) 'Primary health care comes full circle', *Bulletin of the World Health Organization*, vol 86, no 10, pp 747–8.

Health, equity and social justice

Stephen M. Rose

Poor living and working conditions impair health and shorten lives. These associations persist well into the late twentieth century, despite marked improvements in living standards and medical care, and are not substantially explained by known biomedical and behavioural risk factors. In both industrialized and less industrialized countries, socioeconomic gradients are apparent for infant mortality, adult mortality, acute and chronic infectious and non-infectious diseases, and psychiatric morbidity. (Krieger et al, 1997, p 343)

Introduction

The link between poverty and illness has been identified for over 200 years. Daly et al (1998, p 315) conclude, 'It has long been known that the socioeconomic status (SES) of an individual is a pervasive and persistent correlate of that individual's health ... the correlation between SES and health is invariably positive and is often best described as a continuous but nonlinear "gradient".' Exposure to toxic living and working environments (Krieger et al, 1997), elevated unrelenting stress found in societies with higher income inequality (Wilkinson, 1997), and underinvestment in human capital (Navarro, 1999; Coburn, 2004) are acknowledged to be evidence-based, fundamental causes of health inequities (Link and Phelan, 1995) as described by the World Health Organization (WHO) in their publication entitled *The Social Determinants of Health: The Solid Facts* (Wilkinson and Marmot, 2003).

Lynch et al (1997) describe the outcome of these 'solid facts': cumulative impact on population health derived from unrelenting immersion in severe economic hardship. They link this cumulative impact over the life course to major deficits in adult physical, cognitive, psychological and social functioning. The connection to elevated levels of morbidity and mortality is equally well-documented (Kaplan et al, 1996; Wilkinson, 1999; Blackwell et al, 2001; Isaacs and Schroeder, 2004). Population health, or its absence, is socially constructed, a historical outcome of the distribution of population wealth. Social work could acknowledge, incorporate and act on the structural sources of harsh, cumulative health impact to advance our advocacy and clinical practices in health.

Acknowledging my standpoint for this discussion, a structural focus, and its link to empowering paradigms for social work practice, has been the purpose of my work for more than 35 years (Rose, 1972; 1990; 1992; 2005; Warren et al, 1974; Rose and Black, 1985). This chapter directs attention to the social causes of chronic disease and possible avenues for social work practice. This focus is required because chronic disease, at least in the US, already accounts for 75% of all health care interactions. While the analysis derives from more advanced capitalist countries, evolving data about such diseases as Type 2 diabetes and coronary heart disease in developing nations (see Chapter 9), suggests a more global relevance may also exist. Clearly, chronic disease incidence replaces communicable diseases as per capita income rises – perhaps a previously unanticipated outcome of global economic colonisation. As Coburn (2004) demonstrates, inequity in population wealth inevitably brings with it a rationalising neoliberal ideology, its reliance on market rather than government intervention and the reallocation of resources needed for human development. Social policy and social welfare benefits and services, globally, will either move in this direction or be challenged. Social work has a role to play in this struggle; the scope, nature and validity of that role depends on the degree to which the profession incorporates population health and the health impact of poverty nationally and globally. As pointed out by Global Health Watch (2007), worldwide, poverty and ill-health are inseparable; income inequality within and between nations contributes to avoidable morbidity and mortality; and both produce breakdowns in social cohesion, redistributive social policies and political participation – all prerequisites for democratic societies.

Conceptualising health: a beginning

Accumulating health impact – the embodiment of inequality or class position (Krieger, 2001a) – leads to higher or lower levels of morbidity, co-morbidities and mortality, disability, and level of responsiveness to health care when it is available. These empirically validated, socially produced outcomes of inequity in the distribution of health suggest the need for a broad definition of health to guide our thinking as social workers practising in health.

Conceptualising health is a daunting but necessary task for social work to enhance our role in health policy, research and practice (Graham, 2002). Studies in social epidemiology (Kuh and Ben Shlomo, 1997; Krieger, 2001a; 2001b; Kawachi, 2002) demonstrate that population health and societal patterns of distributing wealth are indivisible (Feachem, 2000; Marmot, 2002). Health, like wealth, is distributed in gradients (Gorin, 2000; Wilkinson and Marmot, 2003). Gradients in health closely parallel each society's historically evolved form of distributing resources necessary for human development and well-being. Access to health care, while vitally important in the lives of individuals and families, does not significantly overcome inequality in the distribution of wealth or its impact on population health. Isaacs and Schroeder found that, 'Medical care has been estimated to account for only about 10 to 15% of the nation's premature deaths. Thus, ensuring adequate medical care for all will have only a limited effect on the nation's health' (2004, p 1141). Further, Poulton et al (2002), studying the impact of children's exposure to socio-economic disadvantage on adult health in the UK, concluded that there was a detrimental impact on physical, dental and mental health despite a universally accessible and subsidised health care system.

The unequal distribution of material and psychosocial resources and their impact are also unveiled in the differential development and scope of various welfare state investments in human capital (Kawachi et al, 1999; Coburn, 2000; 2004). Societies with lower income inequality gaps have higher levels of investment in health and human services, entitlement programmes and support systems. Health at the population level reflects these interacting societal-scale forces.

This conceptualisation of health is significantly influenced by the work of Krieger (Krieger et al, 1993; 1997; Krieger, 1994; 1999; 2001a; 2001b). She proposes a social epidemiological framework (2001a, p 695) to best understand the wealth–health relationship: 'Lifecourse perspective refers to how health status at any given age, for a given birth cohort, reflects not only contemporary conditions but embodiment of prior living circumstances, in utero onwards.' Additional influences shaping our understanding of health come from other theorists and empirical researchers operating within the same paradigm (Bosma et al, 1999; Holland et al, 2000; Graham, 2002; Halfon and Hochstein, 2002).

A social epidemiological perspective views health as far greater than the presence or absence of disease or access to health care. Its focus, instead, 'is distinguished by its insistence on explicitly investigating social determinants of population distributions of health, disease, and well-being rather than treating such determinants as mere background to biomedical phenomena' (Krieger, 2001b, p 693). Krieger (2001a) transforms individual patient data covering descriptive demographics (for example, age, gender, ethnicity, income, education) and medical-diagnostics from 'mere background information' to the forefront for health professionals' attention (Krieger et al, 1997). This transformation, designed to acknowledge and measure population health, is critical.

Inattention to fundamental structural causes of inequality (Blane et al, 1990; Link and Phelan, 1995) produces an inability to address primary prevention. Additionally, inattention to the life course framework for research and policy development (see Graham, 2002) minimises social work's potential role in health policy, planning and service design.

Inequality and inequity: defining health in social justice terms

Societal patterns of inequality in the distribution of health, income or any other vitally needed resource for human development that persists over time are inequitable (Braverman et al, 2001; Braverman, 2002). Inequity produces patterns of inequality in the distribution of morbidity, co-morbidities, the burden of disease and eventual mortality (Blane et al, 1990; Kawachi and Kennedy, 1997).

Parallel outcomes occur in psychosocial development: harsh exposure to negative environments, particularly in early childhood, have been shown to impair one's sense of self-efficacy (Bandura, 1986; Siegrist and Marmot, 2004), self-esteem and internal locus of control (Kristenson et al, 2004). These impairments obstruct development of the prerequisites for optimal participation in the self-management aspect of chronic illness care – or the primary ingredients for optimal chronic disease management, a point we will consider below.

From this social justice framework, the inequitable distribution of wealth and human resources constitutes an imposed burden of disease and premature death, including the amount and extent or burden of human suffering and the number of years of productive life lost. This pattern precedes and transcends the issue of equity in access to medical care. A substantial amount of sickness and death is avoidable; philosophically, from the standpoint of social justice, it also is fundamentally amoral. Population health, as a cornerstone of social justice, requires social work attention. Social work, concurrently, requires input from social epidemiology to actualise our commitment to social justice.

Population distributions of health: strengthening the dual focus for social work

Focusing on population distributions of health emphasises the need to see health as a political and economic issue – how can we best understand the inequitable distributions of health embedded in the client populations served by social work? Health, in this view, is an outcome: it results from the prevailing relations of production and distribution of a society's resources. Krieger (2001a, p 668) says that the fundamental question is: 'Who and what is responsible for population patterns of health, disease, and wellbeing, as manifested in past, present, and changing social inequalities in health?'

Health is a condition that simultaneously applies to populations and individuals as well as to the social context of their lives. This certainty lodges population health well within the social work profession's long-standing claim to hold a dual (macro/micro) perspective. This can be most clearly seen in Krieger's (2001a; 2001b) concept of embodiment.

Embodiment: a concept for social work theorising

The political and economic context of life is embodied in people's lives. Embodiment is 'a concept referring to how we literally incorporate, biologically, the material and social world in which we live, from in utero to death; a corollary is that no aspect of our biology can be understood [in the absence of] knowledge of history and individual and societal ways of living' (Krieger, 2001b, p 694). Physiological and/or emotional conditions are not unidimensional states; rather, they are multi-level relationships (see Brunner et al, 1996). Lynch (2000) describes this indivisible self–class–society relationship: people live their class positions (as well as ethnicity, gender or other forms of structural patterns of discrimination) of privilege or exclusion in the distribution of those needed resources for living and participating in society through and in their biological beings. People's bodies contain the cumulative impact of their material existence and its meaning.

Health risk behaviours of individuals are inseparable from the circumstances in which their lives are embedded (Lynch et al, 1997; Lawlor et al, 2003). They represent coping mechanisms or adaptations to damaging, imposed social environments. This conceptualisation resonates with social work's interests in resilience and clients' strengths.

Hierarchically organised societies, where status is attached to wealth, where poverty and pejorative judgements about it pervade many lives, and where the gap between the rich and the poor is great or growing, produce inequitable gradients of health risk behaviours and health outcomes (Wilkinson, 1999; Marmot, 2002). These behaviours contribute to gradients in morbidity and mortality regardless of the average standard of living in any given country (Wilkinson, 1997; 1999; Kawachi and Kennedy, 1999). They are becoming more visible recently in data identifying growing chronic illness rates in developing countries.

As Wilkinson (in Kawachi and Kennedy, 1999, p 215) notes: 'the greater the gap between the rich and poor, the worse the health status of citizens'. Everyone, regardless of socio-economic position, reflects the impact of the inequitable distribution of wealth in their own health. Health, as such, is an indivisible social relational component of society, not solely a property of individuals and their behaviours (Raphael, 2002).

Pathways of embodiment

Equally important from this perspective are the *pathways of embodiment* or the processes through which hierarchies of power and property create constraints on and/or possibilities for our health. This is a complex issue over which there is very active debate in the literature of social epidemiology. At its core is the issue that Krieger (2001a) raises about the interaction or bio-psychosocial processes of internalising or embodying inequality in the distribution of material needs and their meaning to personal development. Many researchers in the field of income inequality perceive this internalisation to result in heightened susceptibility to illness as a product of omnipresent stressors that exert negative impacts on individuals in direct proportion to their socio-economic status.

McEwen (1998) and Seeman et al (1997) document the interaction between exposure to poverty, its meaning and expression in the form of impact from stressors. Exposure to poverty or family violence can be directly pathogenic, not just related to later susceptibility to stress-induced illness arising from psychosocial influences. McEwen's (1998; 1999; 2000) concept of allostatic load describes the cumulative impact or wear-and-tear on the body from responding to chronic stress. The result is a vulnerability of the immune system that demonstrates the cumulative, long-term impact of deprivation and reflects embodied inequity and suffering from it (see also Brunner et al, 1996; Hertzman and Wiens, 1996). The impact has direct consequences for physiological, social and emotional functioning – key indicators of acuity of disease, co-morbidities and potential outcomes of care.

An alternative paradigm for health

In 1998, the World Health Assembly of the WHO reaffirmed its conception of health: 'the enjoyment of the highest attainable standard of health is one of the fundamental rights of every human being; in doing so, we affirm the dignity and worth of every person, and the equal rights, equal duties and shared responsibilities of all for health' (WHO, 1998, para 1). This assertion led Halfon and Hochstein (2002, p 435) to conclude: 'Our view of disease causation and predisease pathways has (also) broadened, as it has become clear that health risks are created and maintained by social systems and that the magnitude of those risks is largely a function of socioeconomic disparities and psychosocial gradients.'

The realisation of health depends on the degree to which health-promoting or health-obstructing social structural and political-economic preconditions exist. This understanding of health provides social work with the possibility to measure or assess the extent to which governments are moving towards health promotion or away from it. Daly et al (1998) concluded that an inequitable income distribution may be associated with a set of economic, political, social and institutional processes that reflect a systematic underinvestment in human, physical, health and social infrastructures. The authors believe that: 'political units that tolerate a high degree of income inequality are less likely to support the human, physical, cultural, civic, and health resources needed to maximize the health of their populations' (1998, p 319). Social work's self-interest as a profession, as well as our integrity as it relates to our value base, is tied to this level of analysis.

Equally important, however, are issues that occur at the clinical level. If health is considerably broader than the absence of physical illness or injury, health care can be seen in a similar light. The multifaceted human beings we treat require multi-level interventions to respond to whatever the accumulated impact of their life or embodied stressors have been. Recognition of population-based needs of vulnerable groups could be a social work strength, an asset that we bring to emerging chronic illness care models (see Katon et al, 1999) as it reflects our dedication to cultural diversity and cultural competence.

Very often, as we are now seeing in such chronic illness models as collaborative care (see Anderson, 1996; Aubert et al, 1998; Center for the Advancement of Health, 1999; Katon et al, 1999; Holman and Lorig, 2000, among others), multidisciplinary teams that address the patient as a partner in the illness management and healing process produce evidence-based outcomes far beyond normal medical intervention. Evidence-based research measuring the positive impact of these teams is growing (Anderson, 1996; Von Korff et al, 1997; Aubert et al 1998; Gruman and Von Korff, 1999; Friedrich, 2000; Holman and Lorig, 2000; Von Korff, 2000; Wagner, 2000; Mauksch et al, 2001).

Unfortunately, social work rarely appears in the literature of collaborative care teams (see Sommers et al, 2000, for an exception). Typically, these teams are comprised of physicians, nurses, health educators or another provider of self-management skills education. This reflects the medicalisation of the team's focus – still intent on building a more willing, if somewhat disguised, compliance or adherence regimen. We need to identify population-based evidence to demonstrate an array of population-specific needs for supports far beyond those typically envisioned as part of patient care, for example, related to histories of abuse and trauma, material deprivation in the past and present, social conditions impairing efforts to lose weight or quit smoking, and failures to provide adequate nutrition, clean water or clean up environmental toxins. Siegrist and Marmot (2004) demonstrate the impact of these social conditions or negative psychosocial environments: a lowered sense of self-efficacy, lowered self-esteem and a firm belief in extrinsic locus of control. These embodied characteristics impair people's capacities to participate in self-management of care, to challenge their own involvement with health risk behaviours, or to act on behalf of their own health. Social work's experience with empowering practice (see Rose and Black, 1985; Rose, 1992; 2005, among many others) perfectly positions us to participate in chronic or collaborative care because our practice knowledge and wisdom contain the precise knowledge and skills to confront these socially imposed, yet modifiable, conditions. Empowering chronic illness patients involves turning identification of medical concerns and co-development of every medical decision over to them; documenting and demonstrating their active involvement in their own social production of health-promoting decisions, actions and follow-up; and active participation in mutual aid groups based on clients' commitment to self-help.

Conclusion

Social work has the opportunity to assert our relevance to evolving forms of health policy and health care delivery. Doing so requires that we refocus our attention on the relationship between health, equity and social justice. An alternative theory and research base that includes social epidemiology can contribute to revitalised advocacy for appropriate patient care and for our enhanced involvement in primary prevention. Equally important, globally and locally, is challenging neoliberal reliance on market solutions, whether these exist as forms of privatising health care or World Trade Organization involvement in promoting poverty.

Empowering theories of practice at the clinical or direct service level that are grounded in social epidemiological theory and evidence embody social justice and embed it in health and mental health services. They provide the opportunity for social work leadership and professional survival, particularly with vulnerable population groups.

References

Anderson, J. (1996) 'Empowering patients: Issues and strategies', *Social Science and Medicine*, vol 43, no 5, pp 697–705.

Aubert, R., Herman, W., Waters, J., Moore, W., Sutton, D., Peterson, B., Bailey, C. and Koplan, J. (1998) 'Nurse case management to improve glycemic control in diabetic patients in a health maintenance organization: A randomized, controlled trial', *Annals of Internal Medicine*, vol 129, no 8, pp 605–12.

Bandura, A. (1986) *Social Foundations of Thought and Action: A Social Cognitive Theory*, Englewood Cliffs, NJ: Prentice-Hall.

Blackwell, D., Hayward, M. and Crimmins, E. (2001) 'Does childhood health affect chronic morbidity in later life?', *Social Science and Medicine*, vol 52, pp 1269–84.

Blane, D., Davey Smith, G. and Bartley, M. (1990) 'Social class differences in years of potential life lost: Size, trends, and principal causes', *British Medical Journal*, vol 301, pp 429–32.

Bosma, H., van de Mheen, H. and Mackenbach, J. (1999) 'Social class in childhood and general health in adulthood: Questionnaire study of contribution of psychological attributes', *British Medical Journal*, vol 318, pp 18–22.

Braverman, P. (2002) 'Measuring health equity within countries: The challenge of limited information', *Journal of the American Medical Association*, vol 288, no 13, pp 1650–57.

Braverman, P., Starfield, B. and Geiger, H. (2001) 'World Health Report 2000: How it removes equity from the agenda for public health monitoring and policy', *British Medical Journal*, vol 323, pp 678–81.

Brunner, E., Davey Smith, G., Marmot, M., Canner, R., Beksinska, M. and O'Brian, J. (1996) 'Childhood social circumstances and psychosocial and behavioural factors as determinants of plasma fibrinogen', *Lancet*, vol 347, pp 1008–113.

Center for the Advancement of Health (1999) *Patients as Effective Collaborators in Managing Chronic Conditions*, New York: Milbank Memorial Fund.

Coburn, D. (2000) 'Income, inequality, social cohesion and the health status of populations: The role of neo-liberalism', *Social Science and Medicine*, vol 51, pp 139–50.

Coburn, D. (2004) 'Beyond the income inequality hypothesis: Class, neo-liberalism, and health inequalities', *Social Science and Medicine*, vol 58, pp 41–56.

Daly, M., Duncan, G., Kaplan, G. and Lynch, J. (1998) 'Macro-to-micro links in the relation between income inequality and mortality', *The Milbank Quarterly*, vol 76, no 3, pp 315–39.

Feachem, R. (2000) 'Poverty and inequity: A proper focus for the new century', *Bulletin of the World Health Organization*, vol 78, p 1.

Friedrich, M. (2000) 'Enhancing diabetes care in a low-income, high-risk population', *Journal of the American Medical Association*, vol 283, p 4.

Global Health Watch (2007) *Global Health Action 2005–2006*, New York: Global Health Watch, www.ghwatch.org/2005report/GlobalHealthAction0506.pdf

Gorin, S. (2000) 'Inequality and health: Implications for social work', *Health and Social Work*, vol 25, no 4, pp 270–5.

Graham, H. (2002) 'Building an inter-disciplinary science of health inequalities: The example of lifecourse research', *Social Science and Medicine*, vol 55, pp 2005–16.

Gruman, J. and Von Korff, M. (1999) 'Self-management services: Their role in disease management', *Actis International Limited*, vol 6, no 3, pp 151–8.

Halfon, N. and Hochstein, M. (2002) 'Life course health development: An integrated framework for developing health, policy and research', *The Milbank Quarterly*, vol 80, no 3, pp 433–80.

Hertzman, C. and Wiens, M. (1996) 'Child development and long-term outcomes: A population health perspective and summary of successful interventions', *Social Science and Medicine*, vol 43, no 7, pp 1083–95.

Holland, P., Berney, L., Blane, D., Davey Smith, G., Gunnell, D. and Montgomery, S.M. (2000) 'Life course accumulation of disadvantage: Childhood health and hazard exposure during adulthood', *Social Science and Medicine*, vol 50, pp 1285–95.

Holman, H. and Lorig, K. (2000) 'Patients as partners in managing chronic disease', *British Medical Journal*, vol 320, pp 526–7.

Isaacs, S. and Schroeder, S. (2004) 'Class – The ignored determinant of the nation's health', *New England Journal of Medicine*, vol 351, no 11, pp 1137–42.

Kaplan, G., Pamuk, E., Lynch, J., Cohen, R. and Balfour, J. (1996) 'Inequality in income and mortality in the United States: Analysis of mortality and potential pathways', *British Medical Journal*, vol 312, pp 999–1003.

Katon, W., Von Korff, M., Lin, E., Simon, G., Walker, E., Unutzer, J., Bush, T., Russo, J. and Ludman, E. (1999) 'Stepped collaborative care for primary care patients with persistent symptoms of depression: A randomized trial', *Archives of General Psychiatry*, vol 56, pp 1109–15.

Kawachi, I. (2002) 'What is social epidemiology?', *Social Science and Medicine*, vol 54, pp 1739–41.

Kawachi, I. and Kennedy, B. (1997) 'The relationship of income inequality to mortality: Does the choice of indicator matter?', *Social Science and Medicine*, vol 45, pp 1121–7.

Kawachi, I. and Kennedy, B. (1999) 'Income inequality and health: Pathways and mechanisms', *Health Services Research*, vol 34, no 1, pp 215–27.

Kawachi, I., Kennedy, B. and Wilkinson, R. (eds) (1999) *The Society and Population Health Reader: Income Inequality and Health*, New York: The New Press.

Krieger, N. (1994) 'Epidemiology and the web of causation: Has anyone seen the spider?', *Social Science and Medicine*, vol 39, no 7, pp 887–903.

Krieger, N. (1999) 'Embodying inequality: A review of concepts, measures, and methods for studying health consequences of discrimination', *International Journal of Health Services*, vol 29, pp 295–352.

Krieger, N. (2001a) 'Theories for social epidemiology in the 21st century: An ecosocial perspective', *International Journal of Epidemiology*, vol 30, pp 668–77.

Krieger, N. (2001b) 'A glossary for social epidemiology', *Journal of Epidemiology and Community Health*, vol 55, pp 693–700.

Krieger, N., Rowley, D., Herman, A., Avery, B. and Phillips, M. (1993) 'Racism, sexism, and social class: Implications for studies of health, disease, and well-being', *American Journal of Preventive Medicine*, vol 9, no 6, supplement, pp 82–122.

Krieger, N., Williams, D. and Moss, N. (1997) 'Measuring social class in US public health research: Concepts, methodologies, guidelines', *Annual Review of Public Health*, vol 18, pp 341–78.

Kristenson, M., Eriksen, H., Sluiter, J. and Urson, H. (2004) 'Psychobiological mechanisms of socioeconomic differences in health', *Social Science and Medicine*, vol 58, no 8, pp 1511–22.

Kuh, D. and Ben-Shlomo, Y. (eds) (1997) *A Lifecourse Approach to Chronic Disease Epidemiology: Tracing the Origins of Ill-Health from Early to Adult Life*, Oxford: Oxford University Press.

Lawlor, D., Frankel, S., Shaw, M., Ebrahim, S. and Davey Smith, D. (2003) 'Smoking and ill health: Does lay epidemiology explain the failure of smoking cessation programs among deprived populations?', *American Journal of Public Health*, vol 93, no 2, pp 266–70.

Link, B. and Phelan, J. (1995) 'Social conditions as fundamental causes of disease', *Journal of Health and Social Behavior*, Extra Issue, pp 80–94.

Lynch, J. (2000) 'Income inequality and health: Expanding the debate', *Social Science and Medicine*, vol 51, pp 1001–5.

Lynch, J., Kaplan, G. and Salonen, J. (1997) 'Why do poor people behave poorly? Variation in adult health behaviors and psychosocial characteristics by stages of socioeconomic life course', *Social Science and Medicine*, vol 44, no 16, pp 809–19.

Marmot, M. (2002) 'The influence of income on health: Views of an epidemiologist', *Health Affairs*, March/April, pp 31–46.

Mauksch, L., Tucker, S., Katon, W., Russo, J., Cameron, J., Walker, E. and Spitzer, R. (2001) 'Mental illness, functional impairment, and patient preferences for collaborative care in an uninsured, primary care population', *Journal of Family Practice*, vol 50, pp 41–7.

McEwen, B. (1998) 'Protective and damaging effects of stress mediators', *Journal of the American Medical Association*, vol 338, no 3, pp 171–9.

McEwen, B. (1999) 'Stress, adaptation, and disease: Allostasis and allostatic load', *Annals of the New York Academy of Sciences*, vol 840, pp 33–44.

McEwen, B. (2000) 'Allostasis and allostatic load: Implications for neuropsychopharmacology', *Neuropsychopharmacology*, vol 22, no 2, pp 108–24.

Navarro, V. (1999) 'Health and equity in the world in the era of globalization', *International Journal of Health Services*, vol 29, no 2, pp 215–26.

Poulton, R., Caspi, A., Milne, B., Thomson, W., Taylor, A., Sears, M. and Moffitt, T. (2002) 'Association between children's experience of socioeconomic disadvantage and adult health: A life-course study', *The Lancet*, vol 360, pp 1640–5.

Raphael, D. (2002) *Social Justice is Good for Our Hearts: Why Societal Factors – Not Lifestyles – are Major Causes of Heart Disease in Canada and Elsewhere*, Toronto: CSJ Foundation for Research and Education.

Rose, S. (1972) *Betrayal of the Poor*, Boston: Schenkman Publishing Co.

Rose, S. (1990) 'Advocacy/empowerment: An approach to clinical practice for social work', *Journal of Sociology and Social Welfare*, vol 17, no 2, pp 41–52.

Rose, S. (1992) *Case Management and Social Work Practice*, New York: Longman.

Rose, S. (2005) 'Empowerment – The foundation for social work practice in mental health', in S. Kirk (ed) *Mental Disorders in the Social Environment*, New York: Columbia University Press, pp 190–200.

Rose, S. and Black, B. (1985) *Advocacy and Empowerment: Mental Health Care in the Community*, London and Boston: Routledge and Kegan Paul.

Seeman, T., Singer, B., Rowe, J., Horowitz, R. and McEwen, B. (1997) 'Price of adaptation – Allostatic load and its health consequences. MacArthur studies of successful aging', *Archives of Internal Medicine*, vol 157, no 19, pp 2259–68.

Siegrist, J. and Marmot, M. (2004) 'Health inequalities and the psychosocial environment – Two scientific challenges', *Social Science and Medicine*, vol 58, pp 1463–73.

Sommers, L., Marton, K., Barbaccia, J. and Randolph, J. (2000) 'Physician, nurse, and social worker collaboration in primary care for chronically ill seniors', *Archives of Internal Medicine*, vol 160, pp 1825–33.

Von Korff, M. (2000) 'Individualized stepped care of chronic illness', *Western Journal of Medicine*, vol 172, pp 133–7.

Von Korff, M., Gruman, J., Schaefer, J., Curry, S. and Wagner, E. (1997) 'Collaborative management of chronic illness', *Annals of Internal Medicine*, vol 127, no 7, pp 1097–102.

Wagner, E. (2000) 'The role of patient care teams in chronic disease management', *British Medical Journal*, vol 320, pp 569–72.

Warren, R., Rose, S. and Bergunder, A. (1974) *The Structure of Urban Reform*, New York: Lexington.

WHO (World Health Organization) (1998) *Health-for-All Policy for the Twenty-first Century*, Geneva: WHO.

Wilkinson, R. (1997) 'Commentary: Income inequality summarizes the health burden of individual relative deprivation', *British Medical Journal*, vol 314, pp 1727–8.

Wilkinson, R. (1999) 'Health, hierarchy, and social anxiety', *Annals of the New York Academy of Science*, vol 896, pp 48–63.

Wilkinson, R. and Marmot, M. (2003) *The Social Determinants of Health: The Solid Facts*, Geneva: The World Health Organization.

Health and the environment

Margaret Alston

Introduction

The environment is under more sustained threat from human activity in the 21st century than at any other time in history with extensive potential social and health consequences. Human health, broadly defined, encompassing physical, mental and spiritual dimensions, is highly dependent on the context in which we live. Any threat to our environmental certainties, therefore, has a significant impact on human well-being. However, the environmental threats now faced by the whole human race are more significant than any previously known. While health remains a significant focus of practice for social workers (Browne, 2005), links between these global environmental concerns and health outcomes have rarely featured in social work discourse. This is despite a long-standing recognition of the impact of the local environment (especially housing) on people's health (for example, Shaw et al, 1998; Brafield and Eckersley, 2007). The environmental conditions into which children are born and which influence both the length and the quality of their adult life are one of the key mechanisms which generate inequalities in health (Wilkinson and Marmot, 2003).

As a social work researcher specialising in exploring the social conditions of rural people, I have become increasingly concerned about the plight of Australians experiencing the deleterious effects of the long-running drought of the 2000s. During the same period there has been a new global awareness of environmental degradation leading to climate change. The link between the drought and climate change led me to research the social and health impacts of the Australian drought and to place it in the context of global climate change research.

Climate change, or climate variability, results primarily from increased carbon dioxide in the atmosphere and refers to changes in weather patterns including rising temperatures which are melting the earth's ice caps and causing more extreme weather events such as flooding and drought (Australian Farm Institute, 2007; IPCC, 2007). Globally, variability in weather patterns and large-scale environmental events such as the tsunami in Indonesia, Sri Lanka, Bhutan and Bangladesh, flooding in the Indian sub-continent, New Orleans and Myanmar/ Burma, desertification in Africa and drought in Australia are disturbingly frequent and intense. These disasters have led to increasing international concerns that they may be a consequence of climate change/variability and that cataclysmic events may therefore continue and escalate. Not only is climate change already leading to changes in agricultural productivity with resultant impacts on food security, water access and nutrition, it will increasingly impact on economies and services (McMichael, 2003; IPCC, 2007) with flow-on effects to much of the world's population and their health (FAO, 2007).

Just as important as the environmental manifestations of climate change are the likely and widespread people movements and resultant repercussions for humanity. Yet, to date, the climate change debate has been dominated by environmental and economic rather than health and human rights concerns (for example, Stern, 2007). This narrow focus ignores the links between environmental changes and health, and between environmental changes and social and health inequalities. Crudely, those people who have greater income and wealth have both a greater carbon footprint and are in a better position to protect themselves against the impact of climate change on their standard of living and their health. For those with few resources, having little personal global environmental impact, even marginal changes, for example in water for agriculture or in food prices, have devastating consequences, as the growing number of recent food riots testify (Borger, 2008). I argue that this is an area where we as social workers have a significant role to play in bringing the voice and concerns of the people most affected to the international debate on the environment and climate change. There are numerous ways we might do this including joining social movements, assisting in crisis situations, advocating on behalf of those most affected, publicising the deleterious effects of climate change and assisting with shaping policy responses. Additionally we can also act to change the discourse of catastrophe to include information collected through social work research that focuses on people and their situations, their health consequences and human rights expectations.

In this chapter I provide a brief outline of climate change and its social consequences. Space limitations allow me to do little more than provide a sketch of the global realities of climate change. I, therefore, draw largely on the particular social and health impacts on Australians consequent on drought and the links between the local situation and the global construction of climate change. The research has given me the opportunity to walk for a while in the shoes of those on the front line of climate change, to hear their stories and broken dreams, and to know the resilience of the human spirit. Yet I note that global humanitarian responses to climate change have been largely crisis-driven, and this leads me finally to examine a long-term role for social work in this new world of environmental uncertainty.

Climate change and variability

It is arguable that the earth has been irreversibly changed by human activity and production techniques such as the burning of fossil fuels, production of mining waste and overuse of agricultural chemicals. These practices have caused ground and air pollution, groundwater contamination, contaminated fish stocks and the destruction of wildlife corridors placing significant pressures on the environment (McMichael, 2003). Climate change and/or variability results from these activities primarily because they deliver increased levels of carbon dioxide into the atmosphere (IPCC, 2007).

The United Nations Intergovernmental Panel on Climate Change (IPCC, 2007) notes there has been an increase in greenhouse gas emissions of 70% between 1970 and 2004 and that these are likely to grow by up to a further 110% by 2030. These emissions have resulted in global warming with consequential increases in average air and sea temperature, widespread melting of snow and ice and rising sea levels (Working Group 1 of the IPCC, 2007). As a result there have not only been incremental changes in climate typified by increasing periods of droughts, heavy rain, heatwaves and more intense tropical cyclones (Working Group 1 of the IPCC, 2007), but also in cataclysmic events such as floods.

Examples of the incremental changes include increasing desertification in Africa which is affecting the livelihood and well-being of many subsistence families in Africa (FAO, 2007). Desertification refers to the process of the spread of desert conditions into surrounding arid lands and is largely irreversible. The causes of desertification are said to be human activity, increased livestock grazing and climate change. It is strongly linked to poverty because of the need for people to over-exploit the land and leads inevitably to major threats to food security in these regions (UNCCD, 2007). Predictions are that desertification will increase in areas of Africa and that much arable land in developing countries will be lost (FAO, 2007).

The long-running Australian drought is another example of incremental climate change which has had devastating impacts on people (Alston and Kent, 2004; 2006). This drought is unlike any experienced in the recorded history of the continent and has been variously described as 'one of the most severe in the last 100 years' (Howard, 2002) or 'more typical of a one in a 1,000-year drought' (Vidal, 2006). The Australian drought has been unique in its severity because its impact has been across the entire continent. It has been typified by a lack of rain as well as a rise in average temperatures of up to 1.6 degrees (Lindesay, 2003) and has cost the country several billion dollars in lost production (Botterill and Fisher, 2003). While these figures have been readily available, assessing the human consequences of these events was more difficult and led to our research on drought and its social consequences (Alston and Kent, 2004; 2006).

By contrast, cataclysmic events are also evident around the world and arguably the social consequences are more evident because they are immediate. One of the most dramatic in recent times was an earthquake in the Indian Ocean in 2004 which led to widespread tsunamis along the coastlines of several countries bordering the Indian Ocean. Up to a quarter of a million people in Indonesia, Sri Lanka, Thailand and India were killed and their coastal communities devastated (Van Rooyen and Leaning, 2005). Speaking after the event Britain's chief scientist had no restraint in linking the event to climate change noting that this threat to the world's population is caused by our insatiable appetite for fossil fuels (Press Association, 2004).

Further major catastrophic events have occurred across the globe in the past decade. For example, floods devastated large parts of India and neighbouring countries in 2000 and killed at least 300 people and left over five million people homeless in India, Nepal, Bhutan and Bangladesh (Peris, 2000). Again this event has been linked to climate change by various bodies including the Red Cross in its annual report on global disasters (Red Cross, 2000). The increasing frequency and severity of both incremental and cataclysmic events is causing significant social and health crises both at national and global levels.

Social and health impacts of climate change

Perhaps the most disturbing consequence – the 'sleeping giant' of climate change – is the likely long-term impact on access to food and water. Food security is defined by the World Bank (1986, p 1) as 'access by all people at all times to enough food for an active, healthy life'. Climate change poses a real threat to world food security with estimates that the number of hungry and malnourished people will rise by more than 10% in the coming decade and will exacerbate poverty among the most vulnerable (FAO, 2007). Lee (2002) suggests that those disproportionately affected by environmental catastrophes are people of colour, tribal communities and people from disadvantaged socio-economic groups. Further, because women make up the majority of the agricultural workforce in these countries there is a significant gendered element to the burden of climate change. FAO (2007) predicts that climate change is likely to have the most significant impact on poor women in rural areas of developing countries.

What is common with both incremental climate change and cataclysmic events is that there are major impacts on health and well-being. In the developing countries where flooding and desertification have had devastating environmental consequences, there have been significant mortality rates, malnutrition and disease. In the developed countries, such as Australia, the effects of drought include higher morbidity rates and increases in mental health consequences (Alston and Kent, 2004; 2006). Our research on drought showed that while rural people experienced poorer health and well-being on a number of criteria prior to drought, this event had exacerbated these inequalities. In particular, we noted that the drought had increased health inequalities and had significant impacts on the mental health of rural people. Older people and children are particularly affected and there are very evident levels of alienation and disaffection (Alston and Kent, 2004; 2006). At the same time neoliberal policy developments such as the introduction of user-pays principles, privatisation and regionalisation have reduced rural people's access to health services. Our research and the advocacy that followed its publication led to widespread publicity in the media and a new community awareness of the drought's impacts on people. There were also global extensions to the research as it led to collaborations through the UN's Food and Agricultural Organization in Rome in a research proposal examining the gendered impacts of climate change across several countries.

In both developing and developed countries climate change has resulted in an increase in the number of people who are socially excluded, lacking the ability to fully participate in society through no fault of their own (Burchardt, 2000). This underclass (Shucksmith, 2004), so evident in rural and outer urban areas of developed countries, and in refugee camps across the world, breeds discontent, a strong sense of alienation and despair (Valtonen, 1998; Alston and Kent, 2004). Food riots by people whose poverty means that rising food prices cannot be accommodated have been reported in 37 countries during the first five months of 2008, with UN crisis talks set up to prevent what some view as a greater threat to world stability and security than terrorism (Borger, 2008).

In both developed and developing countries affected by cataclysmic events there are other observed commonalities. These include large-scale population shifts. In developing countries this may mean mass migrations as people escape famine and reduced access to water by fleeing to neighbouring countries or refugee camps. In developed countries such as Australia the movement of people away from drought-affected rural areas is also an escape, but one that in the short term involves leaving communities of high unemployment and reduced income for the greater opportunities offered by the capital cities and coastal regions (Salt, 2001).

Rising levels of poverty are also a common and widespread consequence of major cataclysmic events. In Australia for example, low rural incomes are significantly exacerbated by drought conditions (Stehlik et al, 1999; Alston and Kent, 2004). In developing countries increasing poverty is inextricably linked to climate change and declining access to productive land and water (FAO, 2007). In the developing world increasing poverty is linked to malnourishment, disease, a lack of education and death – an estimated six million children under five die as a result of hunger each year (Care, 2007). My own research across drought-affected parts of Australia indicates that the health effects include stress-related illnesses, higher levels of morbidity and increased mental health impacts (Alston and Kent, 2004).

While health consequences of major events are evident, those resulting from incremental climate change are not as visible but just as deadly. Across the world climate change is predicted to have direct health effects as a result of changes in exposure to extremes of weather (heatwaves or cold snaps); increased production of airborne pollutants and aeroallergens; and indirect effects as a result of the transmission of water and airborne infectious diseases such as malaria and cholera; decreased food production yields both on land and in the sea; decreased access to fresh water; and loss of biodiversity (McMichael, 2003). Climate change events which destabilise agricultural areas can only exacerbate these conditions.

Why are people silenced? Why a need for social work?

When addressing the issue of the silencing of local populations it is instructive to differentiate between: a) areas where there have been catastrophic climate events; b) areas dependent on environmentally destructive practices which create greenhouse gas emissions into the environment – the precursor of climate change; and c) those suffering the results of incremental climate change. A distinction can be drawn between the humanitarian responses that usually follow catastrophic events and responses to more insidious outcomes of environmental degradation and climate change.

Cataclysmic events tend to result in a significant mobilisation of international humanitarian activity. Post-tsunami, for example, the laudatory worldwide response from agencies from the UN down to the smallest non-government organisation was such that there were significant bottlenecks at airports and on the ground and aid was slow getting to the people most affected (Barker, 2004). The more dramatic the event and the more publicity it is given, the more likely that the world will respond in kind. Sometimes, however because of the ad hoc nature of the relief, the response can be inappropriate. For example, post-tsunami, Sri Lanka's Foreign Minister, Laxman Kadirgamar, noted that one container of aid had contained only teddy bears (BBC, 2005).

In areas where environments are contaminated as a result of our insatiable demand for fossil fuels or because of unsustainable industrial processes, people nonetheless need to find work and it is this need that leads people to overlook both the environmentally destructive practices and the long-term health consequences. Because of the significance of these industries to local economies, the impact of their activities on the environment and the health of the people are largely ignored both within the countries themselves and in the international arena. Space limitations allow me only one example of environmental 'dead' zones to illustrate the silencing of the local populations.

The region along the Mississippi Delta in the US has more than 50 petrochemical plants and is euphemistically called 'chemical alley' or 'cancer alley' because it has one of the highest rates of cancer deaths in the country. Because people are dependent on the companies for employment, their ability to address the health consequences flowing from the plants is reduced and people and their governments remain silent on the obvious health impacts (Griscam Little, 2005).

In areas slowly strangled by environmentally destructive practices, as in those affected by incremental climate change events such as drought, humanitarian responses are not so evident. If the event takes place over a long period of time – for example 'chemical alley', the Australian drought or desertification in Africa – there is less world attention and less likelihood that a similar response will occur. In the vast drought-affected areas of rural Australia, our research reveals that people have been silenced by the slow drip of change, the steady but inevitable slide into poverty and the erosion of personal expectations and community cohesion leading to significant health and mental health consequences (Alston and Kent, 2004; 2006).

This slow erosion of health and well-being that takes place over a long period of time produces a less dramatic media event despite it being no less worthy of attention. The widespread health consequences of the drought did not result in world aid into Australia and policy responses even at national levels were slow in addressing the issues. The consequence is that aid for incremental climate change events can be at best patchy, ad hoc and crisis-driven. This suggests the need for attention to the likely long-term health and human rights impacts of environmental degradation and climate change – an area where social work could provide a global lead.

The need to bring the concerns of the people most affected to the debate on the environment and climate change is evident. Social workers, working in the international arena, have the skills to mobilise people, to advocate on their behalf and to lobby for health and human rights outcomes to be part of the environmental debate.

The social work role

Individual social workers have been prominent in the humanitarian responses to catastrophic events and in aid agencies. However, social work involvement in more long-term attention to the consequences of environmental destruction and climate change is not so evident. This may well be because public health concerns and the institutional structures that address them – the places where social workers are found in large numbers – have had little engagement with environmental agencies. As a result there is a lack of widespread acknowledgement of the impact of environmental issues on human health and of the significance of environmental events to social work practice. This bifurcation of concerns impacts on professionals working in the health and human services field and results in social workers not necessarily seeing the linkages between health and the environment. It may also be because neoliberal policy has reshaped the welfare state through user-pays principles, privatisation and the withdrawal of services in such a way that social workers are under-represented in poor areas of low population but high need – such as Australia's drought-affected rural areas.

Thanks to the efforts of environmental activists and concerned scientists, the world is beginning to wake up to the consequences of environmentally destructive practices. However while there has been a necessary focus on the environmental and economic consequences of potential climate change, there is less systematic attention to the health and human rights outcomes. There is a clear role for social workers at national and international levels to build alliances with and participate in global grassroots organisations and social movements, to undertake research that exposes the plight of the people most affected, to undertake long-term planning, policy development, crisis intervention and community development, and to lobby and advocate to raise the profile of the human rights aspects of these issues. Because human-created environmental destruction and climate change events impact so crucially on people's lives and health, and because of the social justice implications, it would therefore appear evident that the social and health impacts of climate change and environmental consequences are significant emerging areas of social work practice.

As Ife (2001) argues, it is social work's brief to bring the voice of the marginalised into mainstream discourse. The climate change discourse with its current dominance by economic and environmental concerns lacks a people focus. At the international level, member associations of the International Federation of Social Workers (IFSW) might lobby for the appointment of social workers to transnational agencies and national climate change policy units. At national levels, as social workers we might lobby national policy-making bodies to include a social perspective on climate change in policy development. While our work in crisis intervention must continue, there is also a significant role for social work to bring a human rights perspective providing a credible voice in these areas, one that is culturally appropriate to various circumstances and locally embedded across the globe, and one that brings a balance to the disturbing global trend to prioritise market concerns over health and environmental consequences.

Conclusion

There is no doubt that we are witnessing significant challenges to our environmental certainties. These include the slow erosion of our rivers and waterways, downgrading of our productive areas and rising temperatures which are leading to more insidious challenges to our environment, our climate and ultimately to our health and well-being. The rise in greenhouse gas emissions has resulted in unusual changes in our weather patterns, and one manifestation is the increasing intensity of cataclysmic as well as incremental events. Potentially of great consequence are the possible dramatic shifts in agricultural productive

Peris, V. (2000) 'Hundreds killed by floods in India, Bhutan, Nepal and Bangladesh', www.wsws.org/articles/2000/aug2000/indf-a12.shtml

Press Association (2004) 'Tsunami highlights climate change risk, says scientist', *Guardian Unlimited*, 31 December, www.guardian.co.uk/education/2004/dec/31/highereducation.uk1

Red Cross (2000) *World Disasters Report*, www.ifrc.org/publicat/wdr2000/

Salt, B. (2001) *The Big Shift: Welcome to the Third Australian Culture*, South Yarra and Victoria: Hardie Grant Books.

Shaw, I., Thomas, S. and Clapham, D. (1998) *Social Care and Housing*, London: Jessica Kingsley.

Shucksmith, M. (2004) 'Young people and social exclusion in rural areas', *Sociologia Ruralis*, vol 44, no 1, pp 43–59.

Stehlik, D., Gray, I. and Lawrence, G. (1999) *Drought in the 1990s: Australian Farm Families' Experiences*, Kingston ACT: Rural Industries Research and Development Corporation.

Stern, N. (2007) *The Stern Review: The Economics of Climate Change*, London: HM Treasury.

UNCCD (United Nations Convention to Combat Desertification) (2007) *Combating Desertification in Africa*, www.unccd.int/publicinfo/factsheets/showFS.php?number=11

Valtonen, K. (1998) 'Resettlement of Middle Eastern refugees in Finland: The elusiveness of integration', *Journal of Refugee Studies*, vol 11, no 1, pp 38–60.

Van Rooyen, M. and Leaning, J. (2005) 'After the tsunami – Facing the public health challenges', *New England Journal of Medicine*, vol 352, pp 435–8.

Vidal, J. (2006) 'Australia suffers its worst drought in 1,000 years', *The Guardian*, 8 November, www.guardian.co.uk/australia/story/0,,1941942,00.html#article_continue

Wilkinson, R. and Marmot, M. (2003) *The Solid Facts: The Social Determinants of Health*, Copenhagen: World Health Organization.

Working Group 1 of the IPCC (Intergovernmental Panel on Climate Change) (2007) *Summary for Policy Makers*, Geneva: IPCC Secretariat.

World Bank (1986) *Poverty and Hunger: Issues and Options for Food Security in Developing Countries*, Washington DC: World Bank.

The health impacts of political conflict: new engagements for social work?

Shulamit Ramon

Introduction

Both violent and non-violent political conflicts have negative health consequences. They are observed so clearly in the destructive impact of violent conflict on the basic infrastructure on which everyday existence relies. Shortages of clean water lead not only to dehydration, but also to a number of illnesses (Jean, 1993). Shortages of food impact within a few days on the more vulnerable members of any society, such as children and older people. Many of them will die if they continue to lack basic food. The destruction of the infrastructure also destroys the economic viability of an area.

The death of children, parents and grandparents; the death of soldiers who are children, brothers (at times also sisters), husbands and boyfriends, as well as friends to many other people in the same society, leaves a mark which takes years to overcome, if at all, though it is not observable. Those unable to live with the loss of their loved ones are likely to die earlier than would have been the case otherwise. They experience mental illness, or live an emotionally reduced life with the scar of loss.

Lack of shelter due to the destruction of houses – an all too typical reaction of a victorious army, or of an underground movement against those deemed to be informers and collaborators – leads not only to adverse health problems in the short term, but also to long-term difficulties in leading a stable life, in having a reasonable working environment and in resolving social protection issues. These can take many years to undo. Figures from Bosnia highlight that 10 years after the end of the war 70% of all housing stock is either heavily damaged or destroyed (Kljajic, 1999) and 30% of households do not have even one breadwinner (FOS, BHAS and RSIS, 2005). These figures illustrate the long-term socio-economic effects such a conflict has on the health of the population.

The health consequences of violent political conflict are socially constructed, and are interrelated to the personal, psychological and social outcomes, too. However, at times a conflict brings with it a positive health outcome, as such events make people reconsider key options. For example, as a result of a direct hit of the psychiatric hospital in Sarajevo during the 1992–95 war, it was decided not to rebuild another hospital but to opt for a network of community mental health centres instead, freeing Sarajevo from the institutionalisation that would have taken it years to achieve otherwise.

Meeting health challenges in political conflict contexts

Most of the existing literature and the world media tend to focus on observable health consequences of a violent political conflict. Much less attention has been paid to consequences which cannot be directly observed, such as family preservation, mental well-being and community cohesion. A lot more attention has been paid to erupting violence, with less to ongoing violent political conflict and much less to non-violent conflicts. Perhaps this is the case because we feel we can do so little about such situations.

For example, the impact of the treatment of Australian Aborigines by white Australians over the last few hundred years has highlighted the effect of the cumulative physical, psychological and social oppression on Indigenous peoples (Coates, 2004). This has resulted in a much higher rate of physical ill-health, considerably lower life expectancy, higher rates of alcoholism and other substance misuse, lower levels of education, poorer schools, higher levels of poverty, community disintegration, forcible removal of children from their parents, poor housing conditions, and lower levels of participation in civic activities (ABS/AIHW, 2008). Recent research has further demonstrated a considerable gap in expectations and understanding between social workers and their Indigenous clients (Whyte, 2006), with social workers being unaware that clients viewed them as lacking in knowledge of Indigenous people and a commitment to treating them with respect. The social workers were sure that they understood the clients well and had a good working partnership with them. These identified gaps inevitably led to working at cross-purposes and to difficulties in the partnership.

A second example pertains to the health of refugees. Thirty-six million refugees inhabit the world today. Seventy-five per cent of them (27 million) are internally displaced people (IDP), as a result of the large number of violent political conflicts of the last 20 years (UNHCR, 2007). Being an internally displaced person implies living in one's own country, but having considerably fewer rights than other citizens: one is not allowed to work, have a business, buy a property and live where one chooses. Often, IDP live in sub-standard housing conditions. Many remain unemployed and as a consequence are poor, experiencing considerable physical and psychological ill-health, as well as lack of hope. They are clearly pawns in the political games played by their own governments and those on the opposite side of the political conflict.

The recent eruption of the Kenyan violent political conflict, following the close election results of December 2007, is a repeat of similar eruptions that followed previous elections. It will no doubt add to the number of IDP in Kenya. This creates havoc for many people whose health and economic life has been blighted for a long time already. The current round of the conflict cannot be understood outside of the Kenyan socio-economic and cultural context, where tribes compete for fertile land and inter-ethnic conflicts reinforced by British colonial rule continue to be re-enacted.

Social workers have focused their efforts on mediating in such conflicts; at times they have risked their own lives in the process, as their loyalty to their own tribe is tested, while the government systematically has failed to defend them (Wairire, 2008).

The situation of migrant workers in New York provides a third example. The advocacy programme developed by the Mount Sinai Hospital social work department for migrant workers, who were injured by cleaning the World Trade Center in the post-September 11th, 2001, aftermath, placed a clear focus on securing the right to health care. About 3,500 such workers, most of whom were legal migrants, were caught as having no entitlement to health care, a right that is not automatic in the US. Although injured due to lack of attention to their safety during their involvement in the cleaning work, this too did not entitle them to health care, which few cleaners could afford. The social workers created a lobbying coalition with trade unionists and not-for-profit organisations and managed to win the entitlement from the Federal government (Hill et al, 2008). However, those migrants who recovered sufficiently from their injuries found that they had lost the right to work in the US because they were out of work for so long. Injury, loss of earnings, being unwell without family support, loss of status as the breadwinner, will no doubt take their toll further on the health of these migrant workers. This case illustrates well the socially constructed disadvantage caused by a specific interpretation of the context of political conflict.

A further example of health-related social work challenges is the extensive – and at times intensive – work with asylum seekers, currently widespread in the UK and continental Europe. Asylum seekers often arrive in a poor state of health, especially if their journey to the place of asylum they hope for has been difficult and followed on from experiencing political conflict. They include people defined as 'economic migrants' and those defined as 'refugees'. While the status of the latter is less ambiguous and evokes a little more sympathy in Fortress Europe, those deemed as economic migrants are perceived as exploiters and scroungers. An attempt to improve one's life and get out of poverty is not perceived as morally acceptable anymore.

People in both categories are not allowed to work, are not entitled to health and welfare services, can be segregated into special camps and may be deported. Both their physical and mental health needs are usually denied, especially the latter. Furthermore, basic universal human rights, such as the right to family life, are denied to children and adult asylum seekers.

Social workers tend to work alongside immigration officers, whose job is to enforce the segregation of asylum seekers during the asylum application process, and to assess the truth of their claims. The assessments are often carried out without adherence to basic human respect, treating asylum seekers as though they were convicted offenders. For example, Crawly (2007) describes how children separated from their parents are interviewed via a glass divide, with the social worker and the immigration officer sitting on the other side. The aim of the immigration officer is to disprove the claim of young people that they are under 18, the cut-off point for the definition of who is a child and who is an adult.

Being an immigrant in a country such as the UK is at the best of times challenging in terms of finding one's place in a new environment, one which often presents as superior to the one from which the immigrant has come. The need to find tangible physical, social, psychological and financial solutions is pressing. This is made impossible for an asylum seeker. Moreover, the media in the UK often portrays asylum seekers as scroungers and offenders, and the Home Office has the final decision as to whether going back to one's country is or is not putting lives at risk. Recent cases include Iraqi refugees being told it is safe to go back to Iraq (Cemlyn, 2008), and a Ghanaian woman deported back to Ghana even though she had been on kidney dialysis, to which she would not have access in her own country.

There is anecdotal evidence of some social workers refusing to take part in the assessment interviews described above, and of local communities supporting the occasional asylum seeker in their objection to deportation. At times they succeed in overturning these decisions. However, as Humphries (2004) has highlighted, most social workers continue to carry out the job as prescribed by the immigration authorities, and do not resist it, even though a number of its elements are going against the grain of basic social work values. No doubt the fact that this work is carried out within the legal frame adhered to by the UK government sanctions it for both immigration officers and social workers, who also tell themselves that it would be worse without social work intervention. At times this is likely to be the case. While those who object to this type of work do not opt for it in the first place, it requires further investigation to understand which situations would lead a national association of social workers advising its members to leave their place of work, and what prevents social workers from doing so.

Health needs and social work at the post-conflict stage

The post-acute political conflict stage both necessitates and enables focusing attention on meeting less urgent needs. South Africa provides a case in point. As Gray and Mitchell (2007) highlight, the reconstruction and development plan (RDP) of the first post-apartheid government included the following five objectives, out of a list of seven:

- extending the school feeding scheme from 3 to 5 million pupils;
- increasing the nutrition and social development scheme from 1.3 to 1.5 million people;
- building 200,000 houses for those who qualified for subsidies;
- extending the community water supply and sanitation programme to reach a further 1.7 million people in 1997 and 2 million in 1998;
- establishing or upgrading 600 mobile clinics and providing another 100 clinics (Gray and Mitchell, 2007, p 83).

These are all health objectives, related to survival, such as nutrition, shelter and sanitation. Simultaneously these are also fundamental conditions with which to begin to tackle poverty; as poverty in turn prevents people from being able to participate in the social life of their community and country.

Gray and Mitchell do not expand on the role social workers may play in achieving these objectives, but Sewpaul and Holscher (2007), writing about community-based interventions for children in South Africa, acknowledge the country's background of political conflict and offer examples of good practice. These begin with family preservation, focused on time-limited home care, where the social worker, the social auxiliary worker and community facilitator are involved. The focus is on the roles of the social worker as mediator, facilitator and coordinator within a programme aimed at keeping the family intact and enabling the family to look after its members, to be empowered and to reconnect to existing social networks. While family preservation is not a physical health need, this objective includes meeting the health needs of different family members.

Meeting mental health needs

Political conflict often increases the level of stress participants have to live with; some may experience mental ill-health as a consequence. The rate of severe mental illness, such as psychosis, does not necessarily increase during an acute political conflict; in some instances it will remain below the level of non-acute conflict. Nevertheless, depression and suicide do increase considerably among those more vulnerable – for example, depression among the civilian population and rage and suicide among soldiers (Hoge et al, 2004). The peak of mental illness related to political conflict surfaces after acute conflict has ended, when people become aware that they may have survived physically, but now have to face the largely irreversible losses of significant others and a way of living. The sheer loss, the guilt of surviving and the doubts about the meaning of one's life may become overwhelming for some people.

Current mental health literature pays attention to post-traumatic stress disorder (PTSD), a syndrome in which people are unable to function due to reliving the difficult experience they went through in the acute conflict. There are effective ways to overcome PTSD which are derived largely from cognitive behavioural therapy; but also working with individuals and families to understand PTSD and to reconnect them to areas of their lives can regenerate meaning and belonging – a natural role for social workers. Much less attention is being given to the many more depressed, disaffected people, who do not demonstrate PTSD symptomatology, but instead under-function and seem indifferent, unable to enjoy and share life with others as before.

There are many examples of mental health projects aimed to support specific target populations after an acute political conflict and sometimes during one that is prolonged. Very few of the writers are social workers, though it is clear that a number of the activities provided were likely to be offered by them, or by their substitutes, in societies without qualified social workers. A large number of projects focus on children (Pfefferbuam, 2003; Shaw and Harris, 2003). This is understandable. Children are highly vulnerable both physically and emotionally in situations of political conflict, especially if they lose their parents. The future of the society that they symbolise is thus affected. Many children also find themselves being forcibly recruited to participate as soldiers, adding to the trauma of being a victim that of being a perpetrator of violence.

Beyond shelter and food, children are offered opportunities for offloading the traumatic experience they have gone through, for example war, unexpected bombing, rape, torture and loss of significant others, of home and of orderly schooling. They may be provided with largely non-verbal group counselling and at times with individual counselling and essential medication. The work of finding out what has happened to their families, breaking bad and good news, and reuniting them with relatives where possible, is usually the domain of social workers.

Most adult groups, apart from soldiers, are usually neglected in terms of being provided with mental health support during and after a political conflict, unless they harm themselves or others, or break down into a psychosis. It would be good if social workers were able to provide support to prevent a massive breakdown, but often they are 'too busy' in the turbulent context, or insufficiently trained, to recognise the signs of impending mental distress breakdown. The tendency to offer debriefing goes against the cultural grain of a number of societies, for example Cambodia (Strober, 1994) and Mozambique (Hayner, 2001). It is perceived as a Western input. While traditional healing techniques will be used, these will not include talking about the traumatic experience.

A further difficulty may arise in the case of rape in societies where the shame of rape of women is too much for the men to acknowledge. Zavirsek (2008) discusses this issue briefly in the context of Bosnia, where rape was a systematic means of torture and humiliation, but where nevertheless women were and are expected to keep silent about it being done to them. Taking into account local attitudes is indispensable for social workers, yet this may clash with some of the more universal values of the profession, namely treating the more vulnerable members of society with respect and individuality.

An interesting example of focusing on the well-being of forced migrants in the UK is a mentorship system provided by retrained doctors from their own original culture. The project offers migrant doctors an opportunity to understand and work within a social approach to mental health with their new country while they in turn offer mentorship to people with identified mental health needs. The mentorship reads like a classical social work script – listening, enabling people to understand and improve their coping skills in the new situations in which they find themselves, while enabling them to connect to useful networks (Palmer, 2007).

The effect of political conflict on social workers

Living and working in an acute political conflict and its aftermath is likely to leave its mark on social workers themselves. A Bosnian social worker describes what it was like for her:

> I think we needed help as well. Some initiatives offered support by specialised doctors and counsellors. I was a refugee too, I experienced different traumas and I needed to be involved somewhere, to receive support and help. I think we accumulated strength out of a need to work and our wish to help others. I wouldn't go to work, trust me. I wouldn't expose my life to everyday danger if I wouldn't have a need to help other people. In a way, probably that work was therapeutic, too – you did not have time to think about yourself. (Muminovic and Mustafovski, 2000, p 37)

While the existing meagre research evidence does indeed highlight signs of distress and anxiety, it does not stop most social workers in these circumstances from functioning well professionally in countries such as Northern Ireland, Israel and Palestine, where the acute phase of the political conflict has been enduring (Ramon et al, 2006). Indeed, there is some evidence to indicate that when offered adequate training and support, social workers experience growth of their professional capacities (Ramon et al, 2006). Pinkerton and Campbell (2002) highlight that social workers took pride in their neutral professionalism, as if to indicate that in their professional capacity they acted beyond the sectarian divide, even though each of them worked within a service structure aimed at only one of the two communities affected by that divide. It is questionable if the separation of the personal, the political and the professional is either realistically possible or desirable for the well-being of the worker, but it is one of the key issues that confront social workers serving members of both sides of a political conflict. For example, Israeli Jewish and Arab social workers share the service on offer at Hadasa, a teaching hospital in Jerusalem, which would regularly admit the dead and injured of terror attacks and army reprisals from the mixed Israeli and Palestinian hinterland. At times Israeli Arab social workers were told by Jewish patients that they did not wish to be treated by them, while during visits to Arab families they would be accused of serving 'the enemy', who is for them the Jewish state and its population (Rosen, 2004).

Implications for social work practice and social work education

It has been established that political conflict is very likely to create physical and mental health needs for the many ordinary citizens who find themselves involved in such a conflict. Some of these needs relate to actual physical survival, while other needs are less observable and less likely to be met in either the short or long term. Health needs of children and soldiers are more likely to receive a response than those of other groups. Most health needs come together with social care needs, and the separation of the two in the case of political conflict is artificial. While social workers often contribute in ways that are useful and much needed by the population affected, the work required in meeting health needs is multidisciplinary and other professions are needed no less than social workers. Yet the uniqueness of the social work contribution lies in the ability to relate to more than one group and at more than one level, namely to individuals, families and communities, and to the very practical and the emotional aspects of our being.

Therefore, social work in political conflict, including meeting the health challenges that such conflict brings, has to encompass more than one method: community and casework must coexist. Yet understanding the role of social workers in political conflict and acquiring the knowledge and the skills to act hardly feature on the curriculum of most schools of social work. Even countries such as the UK, which lived with an acute political conflict in Northern Ireland for nearly all of the last 30 years, are yet to acknowledge that the knowledge and skills are worthy of attention in the training on offer to qualifying social workers and to post-qualifying social workers in in-service training.

However, there are positive examples to learn from, where such an attempt has taken place, including:

- Social work students at Queens University Belfast, Northern Ireland, meet with victims of 'The Troubles' and with social workers who were involved in this type of work as an integral part of their social work training (Campbell and Duffy, 2008).
- Social work students at Plymouth University, UK, are involved in a project with refugees and asylum seekers as mentors, rather than as social workers, in an effort to understand the perspective of these clients (Butler, 2005).
- The School of Social Work at Melbourne University, Australia, has undertaken a thorough evaluation of their teaching concerning Indigenous people (Harms et al, 2008, Ch 14). As a result they have begun to require that at least one of the field education placements undertaken by their students will be in an Indigenous community, following an introduction on campus to understanding these communities and their history.

These examples highlight what can be done, though they do not respond to the question of why this strand is not an integral part of basic social work education, in-service training and everyday work. Social work responses to the health challenges which political conflict brings with it are not new, but the need to include them as part and parcel of social work practice and education has perhaps become more acute, due to living in a globalised world in which political conflict is an all too frequent occurrence.

References

ABS/AIHW (Australian Bureau of Statistics/Australian Institute of Health and Welfare) (2008) *The Health and Welfare of Australia's Aboriginal and Torres Strait Islander Peoples*, Canberra: ABS/AIHW.

Butler, A. (2005) 'A strengths approach to building futures: UK students and refugees together', *Community Development Journal*, vol 40, no 2, pp 147–57.

Campbell, J. and Duffy, J. (2008) 'Social work, political violence, and citizenship in Northern Ireland', in S. Ramon (ed) *Social Work in the Context of Political Conflict*, IASSW, Birmingham: Venture Press, pp 57–76.

Cemlyn, S. (2008) 'Social work education response to political conflict issues in the UK', in S. Ramon (ed) *Social Work in the Context of Political Conflict*, IASSW, Birmingham: Venture Press, pp 189–213.

Coates, K. (2004) *A Global History of Indigenous Peoples: Struggle and Survival*, New York: Palgrave Macmillan.

Crawly, H. (2007) *'When is a Child not a Child?' Asylum, Age Disputes and the Process of Age Assessment*, London: Immigration Law Practitioners Association.

FOS, BHAS and RSIS (Federal Office of Statistics, Agency for Statistics of Bosnia and Herzegovina and Republika Srpska Institute of Statistics) (2005) *Living in Bosnia and Herzogovina, Panel Study Final Report*, Sarajevo: Ware 4.

Gray, M. and Mitchell, B. (2007) 'The road less travelled: Reconstruction, welfare and social development in South Africa', in L. Dominelli (ed) *Revitalising Communities in a Globalised World*, Aldershot: Ashgate, pp 79–94.

Harms, L., Clarke, A. and Whyte, J.D. (2008) 'Preparing social work students to work with Indigenous Australian communities', in S. Ramon (ed) *Social Work in the Context of Political Conflict*, Birmingham: Venture Press, pp 245–70.

Hayner, P. (2001) *Unspeakable Truths: Confronting State Terror and Atrocity*, London: Routledge.

Hill, E., Mora, L. and Garcia, L. (2008) 'The role of social security social workers in the aftermath of 9/11', in S. Ramon (ed) *Social Work in the Context of Political Conflict*, IASSW, Birmingham: Venture Press, pp 169–88.

Hoge, C.W., Castro, C., Messer, S., McGurk, S., Cotting, D. and Koffman, R. (2004) 'Combat duty in Iraq and Afghanistan, mental health problems, and barriers to care', *New England Journal of Medicine*, vol 351, pp 13–22.

Humphries, B. (2004) 'An unacceptable role of social workers: Implementing immigration policy', *British Journal of Social Work*, vol 34, pp 93–107.

Jean, F. (ed) (1993) *Life, Death and Aid: The Médicin Sans Frontière Report on World Crisis Intervention*, London: Routledge.

Kljajic, V. (ed) (1999) 'Social work at the verge of the 21st Century', Presentation from the Scientific Seminar, Sarajevo: Department of Social Work, University of Sarajevo.

Muminovic, A. and Mustafovski, F. (2000) *Thesis for the Education of Supervisors in Psychosocial Work*, Sarajevo: University of Sarajevo.

Palmer, D. (2007) '"Face to face": A mentoring project for forced migrants, a life in the day', *Mental Health and Social Inclusion*, vol 11, no 4, pp 16–21.

Pfefferbaum, E. (2003) 'The children of Oklahoma City', in R.J. Ursano, C.S. Fullerton and A.E. Norwood (eds) *Terrorism and Disaster: Individual and Community Mental Health Interventions*, Cambridge: Cambridge University Press, pp 58–70.

Pinkerton, J. and Campbell, J. (2002) 'Social work and social justice in Northern Ireland: Towards a new occupational space', *British Journal of Social Work*, vol 32, pp 723–37.

Ramon, S., Campbell, J., Lindsay, J., McCrystal, P. and Baidun, N. (2006) 'The impact of political conflict on social work: Experiences from Northern Ireland, Israel and Palestine', *British Journal of Social Work*, vol 36, pp 435–50.

Rosen, H. (2004) 'The experience of Arab and Jewish hospital social work students and their supervisors', poster presented at the European Association of Schools of Social Work Conference, Nicosia, Cyprus.

Sewpaul, V. and Holscher, D. (2007) 'Against the odds: Community-based interventions for children in difficult circumstances in post-apartheid South Africa', in L. Dominelli (ed) *Revitalising Communities in a Globalised World*, Aldershot: Ashgate, pp 193–206.

Shaw, J.A. and Harris, J.J. (2003) 'Children of war and children at war: Child victims of terrorism in Mozambique', in R.J. Ursano, C.S. Fullerton and A.E. Norwood (eds) *Terrorism and Disaster: Individual and Community Mental Health Interventions*, Cambridge: Cambridge University Press, pp 41–58.

Strober, S. (1994) 'Social work interventions to alleviate Cambodian refugee psychological distress', *International Social Work*, vol 37, pp 23–35.

UNHCR (United Nations High Commissioner for Refugees) (2007) *Information about IDP: Questions and Answers*, Geneva: UNHCR Media Resource and Public Information Service.

Wairire, G. (2008) 'The challenge of social work in the Kenyan context of political conflict', in S. Ramon (ed) *Social Work in the Context of Political Conflict*, IASSW, Birmingham: Venture Press, pp 101–22.

Whyte, J.D. (2006) 'Contesting paradigms: Indigenous worldviews, Western science and professional social work', Melbourne: University of Melbourne.

Zavirsek, D. (2008) 'Social work as memory work in times of political conflict', in S. Ramon (ed) *Social Work in the Context of Political Conflict*, IASSW, Birmingham: Venture Press, pp 147–67.

Reproduction in the global marketplace

Eric Blyth

Introduction

This chapter discusses the implications of the development of a global marketplace in reproduction services and proposes new directions for social work action based on the perspective that reproduction is an issue of human rights. Social work engagement with issues of reproduction – family planning, fertility, pregnancy and birth – varies both within and between countries. Sometimes services focus on a particular policy such as planned parenthood and population control, sometimes on particular groups considered vulnerable or 'dangerous' such as young parents, sometimes on decision making, for example around termination of pregnancy, and sometimes on the support of parents and children facing particular health challenges. There is no established pattern of provision. The global commodification of reproduction exacerbates health inequalities embedded in the processes of reproduction. There are inequalities in access to services which depend on people's ability to pay and inequalities in risk in an unregulated market. Financial and social inequalities provide the context in which women can be exploited, for example, as 'donors'[1] or surrogates, because of their poverty.

Estimates of the prevalence of infertility worldwide vary considerably. The World Health Organization (2003) suggests at least 186 million couples in the world's poorest countries alone experience infertility. Boivin et al (2007), analysing published population surveys, identified a global population of between 40.2 million and 120.6 million women aged 20–44 living in married or consensual relationships, failing to conceive after 12 months of unprotected sexual intercourse. Between 12 million and 90.4 million of these are likely to seek medical help for their fertility problems. In the US approximately 12% of women of childbearing age have received an infertility service at some time in their lives (Centers for Disease Control and Prevention, 2007).

The centrality of reproduction to the 'human condition', self-evidently essential for the long-term survival of any species, is enshrined in cultural and religious practices and human rights codes, providing a key marker for adult identity, particularly for women. A number of commentators have highlighted the central importance of 'reproductive autonomy' and reproductive choice for the individual's sense of identity (for example, Jackson, 2007, p 48). The reproductive rights of individuals are reflected in both international conventions (for example, the Universal Declaration of Human Rights, the American Convention on Human Rights, the European Convention on Human Rights and Fundamental Freedoms) and national laws respecting individuals' reproductive autonomy. Such rights have conventionally been interpreted not as positive rights obliging the state to provide a service, such as assisted conception, but rather as a negative right against state interference, that is justified only where an individual's reproductive choices and decisions infringe the rights of others.

Adults who fail to conform to reproductive expectations face psychological, social and cultural sanctions of varying severity. History provides evidence of pronatalist demands and expectations, often buttressed by underlying cultural, religious and social ideologies, that impact adversely on individuals – and especially, but not exclusively, women – who are unable to produce a child. Documented consequences of the failure to meet these expectations range from internalised feelings of shame and inadequacy, loss of control over one's life and body and diminished self-esteem, to social sanctions that include social exclusion, economic deprivation, psychological and physical abuse, murder, violence-induced suicide and a lack of respect afforded to a childless person after her or his death (Daar and Merali, 2002).

As a corollary, different societies have devised a range of culturally-valorised interventions to procure children for the childless, including: religious rites and supplications to supernatural or divine powers; the application or ingestion of herbal and other preparations; various mind/body therapies (for example, meditation, relaxation, yoga); instruction on the most propitious location, timing and positioning for sexual intercourse; finding a new sexual partner – typically following divorce or through polygamous marriage (the latter option usually restricted to males); conception of a child on behalf of an infertile woman by a family member (often a younger sister); impregnation of the wife of an infertile man – or provision of sperm for insemination – by a family member (often the man's brother); provision of a child for a childless couple either through the 'adoption' or 'gifting' of an existing child or conceiving a child specifically for the childless couple by another couple within the kinship network; and purchase of a child.

Contemporary forms of assisted conception, such as donor insemination (DI) and surrogacy, have clear links with some traditional practices. Modern technology has enabled expansion of the repertoire of procedures to include use of 'donated' eggs or embryos as well as procedures that do not involve the provision of reproductive tissue or reproductive services by a third party. The successful fertilisation of a human egg outside the human body in the 1970s has resulted in the subsequent births of over 3 million children worldwide using in vitro fertilisation (IVF) and derivative reproductive technologies (Horsey, 2006). Annually, approximately 200,000 children are born as a result of various reproductive technologies (Adamson et al, 2006). Births from reproductive technologies represent around 1% of all live births in developed countries, although higher proportions have been reported in some countries (Andersen et al, 2007). These proportions could rise if declining global fertility rates (especially in developed countries) are maintained (United Nations, 2003) even in the absence of any increased recourse to technological interventions.

A globalised market in reproduction services

A key characteristic of services for fertility difficulties in the 21st century is that they have become a globalised endeavour in the world marketplace that has prospered in the age of 'free trade' and opening up of world markets. In the US alone, IVF and fertility drugs comprise a market worth several billion dollars annually – even excluding egg, sperm and surrogacy brokerage (Spar, 2006). In 2000, the annual global market for sperm exports was estimated to be worth between US$50–100 million (Zachary, 2000, cited in Spar, 2006). Cryos, based in Denmark, operates the world's largest sperm bank, offering worldwide express delivery by air courier and exporting sperm from its 300 donors to over 60 countries. Cryos (2007) claims that it has achieved more than 13,000 pregnancies since 1991.

The internet has brought the world of reproductive technology into the homes of prospective customers,[2] surrogates and donors, a world characterised by a bewildering extent of choice. A Google search undertaken for this chapter[3] identified 482,000 websites for 'sperm donor clinics', 974,000 for 'egg donor agencies', 1,760,000 for 'surrogacy agencies', 778,000 for 'IVF clinics' and 568,000 for 'IVF holidays'. Prospective customers can review the services offered by different clinics and other providers of reproductive services (such as surrogacy agencies, egg brokers and laboratories offering embryo sex identification), their claimed success rates, browse agencies' and brokers' profiles of prospective donors and surrogates, and compare fees and charges, while potential donors or surrogates can advertise their services directly to prospective customers or register with agencies or brokers. Online chatrooms and blogs enable individuals to share experiences and pass on recommendations; online deals can be sealed using credit card payment facilities; and cheap and extensive international flight schedules enable prospective customers, gamete providers, surrogates, sperm, eggs and embryos to be transported to virtually any part of the world. In recent years, the media have reported an apparently increasing number of people travelling to another country specifically to access reproductive services because the services they want may not be available at all in their home country, certain individuals or groups (for example, single women and lesbian couples) may be prohibited from accessing services in their home country, waiting lists may be shorter elsewhere, services may be cheaper and/or offer better success rates, and legislation/regulation may be less restrictive (for example, Leigh, 2005; France, 2006; Graham, 2005). Service providers enthusiastically promote their wares.

Some clinics explicitly emphasise the concept of 'fertility tourism', despite some commentators' criticism of the term (see, for example, Pennings, 2005). Barbados Fertility Centre (2008) markets its favourable location, explicitly drawing on research that correlates stress reduction with improved outcomes of fertility treatment:

> We would never pretend that going through an IVF program would not be stressful. But with a number of recent studies psychologists have established that by reducing a couples [sic] stress levels while they undergo fertility treatments, a marked increase of a successful outcome is achieved. With that knowledge what better place in the world to reduce your stress than in the exotic island of Barbados in the Caribbean.... In between your appointments, you have constant access to our team of experts by cellular phone but with the freedom of being on holiday. You can enjoy the soothing sound of the lapping Caribbean Sea, go for a long romantic walk along the white sandy beaches and then enjoy the tantalizing tastes of the Caribbean's cuisine. Barbados is famous for its world class luxury hotels and we have selected some of the best the island has to offer.

The Centre offers four different 'packages' in ascending order of facilities and cost, according to customers' budgets: 'Comfort', 'Luxury', 'Premium' or 'Elite'.

Cross-border reproductive services: cause for concern

It goes without saying that if individuals choose to spend their resources in a particular way in order to exercise their reproductive autonomy, it does not behove others or a democratic society operating collectively to stand in their way, save – as noted above – where this harms others. It is precisely in this respect that some specific activities related to the global reproductive marketplace give cause for concern. Underlying these concerns are socio-economic inequalities that, in particular, put at risk the physical and mental health of poor women living in developing countries.

At the outset, the difficulty of discerning the prevalence of such practices should be noted, since even where they are not formally prohibited, they may be conducted surreptitiously because of a lack of community endorsement (Nanda, 2007), thus precluding systematic recording or empirical study.[4] Such evidence as currently exists is derived from anecdotal accounts in the media or shared on websites and reports undertaken by investigative journalists posing as prospective customers. These have highlighted the plight of financially disadvantaged young women, primarily in economically impoverished countries in Eastern Europe and South Asia, acting as surrogates or egg donors for comparatively wealthier citizens of other countries (Abrams, 2006; Barnett and Smith, 2006; Foggo and Newell, 2006).

Typically in countries where these practices are reported, reproductive technologies are largely unregulated and no systems exist to ensure the protection of participants' interests (Barnett and Smith, 2006; Braid, 2006; Chopra, 2006; Mukherjee, 2007). Remuneration of donors and surrogates is an essential element of such arrangements, without which they would not exist. Where third-party-assisted conception procedures are permitted, there is a general global acceptance for a prohibition on the outright sale and purchase of human embryos and gametes. However, there is some institutionalised support for the 'compensation' of donors in recognition of the 'inconveniences' (European Union, 2004) or the time, stress, physical effort and risk (ASRM, 2007) related to the 'donation'. At the same time, the risk that high levels of remuneration may encourage a prospective donor to discount the potential physical and emotional risks involved has been recognised, with the Ethics Committee of the American Society for Reproductive Medicine (ASRM) recommending maximum fees for US egg donors (ASRM, 2007). There is less formalised agreement on the compensation of surrogates, although constraints on 'compensation' are mandated in some jurisdictions (for example, the UK's 1990 Human Fertilisation and Embryology Act).

Given these considerations, while remuneration for prospective surrogates and egg donors in destination countries may be low compared to remuneration in the recipient's home country (where such payment is permitted at all), relative to income levels in the destination country, remuneration offered to surrogates and donors may be at a level that compromises their ability to give informed consent. The financial rewards for service providers in both home and destination countries may compromise the information and advice given to prospective surrogates and donors, especially if the provision of complete advice and information about potential risks is likely to discourage their participation.

A surrogacy and egg procurement cottage industry has been reported in the Gujerat village of Anand, mainly catering for non-resident Indian couples living in Japan, Southeast Asia, the UK and the US. While remuneration for both surrogates and egg donors may be high by Indian standards – a surrogate could receive the equivalent of six years' salary of a school teacher (Chu, 2006) – these are a fraction of what surrogates and donors could earn in more affluent countries that permit commercialised reproductive services. A surrogacy 'package' costing around US$45,000 in the US would cost between US$2,500 and US$6,500 in India (Chopra, 2006; Mata Press Service, 2006). Eastern European countries have been identified as sources of 'donor egg bargains'. Barnett and Smith (2006) report the case of a Ukrainian egg donor offered US$300 for her eggs – which could be sold on for more than $6,000 each to Western customers. When the young woman produced 40 eggs, she was given a $200 bonus. However a leading British fertility specialist invited to comment on this case suspected that the woman would have been exposed to excessive levels of ovarian stimulation drugs in order to produce such a high number of eggs, thus placing her at risk of ovarian hyperstimulation, a potentially lethal condition. Abrams (2006) reports a Romanian factory worker paid the equivalent of three months' wages to act as an egg donor and whose subsequent health problems adversely affecting her own future fertility were ignored by the clinic with whom she contracted to sell her eggs.[5] According to the owner of a surrogacy centre in Georgia (cited in Rimple, 2006) most of the women offering their services to them were desperate, with children to support and living in poverty.

What can be done by social workers?

The role of social workers in combating the excesses of international reproductive services may not be immediately evident, especially given the range of apparently more pressing concerns demanding social workers' efforts and energies. In practice, few social workers appear to be directly engaged in providing or regulating reproductive services. In a number of developed countries where reproductive services are well-established, some social workers are engaged as counsellors, either employed directly by fertility clinics or as private practitioners contracted to provide counselling services. Some social workers may be employed by regulatory bodies (one is known to be employed by the Canadian regulatory body, Assisted Human Reproduction), or appointed as members of regulatory bodies (currently one social worker is a member of the UK's regulatory body, the Human Fertilisation and Embryology Authority [HFEA], while a social worker, Dame Suzi Leather, was HFEA chair between 2002 and 2006). In Israel, membership of the Special Committee to Authorize Surrogacy Agreements established under the 1996 Surrogacy Arrangement Act includes a social worker. Otherwise, a few social work academics and practitioners have undertaken research in the field of reproductive health (see, for example, Sewpaul, 1999; Bergart, 2000; Blyth et al, 2001; Daniels and Thorn, 2001; Gagin et al, 2004; Landau, 2004; Robinson and Miller, 2004; Schneider and Forthofer, 2005; Covington and Burns, 2006; Wincott and Crawshaw, 2006; Crawshaw et al, 2007; Paul and Berger, 2007).

The case I advocate for social work to at least begin to think about engaging in the debate on globalised reproductive services is derived from key policies agreed by the International Federation of Social Workers (IFSW, undated; 1996; 1999; 2008; IFSW/IASSW, 2004) and their reference to major international human rights codes (United Nations, 1948; 1979; 1989; 2000). These provide a basis for sketching out actions that social workers and social work organisations might legitimately take to ensure an appropriate balance between the rights of involuntarily childless adults seeking to build a family through forms of assisted conception that are dependent on the involvement of a third party as a donor or surrogate, and safeguarding the interests of potential donors and surrogates (especially where these are indigenous and/or poor women) and any child who may be conceived or affected by the procedure.

At a general level, social workers should:

- advocate for full implementation of international human rights declarations and conventions;
- pressurise their own governments to meet their obligations to such conventions and to ratify and implement such conventions where they have not done so;
- advocate for respect for the inherent worth and dignity of all people;
- promote gender equality, to ensure that women and girls are treated equally with men and boys in all areas of life.

At the more specific level of reproductive services, they should seek to participate in all appropriate aspects of reproductive health, including fertility clinics, regulatory bodies and government departments to:

- promote individual reproductive choice and decision-making (that is consistent with avoiding harm to vulnerable third parties) and challenging reproductive health policies and practices that facilitate forms of reproductive duress, and restricted access to services;
- seek representation on bodies that monitor and/or regulate reproductive services;
- promote the development of safe and affordable reproductive health services;
- promote community education in respect of fertility and reproductive health issues;
- challenge practices that exploit materially disadvantaged women for reproductive purposes;
- advocate for regulation and/or legislation in individual jurisdictions to ensure the necessary protection of all individuals affected by reproductive services, in particular those seeking reproductive services, donors, surrogates and children;
- (where financial compensation of surrogates and donors is permitted) promote and engage in debate to ensure that such provisions do not exploit potentially vulnerable participants, or commodify children or women's reproductive capacities;
- engage with other organisations, including those that are more centrally involved in the provision of reproductive services and those with a specific remit to promote human rights, to explore the feasibility of coordinated joint action (for example, the International

Federation of Gynaecology and Obstetrics [2008] and the European Society for Human Reproduction and Embryology [see note 4]).

At a national level, work in this area, especially emphasising the rights of donor-conceived people to information about their origins and the importance of quality care and counselling provision for people directly affected by fertility concerns, has been undertaken by the British Association of Social Workers Project Group on Assisted Reproduction since the early 1980s (Wincott and Crawshaw, 2006). While this remains the only such group operating under the auspices of a national professional social work association, the international social work community has taken the first step in engaging with the risks of exploitation inherent in globalised reproductive services. In August 2008 the International Federation of Social Workers adopted a policy on cross-border reproductive services focusing on the issues discussed in this chapter (IFSW, 2008).

This chapter has outlined the capacity for cross-border reproductive services to both enhance and diminish human rights. The challenge for the global social work community is to transcend local and national differences and to engage in activities that ensure that the promotion of the rights of some individuals to reproductive health care is not achieved at the expense of the rights of others. Such a remit is entirely consistent with social work's mandate to combat social inequalities wherever they exist and can be best achieved by working in partnership with similarly concerned and motivated partners among other professional groups and multinational organisations.

Notes
[1] In practice, many 'donors' of eggs or sperm receive remuneration. My use of terms such as 'donor' and 'donation' follows conventional usage; however, readers should be aware of this caveat.

[2] The commercialisation of much reproductive technology provision and, in particular, the specific aspects discussed in this chapter, questions the appropriateness of traditional medical discourse. Since this chapter is primarily focused on the purchase of reproductive services, I have deliberately chosen to use the terms 'customer(s)' and 'service(s)' in preference to 'patient(s)' and 'treatment'(s).

[3] Undertaken on 7 April 2008. However, significantly different results have been obtained from conducting this exercise on different occasions.

[4] This is beginning to be addressed. In 2007, the European Society for Human Reproduction and Embryology (ESHRE), a multidisciplinary body with a membership extending to 114 countries, established an investigation into cross-border reproductive care, although its remit is confined to Europe in the first instance. Also in 2007, a Global Forum on Reproductive Health Care (an international body representing professionals and regulatory bodies in Belgium, Canada, Norway, Spain, the UK, the European Commission and the World Health Organization) was established. In 2008, two surveys of patients' experiences of overseas fertility services were undertaken (Blyth, 2008; Infertility Network UK, 2008) and in January 2009 the first International Forum on Cross-Border Reproductive Care, hosted by the Canadian government, brought together, for the first time, national regulators, representatives of national and international professional bodies and consumer groups, the European Union and the World Health Organisation.

[5] In response to extensive disquiet resulting from this case and a campaign supported by several Members of the European Parliament, on 10 April 2005 the European Parliament adopted a resolution banning trade in human cells and embryos (www.europarl.europa. eu/sides/getDoc.do;jsessionid=DFABA61A764E316D78BFACF810 DFD2B8.node1?language=EN&pubRef=-//EP//TEXT+TA+P6-TA-2005-0074+0+DOC+XML+V0//EN).

References

Abrams, F. (2006) 'The misery behind the baby trade', *Daily Mail*, 17 July, www.dailymail.co.uk/pages/live/femail/article.html?in_article_id=396220&in_page_id=1879&in_a_source

Adamson, G., de Mouzon, J., Lancaster, P., Nygren, K.-G., Sullivan, E. and Zegers-Hochschild, F. (2006) 'World collaborative report on in vitro fertilization, 2000', *Fertility and Sterility*, vol 85, pp 1586–622.

Andersen, A., Goossens, V., Gianaroli, L., Felberbaum, R., de Mouzon, J. and Nygren, K.-G. (2007) 'Assisted reproductive technology in Europe, 2003. Results generated from European registers by ESHRE', *Human Reproduction*, vol 22, pp 1513–25.

ASRM (Ethics Committee of the American Society for Reproductive Medicine) (2007) 'Financial compensation of oocyte donors', *Fertility and Sterility*, vol 88, pp 305–9.

Barbados Fertility Centre (2008) 'A holiday with a purpose', www.barbadosivf.org/holidays.htm

Barnett, A. and Smith, H. (2006) 'Cruel cost of the human egg trade', *The Observer*, 30 April, www.guardian.co.uk/medicine/story/0,,1764687,00.html

Bergart, A. (2000) 'The experience of women in unsuccessful infertility treatment: What do patients need when medical intervention fails?', *Social Work in Health Care*, vol 30, no 4, pp 45–69.

Blyth, E. (2008) *Fertility Patients' Experiences of Cross-border Reproductive Health Care: Report to Assisted Human Reproduction Canada*, Huddersfield: University of Huddersfield.

Blyth, E., Crawshaw, M., Haase, J. and Speirs, J. (2001) 'The implications of adoption for donor offspring following donor-assisted conception', *Child and Family Social Work*, vol 6, pp 295–304.

Boivin, J., Bunting, L., Collins, J. and Nygren, K.-G. (2007) 'International estimates of infertility prevalence and treatment-seeking: Potential need and demand for infertility medical care', *Human Reproduction*, vol 22, pp 1506–12.

Braid, M. (2006) 'The donor business: The price of eggs', *The Independent*, 26 March, http://news.independent.co.uk/health/article353598.ece

Centers for Disease Control and Prevention (2007) *2005 Assisted Reproductive Technology Success Rates: National Summary and Fertility Clinic Reports*, Atlanta, GA: US Department of Health and Human Services Centers for Disease Control and Prevention.

Chopra, S. (2006) 'Childless couples look to India for surrogate mothers', *Christian Science Monitor*, 3 April, www.csmonitor.com/2006/0403/p01s04-wosc.html

Chu, H. (2006) 'It's win-win. It's a completely capitalistic enterprise', *Toronto Star*, 20 April.

Covington, S. and Burns, L. (eds) (2006) *Infertility Counselling: A Comprehensive Handbook for Clinicians*, 2nd edn, New York: Cambridge University Press.

Crawshaw, M., Blyth, E. and Daniels, K. (2007) 'Past semen donors' views about the use of a voluntary contact register', *Reproductive Bio Medicine Online*, vol 14, pp 411–17.

Cryos (2007) http://dk.cryosinternational.com/home.aspx

Daar, A. and Merali, Z. (2002) 'Infertility and social suffering: The case of ART in developing countries', in E. Vayena, P. Rowe and D. Griffin (eds) *Medical, Ethical and Social Aspects of Assisted Reproduction: Current Practices and Controversies in Assisted Reproduction*, Geneva: World Health Organization, pp 15–21.

Daniels, K. and Thorn, P. (2001) 'Sharing information with donor insemination offspring. A child-conception versus a family-building approach', *Human Reproduction*, vol 16, pp 1792–6.

European Union (2004) 'Directive 2004/23/EC of the European Parliament and of the Council of 31 March 2004 on setting standards of quality and safety for the donation, procurement, testing, processing, preservation, storage and distribution of human tissues and cells', *Official Journal of the European Union*, L102, pp 48–58.

Foggo, D. and Newell, C. (2006) 'Doctors offer illegal baby sexing: Couples pay £12,000 to get child of choice', *The Sunday Times*, 5 November, www.timesonline.co.uk/tol/news/uk/article625517.ece

France, L. (2006) 'Passport, tickets, suncream, sperm ...', *The Observer*, 15 January, www.observer.guardian.co.uk/woman/story/0,,1684149,00.html

Gagin, R., Cohen, M., Greenblatt, L., Solomon, H. and Itskowitz-Eldor, J. (2004) 'Developing the role of the social worker as coordinator of services at the surrogate parenting center', *Social Work in Health Care*, vol 40, pp 1–14.

Graham, K. (2005) 'It was a big leap of faith', *The Guardian*, 21 June, www.guardian.co.uk/g2/story/0,,1510864,00.html

Horsey, K. (2006) 'Three million IVF babies born worldwide', *BioNews*, 364, 26 June, www.ivf.net/ivf/three_million_ivf_babies_born_worldwide-o2105.html

Infertility Network UK (2008) *The Infertility Network UK Fertility Tourism Survey Results*, Bexhill-on-Sea: Infertility Network.

International Federation of Gynaecology and Obstetrics (2008) www.figo.org

IFSW (International Federation of Social Workers) (2008) *International Policy on Health*, Berne: IFSW, www.ifsw.org/en/p38000081.html

IFSW (1996) *International Policy on Human Rights*, Berne: IFSW, www.ifsw.org/en/p38000212.html

IFSW (1999) *International Policy on Women*, Berne: IFSW, www.ifsw.org/en/p38000218.html

IFSW (2008) *International Policy on Cross Border Reproductive Services*, Berne: International Federation of Social Workers.

IFSW/IASSW (International Association of Schools of Social Work) (2004) *Ethics in Social Work: Statement of Principles*, Bern: IFSW and IASSW, www.ifsw.org/en/p38000324.html

Jackson, E. (2007) 'Rethinking the pre-conception welfare principle', in K. Horsey and H. Biggs (eds) *Human Fertilisation and Embryology: Reproducing Regulation*, London: Routledge-Cavendish, pp 47–67.

Landau, R. (2004) 'The promise of post-menopausal pregnancy (PMP)', *Social Work in Health Care*, vol 40, pp 53–69.

Leigh, S. (2005) 'Reproductive "tourism"', *USA Today*, 2 May 7D, www.usatoday.com/news/health/2005-05-02-reproductive-tourism_x.htm

Mata Press Service (2006) 'Wombs for rent in a hamlet of hope', *Asian Pacific Post*, 9 March, www.asianpacificpost.com/portal2/ff80808109 dc23b20109dc491ba8001a_Wombs_for_rent_in_a_hamlet_of_hope. do.html

Mukherjee, K. (2007) 'Rent-a-womb in India fuels surrogate motherhood debate', *Reuters*, 4 February, www.reuters.com/article/latestCrisis/idUSDEL298735

Nanda, P. (2007) 'Donating motherhood for money', *Hindustan Times*, 2 August, www.hindustantimes.com/Redir.aspx?ID=e918a200-0cfc-4aa5-b0cd-8907fc3f32dd

Paul, M. and Berger, R. (2007) 'Topic avoidance and family functioning in families conceived with donor insemination', *Human Reproduction*, vol 22, pp 2566–71.

Pennings, G. (2005) 'Reply: Reproductive exile versus reproductive tourism', *Human Reproduction*, vol 20, pp 3571–2.

Rimple, P. (2006) 'Surrogate motherhood in Georgia: A chance for cash', EurasiaNet.org, 29 March, www.eurasianet.org/departments/civilsociety/articles/eav032906.shtml

Robinson, C. and Miller, M. (2004) 'Emergent legal definitions of parentage in assisted reproductive technology', *Journal of Family Social Work*, vol 8, no 2, pp 21–51.

Schneider, M. and Forthofer, M. (2005) 'Associations of psychosocial factors with the stress of infertility treatment', *Health and Social Work*, vol 30, pp 183–91.

Sewpaul, V. (1999) 'Culture, religion and infertility: A South African perspective', *British Journal of Social Work*, vol 29, pp 741–54.

Spar, D. (2006) *The Baby Business: How Money, Science and Politics Drive the Commerce of Conception*, Boston, MA: Harvard Business School.

United Nations (1948) Universal Declaration of Human Rights, www.un.org/en/documents/udhr/

United Nations (1979) 'Convention on the Elimination of All Forms of Discrimination Against Women', www.un.org/womenwatch/daw/cedaw/text/econvention.htm

United Nations (1989) 'Convention on the Rights of the Child', www2.ohchr.org/english/law/crc.htm

United Nations (2000) Millennium Declaration, www.un.org/millennium/declaration/ares552e.pdf

United Nations (2003) 'World fertility report 2003: Executive Summary', www.un.org/esa/population/publications/worldfertility/Executive_Summary.pdf

Wincott, E. and Crawshaw, M. (2006) 'From a social issue to policy: Social work's advocacy for the rights of donor conceived people to genetic origins information in the United Kingdom', *Social Work in Health Care*, vol 43, pp 53–72.

World Health Organization (2003) 'Assisted conception in developing countries: Facing up to the issues', *Progress in Human Reproduction Research*, no 63 www.who.int/reproductive-health/hrp/progress/63/63.pdf

Zachary, P. (2000) 'Family planning: Welcome to the global sperm trade', *Wall Street Journal*, 6 January, B1.

Laying the foundations for good health in childhood

Norma Baldwin

Introduction

The common needs of children have been recognised in the United Nations (UN) Convention on the Rights of the Child and accepted within the policies and legislations of almost all countries. The Convention and the UN Millennium Development Goals (UN, 2006) emphasise the importance of global commitments to ensure that all children will be able to enjoy:

• freedom from poverty and inequality
• shelter
• adequate nutrition
• health
• education
• family and social care
• protection from war, violence, abuse and exploitation
• cultural and religious rights.

Yet there are enormous inequalities between countries and regions and within countries in children's life chances (WHO, 2005; 2008; UNICEF, 2005; 2006; 2007a; 2007b).

Many children live in enviable conditions where income, environment, housing, health and education allow them to achieve their potential and enjoy a good quality of life and well-being into old age. Other children experience harsh and brutal conditions, where life is an endless – often losing – struggle for survival. This variable picture needs to be understood in all its complexity if policies and services are to be effective in laying the foundations for health in childhood. Throughout the chapter, health and well-being will be seen as inextricably linked, related to the optimum developmental needs of children. The contribution of social work to health and well-being in childhood depends on a multidisciplinary analysis, within a strategic, inter–agency context.

This chapter will consider major differences in life chances for children. It will argue for holistic approaches, seeing children's needs and rights in the context of their families, social and cultural groups and wider environment. The consequences of wide-ranging policies, for example economic, defence, trade, immigration, housing, health and education, need to be explored as well as narrower more individualised policies. Such policies can ameliorate or aggravate the consequences of inequalities.

The *European Health Report* (WHO, 2005, p ix) argues that 'the inequalities in children's health are unacceptably large, and overwhelmingly affect the countries, societies, communities, families and children with the fewest resources to cope with them'. Even within affluent countries, poverty is the greatest threat to children's health, with lifelong consequences. Poverty may arise from underdevelopment, wars, natural disasters, and political and economic problems. It may be a result of political, economic and social factors, which lead to inequalities and disadvantage for particular groups within a society. The starting point is whether countries have the economic means and the infrastructure to meet the needs of all adults and children. Social and economic policy decisions may then enhance or impede the ability of parents to undertake the difficult task of child-rearing. They have direct and indirect consequences for the capacity of families to promote their children's health and growth, their social, emotional and personal development (Spencer and Baldwin, 2005). Taxes and benefits, health services, education and employment policies affect the opportunities for all adults and children to live in health and safety and to participate in mainstream society.

Wilkinson (1996; 2005) and Wilkinson and Pickett (2006) argue that more egalitarian societies are more socially cohesive and can protect from anxiety, bitterness, stigma and feelings of uselessness present in the most economically divided societies. Stahl et al (2006) argue that health is central to the well-being, safety, and social and educational opportunities of all children. They support the approach of the European Union and World Health Organization (WHO) in moves to consider the health impacts of all social policies. This is a starting point for this chapter: all who are involved in social work and allied fields need to recognise the interconnections of day to day practice with all policies and services which affect the health and well-being of children.

Income across the world

Gross National Income (GNI), expressed in US dollars, varies across the world's regions from an average of $600 to over $30,000. There are also enormous inequalities within regions. Table 7.1 shows this dramatic difference across regions, while Table 7.2 exemplifies individual differences within them. UNICEF reports (2006; 2008) on movement globally towards meeting Millennium Development Goals (UN, 2006) show continuing huge differences in life chances between affluent and developing countries. Poverty and inequality are major, though not the only, influences on survival and health.

Table 7.1: GNI ($) across the regions, 2004

Sub-Saharan Africa	611
Mid-Eastern and North Africa	2308
South Asia	600
East Asia and Pacific	1686
Latin America and Caribbean	3649
Central and Eastern Europe	2667
Industrialised countries	32,232

Source: Adapted from UNICEF (2006)

Table 7.2: GNI ($) in some individual countries, 2004

Afghanistan	250
Australia	26,900
Cuba	1,170
Denmark	40,650
Ethiopia	110
Finland	32,790
India	620
Rwanda	220
Sierra Leone	200
UK	33,940
US	41,400

Source: Adapted from UNICEF (2006)

Maternal and infant health and well-being

The foundations for good health – in fact for survival – are laid before birth. Children's health is dependent particularly on the circumstances of their mother, her income, environment and access to health and social care. She is dependent on her family and social groups, and on the economic and political regime within her country or region.

Across the world the likelihood of dying before reaching the age of five is 72 per 1,000 live births. In sub-Saharan Africa the rate is 160 for every 1,000. In South Asia it is 83. In developed industrialised countries only six per 1,000 children die before the age of five, but there are substantial differences between the most and least affluent groups. Nutrition is crucial to every child's development. There are huge discrepancies across the regions in the adequacy of food supplies. South Asia has the highest level of under-nutrition among regions, with 42% of under-fives being undernourished:

- in sub–Saharan Africa the figure is 28%;
- in the Middle East and North Africa it is 17%;
- in East Asia and Pacific it is 14%;
- in Latin America and Caribbean it is 7%;
- in Central and Eastern Europe it is 5% (UNICEF, 2008).

The figures in this report show at least 25% of children throughout the world to be undernourished. Black et al (2008) claim that the prevalence of under–nutrition in low– and middle-income countries is associated with about 35% of child deaths and 11% of the total global disease burden. As UNICEF has shown (see Table 7.3), there are gross indqualities in under–five mortality; and no improvement in percentage of low birth weight infants in the same countries.

Table 7.3: Under-5 mortality; low birth weight

Under-5 mortality ranking 2006 (The higher the number, the fewer who die under 5)		% of infants with low birth weight	
		In 2006 report	In 2008 report
Cuba	159	6	5
Denmark	172	5	5
Finland	185	4	4
India	52	30	30
Rwanda	10	9	6
Sierra Leone	1	23	24
UK	162	8	8
US	152	8	8

Source: Adapted from UNICEF (2006, 2008)

Maternal health

Poor access to antenatal and maternal care in South Asia and sub-Saharan Africa contributes to high rates of maternal death – with attendant harm for existing children as well as newborn infants (UNICEF, 2008). 'One in 16 women die in pregnancy or childbirth in sub-Saharan Africa compared with one in 2,800 women in developed countries' (id21, 2007, p 2001). The id21 paper stresses the importance of the accessibility of intra-partum care and long-term, multiple approaches to providing it.

Add to the inadequacies of maternal care the high rate of childhood HIV infections in sub-Saharan Africa (accounting for almost 90% of paediatric HIV infections), and the extreme risks to children in developing countries become clear (UNICEF, 2008). Global pharmaceutical marketing is influential here.

The consequences of war

The consequences of civil strife and war, particularly in countries where there may already be problems of poverty and development, are immense. An Oxfam report (2007), comparing African countries experiencing conflicts with those at peace, estimated that they had on average:

- 50% more infant deaths;
- 15% more people who were undernourished;
- 20% more adult illiteracy.

The report suggests that armed conflicts are a major factor preventing achievement of the Millennium Development Goals. It describes the undermining of sustainable development and functioning of institutions, the abuse of human rights, long-term spread of violence and breakdown of social responsibility.

Women and children paid a heavy price, not just through the destruction of war, but also through lack of health services, spread of infections and high levels of sexual violence. *The Shame of War* (UN, 2007) documents extreme brutality against women, girls and boys in African conflicts. It draws attention to sexual violence and exploitation by peacekeepers and aid workers following conflicts, raising global gender issues beyond the harm and degradation of war for combatants.

Health care

Global figures for infant and maternal health show strong correspondence between mortality, morbidity and Gross National Income (GNI). However Cuba's situation (UNICEF, 2008) shows what relatively poor countries can achieve when government policies are strategic, integrated and universal and promote public health and primary care. Cuba has a sophisticated health service with universal support for maternal and child health (Cooper et al, 2006; Kath, 2007). Figures for Cuban infant and maternal health compare well with those of rich, industrialised nations. There appear to be no major differences in the ability of black and white groups to gain access to services.

Cooper et al acknowledge the complexity of drawing comparisons. They probe some of the comparisons with the US: in Cuba 35% of the population are of black/white heritage, yet the infant mortality rate is less than half that of black Americans. They acknowledge that perinatal mortality may be affected by the US's high-tech interventions that result in more live deliveries and survival of very low birth weight babies. They argue that, even so, Cuba's results compare well with the best reproductive health records in the developed world.

Cooper et al argue that the Cuban experience and strategy – educated workforce, public health and universal primary care programmes, government leadership on intersectoral collaboration and neighbourhood organisation to achieve health goals – could be used to transform health experience in low- and middle-income countries. They question a lack of curiosity about this radical and effective approach and criticise international aid and development agencies for neglecting the model and for paying undue attention to privatised health care. They acknowledge that ideological differences may have a bearing on the relative neglect of the Cuban model.

Kath (2007) also discusses the importance of intersectoral cooperation in achieving good maternal and child health outcomes in Cuba, for example the combination of initiatives in public health and nutrition. She acknowledges that some community-based initiatives have elements of surveillance but emphasises the importance attached to collective responsibility. She concludes that Cuba's success in matching low mortality rates for mothers and infants with those of the most affluent nations, in spite of its poverty and difficult circumstances, is facilitated by coordinated effort across sectors for national developmental priorities.

Bhutta et al (2008) identify a range of interconnected interventions which can improve survival rates and the health of children. Many are of relevance to social work and allied fields such as community development and education. They include promotion of breastfeeding, strategies to promote complementary feeding and support for family and community nutrition. These connect with the need to improve women's education and empowerment and the elimination of poverty. In a very different context – discussing issues of relative deprivation in Scotland, where GNI is around 30 times higher than that in Cuba – a Joseph Rowntree Foundation report (2007) also emphasises the importance of strategic integration of policies and operations, if deprivation is to be tackled successfully, mirroring principles of Cuban policies.

Education

Alongside maternal health as a foundation for good health in childhood, the education level of a society – particularly that of females – is also significant. The Millennium Development Goals (UN, 2006) include improvements in female education alongside major health improvements. Table 7.4 shows literacy differences across the world's regions.

Table 7.4: Literacy: (A) adult females as % of adult males; (B) youth (15–24): male and female

Region	A	B	
	Adult: female–male (%)	Youth: male (%)	Youth: female (%)
Sub-Saharan Africa	72	75	64
Middle East & North Africa	77	92	83
South Asia	66	81	65
East Asia & Pacific	92	99	98
Latin America & Caribbean	99	96	97
CEE/CIS	96	99	98

Source: Adapted from UNICEF (2008)

Sierra Leone has the highest rate of under-five mortality in the world (UNICEF, 2008) and a high percentage (24%) of low birth weight babies. It has a percentage of 51% female to male literacy. India, 52nd highest for under-five mortality out of 206 countries, has 30% low birth weight babies. Female to male adult literacy is 66%. Rwanda, ravaged by war and displacement, is the 10th highest country in its under-five mortality rate, yet according to UNICEF (2006) figures it had only 9% of infants with low birth weight and UNICEF (2008) recorded it as having dropped to 6%. Rwanda is recorded as having 85% female to male literacy. Cuba, at the bottom of the lower-middle income group with a Gross National Income (GNI) of 1,170 dollars equivalent (UNICEF, 2008) has, as Table 7.3 shows, a low rate of under-five mortality as well as of low birth weight. It is recorded as having 100% female to male literacy. South Asia has the highest level of under-nutrition among the world's regions and the lowest proportion of female to male literacy (66%).

Current percentages for literacy in industrialised countries are not shown in the UNICEF (2008) figures, but are likely to be among the highest, given almost universal secondary education. There are, however, major differences in the UK and US in levels of educational achievement along the socio–economic gradient. In rich industrial consumer societies, educational failure is associated with lower earnings and increased likelihood of unemployment and social exclusion (Spencer and Baldwin, 2005). Limited career opportunities and poor educational attainment are associated with high levels of teenage births in the UK and US, reflecting economic and social conditions associated with motherhood and with differential earning power and cultural roles of males and females (Spencer, 1994; 2002; Spencer and Baldwin, 2005).

Clearly many factors play a part in these variations, but they raise major questions for social work and allied disciplines about the organisation and accessibility of services. They highlight issues of equality concerning gender, ethnicity and disability. Interconnections need to be understood in attempts to identify and implement effective strategies to promote the health and well-being of children.

Childhood

Gross discrepancies in opportunities for children in different regions of the world are indicated by figures on income, health and education. These cannot adequately show, however, the range and complexity of factors that enhance or blight a child's experience. The extent to which boys and girls are valued equally, attitudes to and opportunities in childhood, and the economic circumstances which dictate whether children and young people can participate in education or will be forced into entering the labour market, will have major physical, social, intellectual and emotional consequences.

Stolen Childhoods (Lent, 2006) documents problems of child labour in the poorest parts of the world. Extreme poverty may force parents to accept bonded labour for their children, or their children's involvement in carpet making, tobacco, coffee and cotton picking, and sugar cane cutting (International Crisis Group, 2005; Lent, 2006; Channel 4, 2007). This prevents children's participation in education and exposes them to physical and chemical hazards. Their labour may be of major benefit to consumers in affluent parts of their own and industrialised countries. Globalisation of trade is a key issue and children's exploitation and suffering is a concern for workers in health and welfare everywhere, as well as for us all as consumers.

Lent (2006) stresses the importance of raising consciousness, of campaigning for financial incentives and support to enable poor families to send their children to school and to use healthcare services, and of supporting micro-finance and credit unions. Even more extreme suffering is caused to children in war zones, some of whom may be pressed into service as soldiers (UNICEF, 2006; 2008; UN, 2007). Global influences are complex and pervasive.

In situations of poverty and economic collapse, environmental disaster, war or political upheaval, children are particularly vulnerable to harm, including abuse and sexual exploitation (UNICEF, 2001; UN, 2007). Street children, runaways and children abducted or trafficked may experience the most traumatic physical and sexual abuse. Experiences may differ across continents, depending on legislation, economic conditions, health and welfare provision, attitudes to children, and child protection systems. Children are, however, at risk from global networks of sexual predators, trafficking, prostitution and pornography. This is an area where social policy, social work, development and campaigning have crucial links with health, education, remedial and promotional programmes. These should focus not only on harm to children, but on attitudes to power, gender and sexuality and the commercially exploitative conditions in which they flourish.

The UN Convention on the Rights of the Child states that the responsibility of States Parties to the Convention is to promote the well-being of all children equally. This involves sensitive and respectful attention to different cultural practices and beliefs, without ignoring the oppression and harm which some may cause. There are issues about the shame and blame attached to victims of rape in some societies, about male attitudes to sexual 'rights' and needs, about beliefs in the healing powers of sex with a virgin and so on. Early and forced marriages raise issues of children's rights and the continuing problem of circumcision and genital mutilation needs to remain high on the agenda of children's health and well-being.

It is not only extreme situations that harm children: more subtle and less obviously harmful experiences may have major consequences for mental health, confidence and self-esteem. For example, bullying and social exclusion are often associated with poverty, gender and disability in affluent, industrialised countries. Being excluded by relative poverty and the lack of clothing, equipment and transport from mainstream activities such as school trips and outings with friends, can be harmful to confidence and self-esteem.

There are substantial differences between the experience of the lowest income groups and those whose income allows for adequate housing, nutrition, leisure and involvement in the mainstream of their societies. Single parents are those most likely to have basic incomes below the average. In the US in the 1990s around 60% of single parents had a basic income likely to leave them and their children in poverty. Tax and benefits made a difference of less than 10% to the total of those living in poverty. By contrast, in the Netherlands tax and benefit availability brought the figure down from more than 70% to just over 20%. In Sweden they brought the 40% of single parents who might be living in poverty down below 5% (Spencer and Baldwin, 2005).

In the UNICEF report on child well-being in rich countries (UNICEF, 2007b), the UK and the US, with the highest numbers living in relative deprivation and poverty, were behind other countries on measures of child well-being, even those countries with much lower disposable incomes. As Wilkinson (1996; 2005) asserts, physical and mental health problems, poor social cohesion, violence and other social harms are associated with the most unequal societies.

Social exclusion, discrimination and racism

Discrimination within societies may be directed against whole groups, such as immigrants, black people, indigenous peoples, minority ethnic or religious groups and disabled people. Individual access to jobs, housing, health and to social and leisure activities may well be reduced, but the consequences will be experienced at the family level, with particular problems for children's development. For example, Veling et al (2007) found that minority ethnic groups in the Netherlands who perceived themselves to suffer discrimination were at higher risk of schizophrenia and other psychotic disorders than those not conscious of discrimination. In an American study, Bresnahan et al (2007) compared the markedly increased rates of schizophrenia among Western European (predominantly black) immigrant groups with the situation in the US. Rates of schizophrenia among African Americans were substantially higher than for whites. They looked at more general effects of race on socio-economic status and concluded that while that was a factor in the elevated rates, it could only partly account for them.

As well as difficulties which children experience when families are coping with the stress of mental illness or other disabilities, they may have parallel stresses from bullying, racism and social exclusion. Given that immigrant, black and minority ethnic children are among the poorest groups in industrialised societies, accumulations of disadvantage may be particularly damaging (Spencer and Baldwin, 2005). Children with impairments, and children who have a family member with an impairment, are also likely to suffer accumulated disadvantages with risk of damage to interpersonal relationships within families (Spencer et al, 2001).

Emotional health and resilience

The foundations for health are laid in the material circumstances of children's early years; the quality of their relationships; the ability of communities, parents and carers to provide emotionally nurturing experiences, affection, warmth and stimulus; a valued social and personal identity; and opportunities to develop skills, responsibility and participation (Glaser, 2003; Bartley, 2007).

Interconnections of economic, environmental, social and interpersonal factors are clear and strong. From the African saying 'It takes a whole village to raise a child', to the Scottish response to child protection concerns *'It's Everyone's Job to Make Sure I'm Alright'* (Scottish Executive, 2002), and throughout the UN Convention on the Rights of the Child, these interconnections are acknowledged. They show a complex and diverse picture, but one in which children's common needs are clear. The assessment triangle (Figure 7.1) indicates factors along three dimensions of a child's world, which are crucial to health, physical and emotional development and resilience.

The triangle – and its accompanying assessment and action planning framework – was developed in Scotland by a multidisciplinary group reporting to Scottish Parliamentary advisers. It now provides the common basis for assessment of individual children and their families throughout Scotland, within policy initiatives requiring integrated responses to children's needs across health, social work, education, justice and other services (Scottish Executive, 2005). The Scottish triangle draws extensively on work done in England and Wales to identify the research evidence of what children need to promote optimum development, personally, in their families and social groups and in their wider environment (Department of Health et al, 2000).

Assessment and planning to meet children's needs has to be able to connect different levels together and work collaboratively across services, disciplines and institutions.

Laying the foundations; repairing harm

This chapter has indicated some key factors in laying the foundations for health in policy, organisation and practice. The complexity and range of global factors involved is matched by regional, population-wide and local particularities as well as by the complexity of individual children's situations and needs.

Figure 7.1: The assessment triangle

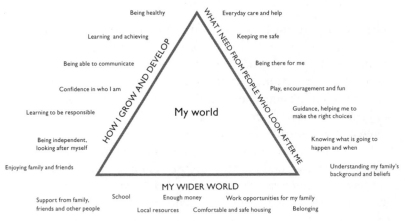

Source: Scottish Executive, 2005

For social work to play an effective role, all involved need to develop understandings of major influences on health, development and well-being by:

• being informed about changing conditions and needs and interconnections of global, regional and local policies and institutional practices;
• contributing to the evidence base in research and practice;
• analysing, assessing and planning policy and interventions;
• forming strategic alliances;
• making realistic plans for intervention at population-wide, organisational and political or local and individual levels;
• evaluating outcomes.

Social work has a key role to play in the radical global movement to achieve progress for all children, particularly the most disadvantaged and vulnerable. Collaborative work across professional groups with communities, families and young people is required to plan and deliver:

• intersectoral initiatives in provision of water, food, shelter, medicines;
• accessible health and social care through local provision;
• transport and funding;
• a continuum of promotional, preventive and remedial services;
• capacity building in localities and communities;
• organisational and service change and development;
• educational and employment opportunities;

- public health education and promotion;
- evidence of need and risks;
- community and family support;
- child protection;
- therapeutic and intensive interventions;
- advocacy and campaigning for human rights and against discrimination.

Initiatives based on humane and equitable principles are needed to lay the foundations for good health in childhood. Social workers see the whole range of human need: from the most individualised and specific, such as a child born with a severe impairment, or a child abandoned or bereaved, through to the most desperate conditions of whole populations following war, disasters, oppression, and rural and industrial decline. We are in a position to speak out, to reach out, to take action.

References

Bartley, M. (2007) *Capability and Resilience: Beating the Odds*, Swindon: ESRC.

Bhutta, Z., Ahmed, T., Black, R., Cousens, S., Dewey, K., Giugliani, E., Haider, B., Kirkwood, B., Morris, S., Sachdev, H. and Shekar, M. (2008) '"What works" interventions for maternal under-nutrition and survival', *The Lancet*, vol 371, no 9610, pp 417–40.

Black, R., Allen, L., Bhutta, Z., Coulfield, L., de Onis, M., Ezzati, M., Mathers, C. and Rivera, J. (2008) 'Maternal and child under nutrition: Global and regional exposures and health consequences', *The Lancet*, vol 371, no 9608, pp 243–60.

Bresnahan, M., Begg, M., Brown, A., Schaefer, C., Sohler, N., Insel, B., Vella, L. and Susser, E. (2007) 'Race and risk of schizophrenia in a US birth cohort: Another example of health disparity?', *International Journal of Epidemiology*, vol 36, no 4, pp 751–8.

Channel 4 (2007) 'Coca Cola', *Dispatches*, 19 November.

Cooper, R., Kennelly, J. and Orduñez-Garcia, P. (2006) 'Health in Cuba', *International Journal of Epidemiology*, vol 35, no 4, pp 817–924.

Department of Health, Department of Education and Employment and Home Office (2000) *Framework for the Assessment of Children in Need and their Families*, London: The Stationery Office.

Glaser, D. (2003) 'Early experience, attachment and the brain', in J. Corrigall and H. Wilkinson (eds) *Revolutionary Connections: Psychotherapy and Neuroscience*, London: Karnac Books, pp 117–35.

id21 (2007) 'Maternal health in poor countries: The broader context and a call for action', *The Lancet*, Maternal Survival Series Research Highlights, January.

International Crisis Group (2005) *The Curse of Cotton: Central Asia's Destructive Monoculture*, Asia Report no 93, 28 February, London: International Crisis Group.

Joseph Rowntree Foundation (2007) *Political Devolution, Regional Governance and Tackling Deprivation*, York: Joseph Rowntree Foundation.

Kath, E. (2007) 'Inter-sectoral cooperation, political will and health outcomes: A study of Cuba's Maternal–Infant Health Programme', *Policy & Politics*, vol 35, no 1, pp 45–64.

Lent, P. (2006) *Stolen Childhoods: Teacher Resource Guide*, Vineyard Haven, MA: Galen Films Inc.

Oxfam (2007) *Africa's Missing Billions*, Briefing Paper 107, Oxford: Oxfam.

Scottish Executive (2002) *'It's Everyone's Job to Make Sure I'm Alright': Report of the Child Protection Audit Review*, Edinburgh: The Stationery Office.

Scottish Executive (2005) *Getting it Right for Every Child: Proposals for Action*, Edinburgh: Scottish Executive, www.scotland.gov.uk/Publications/2005/06/20135608/56164

Spencer, N. and Baldwin, N. (2005) 'Economic, cultural and social context of neglect', in J. Taylor and B. Daniel (eds) *Child Neglect – Practice Issues for Health and Social Care*, London: Jessica Kingsley Publishers, pp 26–42.

Spencer, N. (1994) 'Teenage mothers', *Current Paediatrics*, vol 4, pp 48–51.

Spencer, N. (2002) 'Reducing unintended pregnancy among adolescents: Changes in social, economic and educational policy need to be taken into account', Letter, *British Medical Journal*, vol 325, p 777.

Spencer, N., Taylor, J., Baldwin, N. and Read, J. (2001) 'The impact of poverty and deprivation on caring for children', *Reader for Fragile. Handle with Care*, London: NSPCC.

Stahl, T., Wismar, M., Ollila, A., Lahtinen, E. and Leppo, K. (2006) *Health in All Policies: Prospects and Potentials*, Helsinki, Finland: European Observatory on Health Systems and Policies and Ministry of Social Affairs and Health.

UN (United Nations) (2006) *Millennium Development Goals Report*, New York: United Nations.

UN (2007) *The Shame of War: Sexual Violence Against Women and Girls in Conflict*, IRIN Nairobi, Geneva, New York: United Nations Office for the Coordination of Human Affairs.

UNICEF (United Nations Children's Fund) (2001) *Profiting from Abuse*, New York: UNICEF.

UNICEF (2005) *The State of the World's Children*, New York: UNICEF.

UNICEF (2006) *The State of the World's Children*, New York: UNICEF.

UNICEF (2007a) *The State of the World's Children*, New York: UNICEF.

UNICEF (2007b) *Child Poverty in Perspective: An Overview of Child Well-Being in Rich Countries*, New York: UNICEF.

UNICEF (2008) *The State of the World's Children*, New York: UNICEF.

Veling, W., Seltzen, J.-P., Susser, E., Laan, W., Mackenbach, J.P. and Hoek, H.W. (2007) 'Discrimination and the incidence of psychotic disorders among ethnic minorities in the Netherlands', *International Journal of Epidemiology*, vol 36, no 4, pp 761–8.

WHO (World Health Organization) (2005) *European Health Report*, Copenhagen: World Health Organization.

WHO (2008) *Closing the Gap in a Generation: Health Equity through Action on the Social Determinants of Health*, Final Report of the Commission on Social Determinants of Health, Geneva: World Health Organization.

Wilkinson, R.G. (1996) *Unhealthy Societies – The Afflictions of Inequality*, London: Routledge.

Wilkinson, R.G. (2005) *The Impact of Inequality: How to Make Sick Societies Healthier*, New York: The New Press.

Wilkinson, R.G. and Pickett, K.E. (2006) 'Income inequality and population health: A review and explanations of the evidence', *Social Science and Medicine*, vol 62, no 7, pp 1768–84.

Violence, abuse and health

Lesley Laing

Introduction

Violence against women, also referred to as gender-based violence, is a violation of human rights that occurs in all cultures and in every country across the world (Krug et al, 2002, p 7). It causes profound suffering, limits women's full participation as citizens and is a stark marker of gender inequality. One of its further consequences is to undermine children's health and development (Humphreys, 2007). Recognition of the pervasiveness and profound effects of such violence on women's health has led to violence against women being identified as a public health priority issue by the World Health Organization (2005).

This chapter explores violence against women as an example of gendered health inequality and it is argued that good health policy and practice must address this manifestation of gender inequality. Social work is well placed to contribute to this process because of its commitment to social justice, understanding of the social determinants of health and ability to traverse the 'gap' that often exists between health services and other players essential to a comprehensive response to gender-based violence. These include activist women's groups that have been pivotal to placing this issue on the public agenda. The author draws on her experience as a social worker in the health sector, in various roles that have focused on assisting health personnel to recognise and respond more appropriately to the many 'silent' survivors of gender-based violence they encounter in the course of their work.

Recognition of the extent of violence against women and activism to address it has taken various paths around the world. In Western democracies, this recognition was achieved largely through the activism of second-wave feminists, commencing in the early 1970s and focusing initially on violence against women by intimate partners and ex-partners (domestic violence) and on sexual violence. In countries with strong links to the West, such as Japan and South Korea, feminist activism has also been a driving force, with sex tourism an initial focus of action (Radford and Tsutsumi, 2004; Postmus, 2007). In some developing countries, activism against gender-based violence has been associated with women's empowerment through engagement in other human rights struggles (see, for example, Martins da Silva and Kendall, 2002; Boesten, 2006; Johnson and Brunell, 2006), often influenced by the 'globalisation of human rights discourses' (Radford and Tsutsumi, 2004, p 6), an issue taken up later in this chapter. The common factor in all movements against gender-based violence is their genesis in grassroots women's movements (Fischbach and Herbert, 1997). In many instances the impetus for change has been survivor activism in response to the inadequacy of institutionalised responses to the injustice they are experiencing. This includes the responses of the helping professions, such as social work.

A gendered phenomenon

Defining violence against women is difficult because of the many forms that it can take. The United Nations definition of violence against women explicitly centres gender as the key lens through which diverse violent and abusive behaviours towards women are understood. Hence, in much of the literature, as here, the terms 'gender-based violence' and 'violence against women', are used interchangeably. The definition developed by Heise et al (cited in Heise, 1994, p 136) is used here because it captures the diversity of forms of violence against women and emphasises that women and girls are vulnerable to these violations because of their subordinate gendered position.

Gender-based violence includes a host of harmful behaviours that are directed at women and girls because of their sex, including wife abuse, sexual assault, dowry-related murder, marital rape, selective malnourishment of female children, forced prostitution, female genital mutilation and sexual abuse of female children. Specifically, violence against women includes any act of verbal or physical force, coercion or life-threatening deprivation directed at an individual woman or girl that causes physical or psychological harm, humiliation or arbitrary deprivation of liberty and that perpetuates female subordination.

Gender-based violence is gendered both in its pattern of victimisation and perpetration: the majority of victims are women and girls and men are the perpetrators in the majority of cases (Kelly and Lovett, 2005; Ellsberg, 2006). A gendered lens is concerned with gender as a marker for patterned and systematic inequalities (Humphreys, 2007), rather than inequalities solely between individuals, and hence requires attention to the operation of power. Understanding gender inequality as the underlying cause of violence against women helps to address the many paradoxes that confront us about it. For example, why do attitudes that blame the victim of domestic violence remain entrenched after several decades of community education campaigns (Gracia and Herrero, 2006)? Why, despite several decades of law reform and the development of networks of support services, is there such a high attrition of rape cases from the criminal justice system, resulting in declining conviction rates in many jurisdictions (Kelly et al, 2005; Fitzgerald, 2006)? These conundrums point to the ongoing social acceptance of violence against women that is expressed not only by some individuals, but through social and cultural attitudes that fail to hold perpetrators of violence accountable while blaming the victims for their own violation. This tolerance of violence against women includes inadequate and at times abusive institutional responses, including those by health services (Stark and Flitcraft, 1996a; Astbury and Cabral, 2000).

Highlighting the importance of gender, however, must not exclude attending to other forms of difference that are similarly used to justify, pattern and reproduce social inequalities – such as race, ethnicity, class, caste, immigration status, ability and sexuality. In understanding the effects of multiple, interlocking patterns of inequality, Crenshaw's (1991) concept of 'intersectionality' is helpful. This concept implies more than a notion of cumulative disadvantage; it attempts to draw attention to the complex interactions of multiple coexisting oppressions. Thus, while all women are vulnerable to gender-based violence, their social location shapes and contextualises their experience of violence, their vulnerability to it, the meanings they make of it (including whether the experience, in fact, is named as violence), their options for responding and the responses they receive from both formal and informal supports in their communities. The situation of refugee women exemplifies the ways in which race and gender intersect, resulting in multiple, compounding discrimination and abuse both in the situations that precipitate their displacement, their experiences as refugees and in their access to resettlement. Pittaway and Bartolomei (2002) have documented the many ways in which these intersections result in gross human rights violations of refugee women. For example:

> Refugee women are actively discriminated against on the grounds of their ethnicity and their gender. In terms of racial discrimination they are often devalued or 'othered' on grounds of their race, and this effectively removes any need by the aggressors to respect them by gender. This 'others' them

twice and makes them prime targets for systematic rape and sexual torture for the purpose of shaming the men of their communities. (Pittaway and Bartolomei, 2002, p 19)

Globalisation and violence against women

While violence against women is universal, its various forms are shaped by shifting social, historical, economic and cultural contexts. As noted in the introductory chapter, an important context for the discussions in this book is that of globalisation. Globalisation affects violence against women in complex and contradictory ways. For example, Radford and Tsutsumi (2004, p 2) explore the ways in which in two developed countries, Japan and the UK, which have benefited economically from globalisation, it has provided 'different and more opportunities' for male violence towards women:

> Men in Japan and the UK have exported the risks associated with violence against women by increasingly targeting women and children who occupy the poor 'peripheral' regions. In peripheral regions women are 'outsiders' as they lack rights to protection and often carry both the responsibility and blame for men's violence. (Radford and Tsutsumi, 2004, p 2)

Examples of new and increasing forms of violence against women include sex tourism, trafficking of women for prostitution and use of the internet to transmit pornography and to entrap women in abusive and exploitative relationships. Relatively underdeveloped and poorly enforced sanctions for these forms of transnational violence benefit men at the expense of women and girls in less advantaged regions. However, Radford and Tsutsumi's notion of 'peripheral' encompasses not merely women in geographically distant and poorer nations. It also encompasses women who lack citizen status or whose status is insecure or partner-dependent, putting even well-established legal protections in developed nations beyond their reach.

On the other hand, globalisation has enabled the sharing of knowledge and the development of transnational coalitions of women activists working towards the common goal of eliminating violence against women. At its simplest level, women's increasing access to information that names certain behaviours as violence and challenges taken-for-granted notions about responsibility for it, can be a powerful force for change. For example, writing about grassroots women's groups in Peru, Boesten (2006, pp 371–2) describes how information about women's rights provided by non-governmental organisations (NGOs), can contribute to women's empowerment:

> In this way, some groups of the poorest women, who are situated at the bottom of a very hierarchical social ladder, learn different ways to combat violence.... It proves that they are not 'illiterate indigenous women' or 'uneducated cholas', but Peruvians with rights and obligations, i.e. citizens in their own right.... By speaking up among themselves, women push back the boundaries of what is accepted as 'legitimate' violence.

At the international level, the impact of women's activism is seen in the acknowledgement of violence against women as a human rights violation through the United Nations' Declaration on the Elimination of Violence against Women (United Nations General Assembly, 1993). The subsequent 1995 United Nations World Conference on Women in Beijing produced a Platform for Action that included measures against gender-based violence. Indeed, the elimination of violence against women is regarded as essential to the achievement of the United Nations' Millennium Development Goals (Ellsberg, 2006).

Nevertheless, there remain many challenges in translating these international instruments into real gains in reducing violence against women and some argue that the patriarchal foundations of international law on human rights limit its utility in protecting and advancing women's human rights, in particular, in relation to multiply disadvantaged women (Craven, 2003). For example, Pittaway and Bartolomei (2002, p 22) have highlighted the ways in which the 'gender-blindness' of international Refugee Law leaves refugee women unprotected.

A challenge for globalised action to prevent and overcome the effects of violence against women is for those with experience in addressing gender-based violence in developed nations to avoid replicating colonial and oppressive power relationships in their collaborations with women in developing nations. For example, unequal donor–recipient relationships can lead to the imposition of inappropriate approaches (Johnson and Brunell, 2006). In fact, countries coming to the issue more recently have tackled some of the challenges that have plagued longer-established movements against gender-based violence. For example, both China and East Timor are developing integrated responses to violence against women. This avoids the 'silos' that have divided different agencies' responses to its various forms in the UK and Australia (Hester, 2004; Kelly and Lovett, 2005; Martins da Silva et al, 2006).

Prevalence and health impacts of violence against women

It has been estimated that 'around the world at least one woman in every three has been beaten, coerced into sex, or otherwise abused in her lifetime' (Heise et al, 1999, p 1). When sexual harassment and all forms of gender-based violence are included, more than half of all women are affected (Kelly and Lovett, 2005).

The example of domestic (or intimate partner) violence, the most common form of violence against women, illustrates the scope of the problem. In 2005, the World Health Organization (WHO), released the first report of the population-based *Multi-Country Study on Women's Health and Domestic Violence against Women* (World Health Organization, 2005). Data on the prevalence of intimate partner abuse and on its health impacts was collected from 19,568 ever-partnered women in 10 countries (Bangladesh, Brazil, Peru, Thailand, United Republic of Tanzania, Ethiopia, Japan, Namibia, Serbia and Montenegro, and Samoa), including both rural and urban areas. This study was designed to address many of the methodological limitations of cross-country comparison of previous studies, for example through the use of a standardised questionnaire and standardised training and data collection techniques (Ellsberg et al, 2008). It measured the prevalence of physical violence, sexual violence, emotional abuse (for example: being insulted or made to feel bad about oneself; being intimidated or scared on purpose) and controlling behaviours (for example restricting contact with the woman's family of birth; insisting on knowing where she is at all times; and controlling her access to health care) by a partner. It also measured women's self-reported physical and mental health and explored the association between domestic violence and health.

The proportion of women who had experienced physical or sexual violence, or both, by an intimate partner in their lifetime, ranged from 15% to 71% (with prevalence for most sites between 29% and 62%). Across the study sites, between 20% and 75% of women reported experiencing emotional abuse and between 21% and 90% reported being subjected to controlling behaviours by a partner (World Health Organization, 2005). The study found a significant association between lifetime experiences of domestic violence and self-reported poor health (Ellsberg et al, 2008).

In considering the health impacts of domestic violence, the most obvious are injuries arising from physical violence. The WHO (2005) study found that rates of injury ranged from 19% to 55% across the 15 study sites and that between 23% and 80% of women reported that they needed health care as a result of injury (regardless of whether this was received). While the majority of injuries were classified as minor (for example bruises, cuts), in some study sites there were high rates of serious injury, such as fractures (44% of injured women in Namibia) (Ellsberg et al, 2008). Nevertheless, even relatively minor injury can lead to severe health impacts in the presence of underlying disease such as malaria (Fischbach and Herbert, 1997).

Injury, however, is only one of many health impacts of domestic violence. Many are long term and continue even when the woman has escaped the abusive relationship (Campbell et al, 2002). Campbell et al (2002) found that women who experience domestic violence have a 50–70% increase in gynaecological, central nervous system and chronic stress-related problems when compared to other women. Domestic violence is also associated with increased risk for HIV/AIDS. Many of the health impacts of domestic violence are associated with violence against women during pregnancy and include late accessing of health care, increased risk behaviours such as smoking and substance misuse, vaginal, cervical and kidney infections, premature labour and inadequate weight gain (Ellsberg, 2006).

Ever-abused women in the WHO study also reported significantly more emotional distress, suicidal thoughts and suicide attempts (Ellsberg et al, 2008). This is consistent with a large body of research that finds an association between women's experiences of domestic violence and psychiatric problems such as depression, anxiety and post-traumatic stress disorder (Golding, 1999).

Summarising the health impacts on women of violence in a major review of the research, Astbury and Cabral (2000, p 75) conclude that 'Women who have experienced violence, whether in childhood or adult life, have increased rates of depression and anxiety, stress related syndromes, pain syndromes, phobias, chemical dependency, substance use, suicidality, somatic and medical symptoms, negative health behaviours, poor subjective health and changes to health service utilization.'

Violence against women as a gendered health issue

It is clear from this discussion that violence against women is a crucial health inequality issue for women. This inequality in not only grounded in the many health effects of violence and abuse, but in the response of the health system. Despite evidence of the impacts of domestic violence on women's health, most women are not asked about abuse by their health care provider (Hegarty and Taft, 2001). The landmark Yale trauma study found that doctors in an emergency setting identified one in 35 women as victims of domestic violence, when medical records indicated that the proportion was one in four (Stark, 1984, cited in Stark and Flitcraft, 1996a). Failure to identify and document domestic violence continues to be identified in more recent studies of emergency, general practice, paediatric and maternity services (Thurston and Eisener, 2006).

However, despite the failure to formally identify domestic violence, the Yale study found that victimised women were treated differently to other patients, their subsequent problems (alcoholism, substance misuse, suicide attempts and so on) receiving no or inappropriate treatment and coming to be seen as the cause of their repeated injury. Stark and Flitcraft (1996b) argue that these medical practices both preclude women from receiving sympathetic and appropriate care, and compound the isolation and control imposed by their abusers. In a similar vein, Judith Herman contends that the diagnostic category of 'borderline personality disorder' (previously 'hysteria') is frequently applied to survivors of sexual and domestic violence in mental health services as 'little more than a sophisticated insult' (Herman, 1992, p 123).

Clearly, institutional rather than individual factors are implicated in this silence and re-victimisation of women. The gendered hierarchical medical system both reflects and reproduces this broader social pattern of inequality (Stark and Flitcraft, 1996b). This highlights the necessity for, and challenges in, promoting institutional change so that the potential of the health system to assist abused women – the sole institution that all women have contact with at some time – can be realised.

The contribution of social work

Building bridges

In addition to the need for change among health care personnel in the health care system, social work can be an ally to women activists in negotiating the tensions inherent in their struggle to gain recognition of violence against women, as an urgent social problem. Typically, activist women's groups initially challenge the state and its institutions, such as health services, from the outside (Hester, 2004). They may then be excluded from ongoing participation in the mainstreaming of responses to violence, for example through claims of superior professional expertise, risking the conversion of political and social justice issues into an individual health issue: 'by medicalising social problems as medical or psychiatric disorders, the sufferers lose the context of the experience, the suffering is delegitimated, and society is precluded from responding appropriately' (Kleinman and Kleinman, cited in Fischbach and Herbert, 1997, p 1171).

Towards Better Practice is a social work action research project that addresses this dilemma. Its goal is to enhance collaboration between women's domestic violence services, primarily based in the community sector, and mental health services (Irwin et al, 2006). The research team had experience of working in and with both the mental health and community domestic violence sectors, giving them 'insider' status with each group and the ability to bring together the two groups of service providers in six research sites. Using focus groups, dialogue was facilitated about the barriers and opportunities for collaboration in work with women affected by domestic violence. Working parties were subsequently established at a number of sites to trial a range of collaborative initiatives that are being evaluated using an action evaluation methodology. These initiatives include, for example, a series of training and information programmes hosted in turn by mental health and domestic violence services, bringing together service providers with a common clientele who previously had no or minimal contact; the development of a formal service agreement; the establishment of effective referral pathways; and the implementation of joint assessment sessions between a community mental health team and local domestic violence services. This research reflects the values of feminist social work research: research that promotes change to improve the situation of women. It recognises that the complexity of domestic violence requires the different respective skills, knowledge and resources contributed by two service sectors that are typically divided by very different understandings about the nature of violence.

Using social group work skills to empower survivors of violence

Group work, with roots in the grassroots activism which brought gender-based violence to public attention, is a potentially powerful intervention with women who have experienced this, and is also an area of social work expertise. However, social work, together with other helping professions, has been critiqued for adopting intervention approaches that locate women's experiences of violence in their individual characteristics or behaviour. An example would be group work that targets women's 'passivity', 'co-dependency' or 'assertiveness', removed from the wider social context of women's lives (Brown and Dickey, 1992; Quinn, 2000). In contrast to what she terms traditional 'therapeutic' or 'clinical' approaches to group work, Quinn argues that good social work practice in group work with survivors of sexual violence must incorporate a social justice agenda:

> The new groupwork practice would lead to a nexus of anti-sexual violence activity where women were consulted about their experiences as if they had some vital expertise to contribute on the subject. Women would eventually be able to use the groupwork as a springboard to social change, exposing some of the social injustices that they had been wanting to correct for a long time. (Quinn, 2000, p 7)

In a similar vein, Flannery et al (2000) identify the benefits of applying this perspective to group work with women who have lived with domestic violence. Group work that positions domestic violence as a social justice issue can counteract secrecy and the ensuing isolation commonly experienced by women as a result of perpetrator tactics, inappropriate service responses, shame, fear and self-blame, and can facilitate empowerment by linking private and public worlds. In this way, work with individual women is linked to the broader project of challenging and changing oppressive gender inequalities.

Conclusion

Violence against women is a violation of human rights that exacts an enormous toll on women's health and well-being. The role of social workers in addressing this form of gendered health inequality can be conceptualised as that of 'bi-cultural' workers. They are knowledgeable within health systems where a biomedical frame is pre-eminent, yet maintain a social view of health, and the ability to work with community partners, thus becoming important players in linking health services into a broader response to violence against women. A commitment to social justice links all social work interventions — whether at local or global levels, or targeting individual, community or policy change — to the broader project of reducing the gender inequality that is both a cause and consequence of violence against women.

References

Astbury, J. and Cabral, M. (2000) *Women's Mental Health: An Evidence Based Review. Geneva, Mental Health Determinants and Populations*, Geneva: Department of Mental Health and Substance Dependence, World Health Organization.

Boesten, J. (2006) 'Pushing back the boundaries, social policy, domestic violence and women's organisations in Peru', *Journal of Latin American Studies*, vol 38, pp 355–78.

Brown, P.A. and Dickey, C. (1992) 'Critical reflection in groups with abused women', *Affilia*, vol 7, pp 57–71.

Campbell, J., Jones, A., Dienemann, J., Kub, J., Schollenberger, J., O'Campo, P., Gielen, A. and Wynne, C. (2002) 'Intimate violence and physical health consequences', *Archives of Internal Medicine*, vol 162, pp 1157–63.

Craven, Z. (ed) (2003) *Human Rights and Domestic Violence, Australian Domestic and Family Violence Clearinghouse, Topic Paper*, Sydney: University of New South Wales, Australian Domestic and Family Violence Clearinghouse.

Crenshaw, K.W. (1991) 'Mapping the margins: Intersectionality, identity politics and violence against women of color', *Stanford Law Review*, vol 43, pp 1241–99.

Ellsberg, M. (2006) 'Violence against women and the Millennium Development Goals: Facilitating women's access to support', *International Journal of Gynaecology and Obstetrics*, vol 94, pp 325–32.

Ellsberg, M., Jansen, H., Heise, L., Watts, C.H. and García-Moreno, C. (2008) 'Intimate partner violence and women's physical and mental health in the WHO Multi-Country Study on Women's Health and Domestic Violence: An observational study', *The Lancet*, vol 371, pp 1165–72.

Fischbach, R.L. and Herbert, B. (1997) 'Domestic violence and mental health: Correlates and conundrums within and across cultures', *Social Science and Medicine*, vol 45, pp 1161–76.

Fitzgerald, J. (2006) *The Attrition of Sexual Offences from the New South Wales Criminal Justice System*, Sydney: New South Wales Bureau of Crime Statistics and Research, Contemporary Issues in Crime and Justice, no 92.

Flannery, K., Irwin, J. and Lopes, A. (2000) 'Connection and cultural difference: Women, groupwork and surviving domestic violence', *Women against Violence*, vol 9, pp 14–21.

Golding, J.M. (1999) 'Intimate partner violence as a risk factor for mental disorders: a meta-analysis', *Journal of Family Violence*, vol 14, no 2, pp 99–132.

Gracia, E. and Herrero, J. (2006) 'Acceptability of domestic violence against women in the European Union: A multilevel analysis', *Journal of Epidemiology and Community Health*, vol 60, pp 123–9.

Hegarty, K.L. and Taft, A.J. (2001) 'Overcoming the barriers to disclosure and inquiry of partner abuse for women attending General Practice', *Australian and New Zealand Journal of Public Health*, vol 25, pp 433–7.

Heise, L. (1994) 'Gender-based abuse: The global epidemic', *Cadre Saúde Pública, Rio de Janeiro*, vol 10, pp 135–45.

Heise, L., Ellsberg, M. and Gottemoeller, M. (1999) 'Ending violence against women', *Population Reports, Series L, No. 11*, Baltimore: Johns Hopkins University, School of Public Health.

Herman, J.L. (1992) *Trauma and Recovery*, New York, NY: Basic Books.

Hester, M. (2004) 'Future trends and developments: Violence against women in Europe and East Asia', *Violence Against Women*, vol 10, pp 1431–8.

Humphreys, C. (2007) 'A health inequalities perspective on violence against women', *Health and Social Care in the Community*, vol 15, pp 120–7.

Irwin, J., Laing, L. and Napier, L. (2006) 'Towards better practice: Enhancing collaboration between mental health and domestic violence services', Santiago, Chile: International Federation of Social Work Conference, 'Global Social Work: Growth and Inequality', 28–31 August.

Johnson, J.E. and Brunell, L. (2006) 'The emergence of contrasting domestic violence regimes in post-communist Europe', *Policy & Politics*, vol 34, pp 575–95.

Kelly, L. and Lovett, J. (2005) *What a Waste: The Case for an Integrated Violence against Women Strategy*, London: Department of Trade and Industry.

Kelly, L., Lovett, J. and Regan, L. (2005) *A Gap or a Chasm? Attrition in Reported Rape Cases*, London: Home Office Research, Development and Statistics Directorate.

Krug, E.G., Dahlberg, L.L., Mercy, J.A., Zwi, A. and Lozano, R. (2002) *World Report on Violence and Health*, Geneva: World Health Organization.

Martins da Silva, M. and Kendall, S. (2002) *Issues for Women in East Timor: The Aftermath of Indonesian Occupation. Expanding our Horizons: Understanding the Complexities of Violence against Women: Meanings, Cultures, Difference*, Sydney: University of Sydney, Australian Domestic and Family Violence Clearinghouse.

Martins da Silva, M., Marcal, L., Kendall, S. and Laing, L. (2006) 'Fatin Hakmatek: The safe room project in East Timor', *Australian Domestic and Family Violence Clearinghouse Newsletter*, pp 11–13.

Pittaway, E. and Bartolomei, L. (2002) 'Refugees, race and gender: The multiple discrimination against refugee women', *Dialogue*, vol 21, pp 16–28.

Postmus, J.L. (2007) 'Comparing the policy response to violence against women in the USA and South Korea', *International Social Work*, vol 50, pp 770–82.

Quinn, T. (2000) 'Challenging sexual violence: Social justice agendas in groupwork practice', *Women against Violence*, vol 9, pp 4–13.

Radford, L. and Tsutsumi, K. (2004) 'Globalization and violence against women: Inequalities in risks, responsibilities and blame in the UK and Japan', *Womens Studies International Forum*, vol 27, pp 1–12.

Stark, E. and Flitcraft, A. (1996a) 'Medicine and patriarchal violence', in E. Stark and A. Flitcraft (eds) *Women at Risk: Domestic Violence and Women's Health*, Thousand Oaks, CA: Sage Publications, pp 3–42.

Stark, E. and Flitcraft, A. (1996b) 'Personal power and institutional victimization', in E. Stark and A. Flitcraft (eds) *Women at Risk: Domestic Violence and Women's Health*, Thousand Oaks, CA: Sage Publications, pp 157–91.

Thurston, W. and Eisener, A. (2006) 'Successful integration and maintenance of screening for domestic violence in the health sector – Moving beyond individual responsibility', *Trauma Violence and Abuse*, vol 7, pp 83–92.

United Nations General Assembly (1993) Declaration on the Elimination of Violence against Women, 85th Plenary Meeting, 20 December, Geneva: United Nations General Assembly.

World Health Organization (2005) *Multi-Country Study on Women's Health and Domestic Violence against Women: Summary Report*, Geneva: World Health Organization.

Long-term illness and disability: inequalities compounded

Barbara Fawcett

Introduction

'Disability' is a wide-ranging concept which generates varying interpretations. In countries such as the UK, the US, Canada and Australia, it has been used to describe and also to challenge the socially created disadvantage and discrimination that people with physical or emotional impairments or illnesses face. In parts of Africa, the Indian subcontinent and Asia, situations of extreme poverty and the lack of adequate resources make daily survival the prime consideration. In this chapter, I will draw from my practice and research experience in the field of disability to examine globalising trends and health inequalities, using heart disease and Type 2 diabetes as core examples, to explore how disabling social, economic and political responses compound inequalities, and to start to map out the parameters for adaptable and flexible social work responses.

Globalising trends and health inequalities

Recent decades have seen some major improvements in population health across the globe. In developed and developing nations, increased income and wealth has resulted in enhanced underlying social conditions for health while clean water programmes, advanced pollution control measures, health education programmes, targeted screening procedures, vaccinations and increasing access to medical treatments, have made a significant contribution. The value of concerted international action by governments and non-governmental organisations to combat long-term and life-threatening illnesses has also been increasingly recognised, not only in response to the fear of global pandemics such as bird flu (Shisana, 2005). The World Health Organization (WHO), United Nations (UN) and other international bodies have also coordinated action on global diseases such as TB (WHO, 2006) and HIV/AIDS (WHO, 2008a). In the case of some diseases, such as smallpox, such co-coordinated action has resulted in the effective eradication of the condition (WHO, 2008b).

However, as this book repeatedly testifies, gross socially created inequalities in health outcomes remain between and within countries. Despite repeated international agreements to address the social determinants of health, for example, through the Millennium Development Goals or the WHO Commission on the Social Determinants of Health, actions remain far behind the rhetoric. Meanwhile, continuing military conflict, such as that in Iraq, Afghanistan and in African nations such as Sierra Leone or Darfur, exacerbates the proliferation of the arms trade, including the use of landmines, and results in both directly caused physical and emotional impairments and illnesses and indirect costs to health (Salahaddin, 2006). Similarly, notwithstanding some ethically directed consumer pressure for fair and sustainable trade, global neoliberal economic policies, commonly supported by international institutions, continue to have multiple negative effects on population health including through hampering the introduction of environmental safeguards (GHW, 2005). Tragedies such as Bhopal or Chenobyl, for example, are not isolated incidents and carry with them long-term health repercussions. But the attention paid to major incidents can mask the cumulative effects of multiple small-scale industrial injuries and deaths especially in poorly regulated developing countries or among poorly protected migrants in developed countries (GHW, 2005). It is also evident that coping with the aftermath of natural disasters not only stretches the capacities of developed nations, as can be seen in the case of New Orleans, but also causes the fragile political and social infrastructure of countries such as Myanmar to crumble with devastating health repercussions.

In countries which lack a health care infrastructure, where even basic social welfare and medical services are in short supply, the coping capacities of those already experiencing economic and social adversity are stretched beyond the limit. Countries with unaffordable health insurance schemes (whether developed, such as the US, or developing, such as China) leave large sections of the population exposed to the consequences of acute and chronic illnesses and impairments. The WHO estimates that each year more than 100 million people face 'financial catastrophe' because they must pay for health care (WHO, 2008c, p 32). Even in nations with basic universal health care schemes such as Australia, factors such as being a lone parent, being unemployed or a recently arrived migrant can multiply the effects of poor social, economic and health circumstances (Australian Bureau of Statistics, 2007).

The difficulties and expense involved in obtaining rudimentary health care and pharmaceutical products also makes more poignant the continued ravages of conditions such as malaria. Despite malaria being an eminently treatable disease, through insecticide treated mosquito nets (ITNs), artemisimin combination therapy drugs and preventive treatment programmes, there are over one million deaths per year worldwide with the majority being children under five and pregnant women from sub-Saharan Africa (African Medical and Research Foundation, 2008). Acute poverty sometimes results in people choosing to sell their ITNs to buy food. Similarly, the generational decimation by HIV/AIDS in parts of Africa and treatable mother to child transmission demonstrate further the inaccessibility of essential drug therapies (Coovadia and Hadingham, 2005) against a backdrop of acute economic inequality.

Heart disease and diabetes: exemplifying inequalities

In developed, developing and transitional nations, it is notable that two conditions in particular stand out as representing health and socio-economic patterns and trends worldwide. These are coronary heart disease/cardiovascular disease (CHD/CVD), which include heart, stroke and blood vessel conditions, and Type 2 diabetes. Ebrahim and Davey Smith (2001) report that CHD/CVD accounts for 30% of deaths worldwide, approximately 15 million deaths a year, 11 million in developing or transitional countries. The International Diabetes Federation (IDF) (2008) reports 246 million people living with diabetes worldwide. Although both CHD/CVD and diabetes, particularly Type 2 diabetes, affect women and men from all classes and ethnic groups, there is a clear social gradient. Ebrahim and Davey Smith (2001) note that although only a small number of epidemiological studies have been carried out in these countries, mortality rates appear to be higher while prevalence rates are lower. Such inequalities are likely to be exacerbated by the activities of increasingly profitable tobacco companies (Liu et al, 1998). These are resulting in a growing concentration of smokers in developing countries where 800 million of the worldwide total of 1.1 billion smokers are now to be found (WHO, 2008c). They draw attention to the relatively young age of these smokers and emphasise that the CHD/CVD consequences are likely to be severe. Similarly links have been made between the global spread of fast food and sugar-rich soft drinks and the increasing obesity and higher levels of Type 2 diabetes experienced in developing and transitional nations (IDF, 2008). The IDF (2008), for example, estimates that by 2025 the largest increase in diabetes will take place in countries such as India and China.

Inequalities in rates of illness also exist within developed nations. In the US, for example, there is a particularly high death rate from CHD/CVD among African American and Hispanic women (American Heart Association, 2007), who are also significantly over-represented in the prevalence of Type 2 diabetes (Robbins et al, 2000). With regard to indigenous communities, inequalities are still greater. In Australia, Aboriginal people are nearly three times as likely as non-Aboriginal people to be hospitalised for conditions such as CHD/CVD (Mathur et al, 2006). Aboriginal women with diabetes also experience a significantly higher risk of conditions such as CHD/CVD than women without diabetes and Aboriginal and Torres Straight Islander deaths from diabetes are up to 17 times higher than deaths for non-Indigenous Australians (Australian Broadcasting Company, 2008). Such inequalities contribute to an overall average life expectancy which is approximately 17 years lower than that for the non-Indigenous population (Pink and Allbon, 2008). These statistics serve as a further demonstration of the interrelationship between health and social factors as Aboriginal communities, particularly those in rural areas, have to contend with a lack of health and educational infrastructure, poor housing, high unemployment, reduced resources and poor socio-economic conditions (Altman and Hinkson, 2007).

Similarly, for indigenous communities in Canada, Kauffman (2003) estimates that deaths from CHD/CVD are two and a half times as high as for non-indigenous Canadians. In relation to diabetes, Young et al (2000) note that before the 1950s, Type 2 diabetes was rare, but that over the past decade a rapid increase has been recorded. Diabetes rates are now estimated to be between three and five times higher for indigenous compared with non-indigenous Canadians (Canadian Diabetes Association, 2008). This has to be set against a backdrop of indigenous people in Canada being reported as having three times the level of chronic diseases experienced by the general population with life expectancy rates, although increasing, being over six years lower than the national average (Treasury Board of Canada Secretariat, 2005). As with Australia, it is also significant that indigenous unemployment, a key social indicator of disadvantage, is high at approximately 24% (Kauffman, 2003).

The WHO (2007) maintains that to bring about change for indigenous communities, economic growth has to proceed hand in hand with well-resourced inclusive community development initiatives which build on and develop infrastructure supports. The health, education, housing and employment consequences of not working in partnership, engaging communities and building on community initiatives that are working well can be seen in the recent Howard-led Federal Government intervention in the Northern Territory in Australia in June 2007. Aboriginal communities in the Northern Territory face disadvantage, discrimination and the lack of infrastructure resources. There is a pervading sense of hopelessness, of not being listened to and of not being respected. There are well-documented gendered issues relating to alcohol consumption and family violence (see, for example, Blagg, 2000; Cunneen and Libesman, 2000; 2002; Pocock, 2003; Tomison, 2004; HREOC, 2006; Australian Institute of Health and Welfare, 2007; Libesman, 2007). However, the picture presented by the Howard government was that all Indigenous communities in the Northern Territory were beset by drunkenness, pornography and child sexual abuse (Altman and Hinkson, 2007; Despoja, 2007; Martiniello, 2007). The national emergency measures rolled out by John Howard placed emphasis on control and compliance rather than on inclusion, participation and capacity building and ignored existing community and individual strengths, particularly those of Aboriginal women community leaders. The result has been a top-down 'crackdown'[1] on Aboriginal communities which, as Dodson (2007) and Calma (2008) among many others have highlighted, is far more likely to entrench rather than to tackle poverty and deprivation, to compound health inequalities and to discourage those subject to violence and abuse from speaking out.

How disabling social, economic and political responses compound inequalities

When placing long-term illness and impairments within a health inequalities framework, it is important not only to consider how social disadvantage and health inequalities are interlinked, but also how disabling social, economic and political responses compound inequalities and how these are exacerbated by power imbalances relating to aspects such as age, sex, 'race' and sexual orientation. In Western nations, disability movements have promoted rights-based approaches and the importance of the social model of disability replacing individualised, medicalised understandings and traditional psychosocial methods of intervention. The former are seen to prioritise the categorisation and classification of conditions, while the latter are regarded as individualising the effect of social factors (Beresford, 2004).

The social model of disability differs from both as it focuses on the ways in which people with impairments and long-term illnesses, such as CHD/CVD and Type 2 diabetes, are disabled by social, political and economic barriers. The influence of the social model of disability has resulted in the term 'disabled people' being redefined and used in a political context to refer to the ways in which individuals have been dis-abled by direct and indirect discrimination. The message and the resulting responses are clear and much can and has been achieved by concentrating on issues of rights in the political domain. As a result disability theorists and disabled rights groups have utilised the concept of citizenship as a means of drawing attention to entrenched inequality and promoting an inclusionist and integrationist agenda (Barnes et al, 1999). Disability rights campaigns based on social model understandings have been influential in the passing of Disability Discrimination legislation in the US, Canada, Australia and the UK. However, it has to be noted that the provision, impact and enforcement arrangements differ considerably between countries.

The achievements of disability rights campaigns based on the social model of disability are substantial. However, critical calls for a greater recognition of difference with regard to age, sex, 'race' and sexual orientation have resulted in a more nuanced orientation. As a result it is increasingly recognised that oppression is multidimensional and that there is a dynamic and changing relationship between the individual, power and structures which needs to be continually challenged on a number of fronts (Williams, 1992; Fawcett, 2000).

The ways in which political campaigns to address dis-abling barriers have tended to ignore the implications of impairment and illness has also been highlighted. Crow, for example, maintains that this failure also contains the ultimate irony in that by only tackling one side of 'our situation we disable ourselves' (1996, p 59). She sees impairment/illness as fundamentally a neutral concept, but recognises that bodily differences can easily become regarded as imperfections and as denoting inferiority. To counter this she advocates that disabled people should apply their own meanings to their experiences of impairment/illness and develop autobiographical accounts in order to both contribute to and to reinforce their sense of self. As part of this process, Crow (1996) identifies three main elements. The first is the actual impairment or illness, the second is the individual interpretation of the subjective experience of the condition and the third is the impact of wider social forces which can include misrepresentation, social exclusion and discrimination. She states:

> External disabling barriers may create social and economic
> disadvantage but our subjective experience of our bodies is
> also an integral part of our everyday reality. What we need
> is to find a way to integrate 'impairment' into our whole
> experience and sense of ourselves for the sake of our own
> physical and emotional well-being, and subsequently, for our
> individual and collective capacity to work against disability.
> (Crow, 1996, p 59)

However, as highlighted in the introduction, it has to be acknowledged
that in many non–Western countries, discussion about models and
anti-discrimination legislation loses momentum when confronted
by a fundamental lack of resources and daily struggles for survival. In
rural areas particularly, illness and impairment form part of everyday
life as families expend their meagre resources trying to survive in
impoverished circumstances (WHO/UNICEF, 2004). Nevertheless,
the social, economic and political barriers faced by those living with
illnesses such as CHD/CVD and diabetes in such countries can be
seen to be just as, if not more, disabling and inequitable. Families and
significant others can also be subject to discrimination with disadvantage
being entrenched as a result of physical, emotional, economic and social
consequences. Similarly, power imbalances relating to age, sex, 'race'
and sexual orientation can further compound inequalities. The daily
challenges faced by a widowed woman from Bangladesh, for example,
living in an isolated rural village with a diabetes-related impairment
will be totally different from those of a male stockbroker in London
with the same condition.

Mapping out the parameters for adaptable and flexible social work responses

In terms of social work practice, it is easy to set up a dichotomy.
On one side of the divide, professionals who operate within systems
which privilege non-experiential knowledge and where policy and
resource constraints mould those operating in the field into gatekeepers
of services and determiners of acceptable need. On the other side,
people with impairments and illnesses, such as CVD/CHD or Type
2 diabetes, who are all too well aware of experiential factors and of
divisive and discriminatory barriers. However, such dichotomies are
too simplistic and fail to take account of mediating factors. In any
practice area there are a variety of influencing components which
include environment, resource availability and communal capacity as

well as professional perspectives and the extent of consumer action and engagement. In some settings, deficit models which focus on problems and what individuals and groups cannot do predominate, while in others, multifaceted perspectives are promoted with an accompanying array of proactive and reactive strategies being put forward (Fawcett and Karban, 2005).

An emphasis on partnership, inclusivity, locally owned, controlled and resourced initiatives as well as on community and individual strengths has worldwide relevance in the face of globalising social, economic, environmental and political forces. In Western nations this means that those operating in the health and social work fields have to challenge existing social relations in order to address inequalities and discrimination. Oliver and Sapey (2006) stress that disabled people need to be regarded by workers as colleagues who have a wealth of information and experiential knowledge about their impairment, illness and disabling factors. They emphasise listening to the experiences of disabled people and highlight the importance of disabled people carrying out their own assessments and having access to resources so that they can determine outcomes that are useful for them. For example, in the UK 'direct payments' (money) to purchase support or personal assistance can be paid to the person with an illness or impairment. Direct payment legislation was introduced in the UK in 1996. Oliver and Sapey see the role of professionals being to work in partnership with disabled people to ensure that resources are creatively and flexibly maximised.

In developing countries, although all of the above considerations apply, it is possible to see inclusive practices having a more pronounced community focus. Accordingly, community centres or local schools can be used as a gathering point for those with illnesses or impairments where, rather than emphasis being placed on individuals being 'looked after', different strengths can be shared to produce, for example, weekly lunches and trips to meet with other groups. These groups then have the potential to develop, with social worker facilitation where available, into focal points for local action to address areas of localised concern. In turn, associated networking activities can make links between groups and formulate strategies for networked responses (Fawcett, 2007). Such community development and capacity-building approaches, which are relevant to communities of interest as well as geographical communities, not only address problems of isolation and condition-induced helplessness, but also foster the utilisation of collective strengths that are culturally sensitive and which have the capacity to develop networks with a variety of individuals, groups and organisations. Building on group strengths also recognises that although an individual's facility to participate will wax and wane as a result of an illness or impairment, the collective contribution will remain strong (Fawcett and South, 2005).

Overall, then, when mapping out the parameters for adaptable and flexible social work responses, there are a number of areas to highlight. These include social workers ensuring that they work in partnership with individuals with impairments or long-term illnesses, focusing on those aspects of greatest importance to them and supporting collective action. It also involves acknowledging that family members may experience disadvantage as a result of the physical, emotional, economic and social consequences of illness and impairment, but that their interests may be different. The importance of utilising negotiating and networking skills to maximise the opportunities and resources available needs also to be emphasised. This means that social workers have to operate at the policy and practice interface and prioritise the tackling of inequalities at the community as well as individual levels. This necessitates knowledge of local as well as national policies, the ability to operate in a wide range of settings and the skills to ensure that the voices of those experiencing impairment inform policy and practice. It is also important for social workers to be able to initiate and coordinate participatory action research/evaluation projects so that what is actually happening and how this is being experienced can inform future action.

Bywaters (2009) emphasises that tackling inequalities in health is a matter of social justice and human rights and that the underpinning social causes constitute a global challenge for social work. Clearly social workers have to contend with practice and policy barriers themselves (Lavalette and Ferguson, 2007). These differ according to setting from prescriptive performance indicators designed to shape practice and promote compliance at one end of the continuum, to social workers being faced with few resources and almost no infrastructure at the other. However, as the WHO points out, 'The devastating health inequalities we see globally are man made. The causes are social – so must be the solutions' (WHO, 2007, p 3). This can be seen to give social workers a remit to take up the challenge, to constructively critique prevailing policies and practices, to operate in an inclusive and open manner at a range of levels and to name and actively address injustice, disadvantage and discrimination.

Concluding remarks

In this chapter, using conditions such as CHD/CVD and Type 2 diabetes as examples, the pervasive links between social and health inequalities have been highlighted. Similarly the restrictions and discrimination encountered in Western nations as a result of impairment can be seen to be compounded and multiplied in non-Western countries as a result of a lack of resources and infrastructure. Where environments are multiply impoverished, families and communities have to manage in a variety of ways. This can lead to innovation and integration, but it can also further entrench impoverishment and social division. However, across the globe, inclusivity, empowering processes and the tackling of disabling barriers remains a central focus for social workers. This is a challenging agenda, but one which promises to constructively engage with material, social and political factors and to tackle health inequalities.

Note
[1] Howard, John (2007) *Sydney Morning Herald*, 22 June, p 1.

References

African Medical and Research Foundation (2008) 'Malaria', www. amref.org/index.asp?PageID=50&PiaID=1

Altman, J. and Hinkson, M. (eds) (2007) *Coercive Reconciliation*, Melbourne: Arena Publications.

American Heart Association (2007) 'Heart facts', www.americanheart. org

Australian Broadcasting Company (2008) 'Rudd, Nelson declare intent on Indigenous Health Group', www.abc.net.au/news/stories/2008/03/20/2195460.htm

Australian Bureau of Statistics (2007) 'Australian social trends', Belconnen, ACT: Australian Bureau of Statistics.

Australian Institute of Health and Welfare (2007) 'Child protection in Australia 2005–06', *Child Welfare Series*, no 40, Canberra: Australian Institute of Health and Welfare.

Barnes, C., Mercer, G. and Shakespeare, T. (1999) *Exploring Disability*, Cambridge: Polity Press.

Beresford, P. (2004) 'Reframing the nurse's role through a social model approach: A rights-based approach to workers' development', *Journal of Psychiatric and Mental Health Nursing*, vol 11, pp 365–73.

Blagg, H. (2000) *Crisis Intervention in Aboriginal Family Violence: Summary Report, Partnerships Against Domestic Violence*, Canberra: Office of the Status of Women.

Bywaters, P. (2009) 'Tackling inequalities in health: A global challenge for social Work', *British Journal of Social Work*, vol 39, pp 353–67.

Calma, T. (2008) 'The role of social workers as human rights workers with Indigenous people and communities', paper presented at the Australian Catholic University, 12 February.

Canadian Diabetes Association (2008) 'The prevalence and costs of diabetes', www.diabetes.ca/Files/prevalence-and-costs.pdf

Coovadia, M.M. and Hadingham, J. (2005) 'HIV/AIDS: Global trends, global funds and delivery bottlenecks', *Globalization and Health*, www.globalizationandhealth.com/content/1/1/13

Crow, E. (1996) 'Including all of our lives: Renewing the social model of disability', in C. Barnes and G. Mercer (eds) *Exploring the Divide: Illness and Disability*, Leeds: The Disability Press, pp 55–72.

Cunneen, C. and Libesman, T. (2000) 'Postcolonial trauma: The contemporary removal of Indigenous children and young people from their families in Australia', *Australian Journal of Social Issues*, vol 35, no 2, pp 99–115.

Cunneen, C. and Libesman, T. (2002) *A Review of International Models for Indigenous Child Protection*, Sydney: New South Wales Department of Community Services.

Despoja, N.S. (2007) 'Northern Territory Intervention Legislation – Second Reading' speech, Federal Parliament, Canberra, www.democrats.org.au/speeches

Dodson, M. (2007) 'Dodson slams federal intervention in NT', *Sydney Morning Herald*, 13 September.

Ebrahim, S. and Davey Smith, G. (2001) 'Exporting failure? Coronary heart disease and stroke in developing countries', *International Journal of Epidemiology*, vol 30, pp 201–5.

Fawcett, B. (2000) *Feminist Perspectives on Disability*, Harlow: Prentice Hall/Pearson.

Fawcett, B. (2007) 'Consistencies and inconsistencies: Mental health, compulsory treatment and community capacity building in England, Wales and Australia', *British Journal of Social Work*, vol 37, pp 1027–42.

Fawcett, B. and Karban, K. (2005) *Contemporary Mental Health: Theory, Policy and Practice*, London and New York: Routledge.

Fawcett, B. and South, J. (2005) 'Community involvement and primary care trusts', *Critical Public Health*, vol 15, no 2, pp 1–14.

GHW (Global Health Watch) (2005) *Global Health Watch 2005–2006. An Alternative World Health Report*, London/New York: Zed Books.

HREOC (Human Rights and Equal Opportunity Commission) (2006) *Ending Family Violence and Abuse in Aboriginal and Torres Strait Islander Communities – Key Issues: An Overview Paper of Research and Findings by the HREOC, 2001–2006*, Sydney: HREOC.

IDF (International Diabetes Federation) (2008) 'Did you know?', www.idf.org/home/index.cfm?unode=3B96906B-C026-2FD3-87B73F80BC22682A

Kauffman, P. (2003) 'Diversity and Indigenous policy outcomes: Comparisons between four nations', *International Journal of Diversity in Organizations, Communities & Nations*, vol 3, www.ijd.cgpublisher.com/product/pub.29/prod.3A.20

Lavalette, M. and Ferguson, I. (2007) *International Social Work and the Radical Tradition*, Birmingham: Venture Press.

Libesman, T. (2007) 'Indigenising Indigenous child welfare', *Indigenous Law Bulletin*, vol 6, no 24, pp 17–19.

Liu, B.-Q., Peto, R., Chen, Z.-M., Boreham, J., Wu, Y.P. and Li, J.Y. (1998) 'Emerging tobacco hazards in China: 1. Retrospective proportional mortality study of one million deaths', *British Medical Journal*, vol 317, pp 1411–22.

Martiniello, J. (2007) 'Howard's new Tampa, Aboriginal children overboard', *Australian Feminist Law Journal*, vol 26, pp 123–6.

Mathur, S., Moon, L. and Leigh, S. (2006) *Aboriginal and Torres Strait Islander People with Coronary Heart Disease: Further Perspectives on Health Status and Treatment*, Canberra: Australian Institute of Health and Welfare.

Oliver, M. and Sapey, B. (2006) *Social Work with Disabled People*, 3rd edn, Basingstoke: BASW/Palgrave/Macmillan.

Pink, B. and Allbon, P. (2008) *The Health and Welfare of Australia's Aboriginal and Torres Strait Islander Peoples 2008*, Belconnen ACT: Australian Bureau of Statistics and Australian Institute of Health and Welfare.

Pocock, J. (2003) *State of Denial: The Neglect and Abuse of Indigenous Children in the Northern Territory*, Victoria: SNAICC.

Robbins, J.M., Vaccarino, V., Zhang, H. and Kasi, S. (2000) 'Excess type 2 diabetes, health and welfare in African American women and men aged 40–74 and socioeconomic status: Evidence from the third Network Health and Nutrition Examination Survey', *Journal of Epidemiology and Community Health*, vol 54, pp 839–45.

Salahaddin, M.-A. (2006) 'Arms trade and its impact on global health', *Theoretical Medicine*, vol 27, no 1, pp 81–93.

Shisana, O. (2005) 'Managing globalisation for health', www.who. int/healthpromotion/hpr_6gchp_speech_shisana.pdf

Tomison, A.M. (2004) *Current Issues in Child Protection Policy and Practice: Informing the Northern Territory's Child Protection Review*, Darwin: NT Department of Health and Community Services.

Treasury Board of Canada Secretariat (2005) 'Canada's performance report 2005 – Annex 3 – Indicators and additional information', www.tbs-sct.gc.ca/report/govrev/05/ann3-eng.asp

WHO (World Health Organization) (2006) 'The stop TB strategy', www.who.int/tb/strategy/en/

WHO (2007) *Interim Statement from the Commission on the Social Determinants of Health*, Geneva: WHO.

WHO (2008a) 'Joint United Nations program on HIVAIDS', www. unaids.org/en/

WHO (2008b) 'Smallpox', www.who.int/mediacentre/factsheets/ smallpox/en/

WHO (2008c) *World Health Statistics 2008*, Geneva: WHO.

WHO/UNICEF (United Nations Children's Fund) (2004) *Meeting the Millennium Development Goals Drinking Water and Sanitation Target: A Mid-Term Assessment of Progress*, Geneva, WHO/UNICEF.

Williams, F. (1992) 'Somewhere over the rainbow: Universality and diversity in social policy', in N. Manning and R. Page (eds) *Social Policy Review 4*, London: Social Policy Association, pp 200–19.

Young, T.K., Reading, J., Elias, B. and O'Neil, J.D. (2000) 'Type 2 diabetes mellitus in Canada's first nations: Status of an epidemic in progress', *Canadian Medical Association Journal*, vol 163, no 5, pp 561–6.

Part Three

Social work intervention: addressing global health inequalities

10

Framing health inequalities as targets for social work

Introduction

Social work is essentially an interventive discipline, as reflected in the contributions to this chapter. They not only pinpoint the adverse impact of social inequalities on health chances and experience, but also how this is an appropriate target for social work. In doing so, they also highlight specific dimensions of how social work policy and practice should identify and engage with global health inequalities.

Section 10.1 goes behind the scenes of the burgeoning Chinese economy, integral to global economic development, to explore adverse health consequences for internal migrant workers. It sets out how such workers are caught up in urban poverty and the fault lines in current health and welfare policy, inimical to health. Nevertheless, it also reveals how the vast scale of such problems need not preclude social work gaining traction on them locally. Student social workers' initiatives show how imaginative community work can highlight and mitigate health disadvantages for micro-populations caught up in extensive social transformations.

Section 10.2 then sets out how sexual orientation as a site of health inequality should be integral to social work analysis and practice addressing global health inequalities. It explores the profound and diverse forms of oppression that lesbian, gay and bisexual (LGB) people have suffered and their adverse health consequences. These range from homosexuality being a capital offence in some countries, to heterosexist barriers to health care. It then considers how recognition of this issue has acted as a springboard for social work policy and practice initiatives internationally, to secure LGB people's physical and psychological health requirements.

Finally, section 10.3 draws on a neighbourhood initiative from the US to argue for greater attention by social work to the insidious effects of homelessness on physical health, via psychological stress. It acknowledges that its social work project does not address the root causes of homelessness as, internationally, an adjunct to poverty.

However, it proposes that boosting social resources through solidarity and advocacy on a one-to-one basis may break into the vicious circle of homelessness–psychological stress–physical exhaustion and thereby constitute a compensatory social work resource for health.

10.1: Poverty and health policy in China

Agnes Koon-chui Law

Introduction

The rapid development of China's economy has attracted worldwide attention as an integral feature of globalisation. However, social issues in China that accompany such development can be overlooked. At present, about a quarter of the total Chinese population live in urban areas, while 900 million have their roots in rural areas with relatively poor living conditions. Among them, 100 million are forced to migrate to the cities seeking jobs. This migrant population is caught up in urban–rural divides and the vast gap between rich and poor. These conditions also feature as the causes as well as the consequences of social inequalities embedded in social policies relating to health care.

This chapter first highlights the relationship between health policy and poverty in China. It then discusses the possible application of social work values and skills in empowering vulnerable groups, especially migrant workers, in dealing with their health needs. In doing so it draws on examples from social work pilot projects including organising outreach health education, self-help groups and leadership training. Finally, it considers the effectiveness and limitations of social work in addressing health inequalities among such marginal groups.

Poverty and health policy

In China, public health and primary health care are the responsibility of the government, while an expanding private sector aims to profit from commercialised health care services. Individual welfare and health care entitlements are mainly determined by three elements, namely, funding distributed by different levels of government, residence registration (hukou),[1] and job status (Shue and Wong, 2007). Social disparities are very evident. Census figures have shown that in urban areas alone there are around 400 million people living below the poverty line and without medical insurance (Liang, 2006a; 2006b). More than 60% of health care resources are allocated to urban areas with around a quarter of the total population, and less than 40% to the rural areas where most poor people live (Pan and Guo, 2007). Moreover, it is mainly people who work in public organisations or large corporations who have the privilege of joining the public medical insurance scheme. They are also encouraged to pay an individual supplement on top of their employer's contribution to increase their level of protection. It is estimated that about 44% of the urban population and 79% in rural areas do not have any medical insurance. Migrant workers and the unemployed are the least protected under the current health care system (Li, 2004; Li et al, 2005; Liu, 2005; Ru et al, 2006; Fang, 2007).

Inadequate health care for the vast number of migrant workers is a thorny social problem (Dai, 2007). In some industrial communities, they often outnumber indigenous residents and social tensions are inevitable because of cultural differences. For example, in Shenzhen, indigenous residents make up only one eighth of the total population (Wei, 2007). Migrants are involved in a great variety of service and manufacturing industries, for example catering, cleaning, construction, electrical goods, pharmaceuticals, vehicle parts, furniture, clothing and welding. Their social characteristics are that they are predominantly young, unskilled, with little education and have to work long hours in unstable jobs, for a low monthly income around RMB500–1200.[2] Without a hukou, they are not entitled to general welfare, medical, retirement and schooling benefits enjoyed by the locals. Despite being required to do so by law, only some employers provide a minimum medical insurance that is usually not enough to cover medical expenses, especially in cases of major sickness or occupational injury (Wu, 2006).

With a national health care budget of around only 3% of GDP, it is government policy to fund only part of the expenditure of public hospitals and clinics. They have to raise other income through fees. Irregular practices such as prescribing superfluous tests and drugs, more prolonged hospitalisation of patients than necessary and profit-sharing with pharmaceutical manufacturers have drawn grave criticisms of the present system (Han and Lou, 2005). In 2006, the central government[3] promised to introduce measures to impose stricter regulations and eventually establish a primary health care system with universal coverage. However, these are long-term goals and not likely in the short term to improve medical facilities that are affordable for the poor. In other words, current health care policies marked by limited coverage of medical insurance, shortage of government funding and a social and political infrastructure based on the urban–rural divide, are inherent factors in health inequalities.

Unmet health needs

It is a common observation that high medical fees are a major factor in making poor people poorer (see, for example, *Information Times*, 20 October 2006; *Nanfang Daily*, 14 November 2006; *South Magazine*, December 2006). Ordinary people without medical insurance are reluctant to seek medical consultations because of the expensive fees. In a study of migrant workers in Nanhai, Guangzhou (Wu, 2006), over 70% of respondents had experienced illnesses such as flu, fevers, gastric or kidney complaints and serious skin problems, at least once in the previous six months. However, they had preferred to consume self-prescribed medicines purchased in nearby drug stores rather than go for a consultation at a nearby clinic. This was simply because it would cost them over RMB200 per consultation at a nearby clinic, which for someone earning RMB800 per month is very expensive; whereas they only paid an average of RMB30 for each purchase of medicine. Only about one third of the workers identified their factories as having compensation policies for work injuries, and only 40% of these employers would compensate medical fees in full. Hospitalisation expenses are also very high: a major operation easily costs between a few thousand to over a hundred thousand RMB. Consequently, when migrants are seriously sick or injured, many have to move back to their home village as they are neither able to continue to work, nor to afford medical expenses (*Nanfang Daily*, 14 November 2006; Fang, 2007; *Nanfang Weekend*, 8 November 2007).

The health status of female migrant workers is another cause for concern. About half of the female workers in Wu's (2006) study of Nanhai, commented that they could not have sick leave even when they felt very unwell during menstruation. Some also described being subjected to harassment and other forms of unreasonable physical demands at work. Although there is specific legislation to protect female workers, many owners fail to comply with this (Song et al, 2005).

The mental health of migrant families is a further problem. Most migrant workers first move to the city alone, leaving their spouse and children behind under the care of grandparents or relatives. They then send for their spouse and children when the children are older or their carers in the home village become too frail to undertake childcare. Owing to prolonged separation, and the social and economic pressures of city living, relationships with spouses and children can be distant and stressful. Also, due to authoritarian patterns of upbringing in the villages, many of these parents have no idea how to express their affection towards their children and resort to physical punishment to discipline children's behaviour. Social exclusion and discrimination, poor family relationships and psychological stress are implicated in domestic violence and mental health problems (Man, 2005).

Evolution of social work practice

Social work is an emerging vocation in China: there are now over 200 higher education institutions enrolling social work students. However, to date, the lack of qualified social work educators, scarce resources and a restrictive policy environment for the development of the non-governmental organisation (NGO) sector have been major obstacles to the development of social work services (Law and Gu, 2008). Traditionally, vulnerable groups like disabled people, women and older people have been taken care of by a range of organisations: the Civil Affairs Department, the All China Women's Federation, the China Disabled Persons' Federation, the Communist Youth League, the General Trade Union and district authority community offices. Nevertheless, noting the shortcomings of what tended to be their top-down administrative approach to human services, in 2006 the central government took the bold step of announcing its intention to develop a strong social work workforce. It is anticipated that, given this new policy direction, government funding and support will be increased to expedite the development of social work in the coming decades (Law and Gu, 2008).

Social work intervention and health inequalities

Despite the fact that social work does not have an official role under the existing health care system, academic institutes and some emerging NGOs have attempted to apply social work concepts and methods to increase social support for disadvantaged populations and improve their health status. Employing a collaborative approach, volunteer experts, drawing on a variety of training resources, have joined forces with local social work academics and students to launch numerous pilot projects in Shenzhen, Guangzhou, Shanghai and Beijing. In Guangzhou alone, experimental projects have spread to over 50 locations, providing a variety of social work services. Primary and secondary schools, hospitals and local communities with high concentrations of migrant workers and their families, are focal points for these services. Some of them have a specific focus on health. Drawn from annual reports of the Centre for Social Work Education and Research (CSWER, 2007), Sun Yat-sen University, Guangzhou, across 2003–07, the following are examples of social work ventures to help poorer groups tackle their health-related problems.

Hospital outreach

Since medical social work is not part of the health care system, it is not easy for social work personnel to have access to hospital inpatients. However, with the consent of some sympathetic hospital authorities, university social work students have been placed in generic and psychiatric hospitals and drug rehabilitation centres (CSWER, 2007). Support groups and individual counselling have been the most common forms of intervention they have employed. Though such services are small-scale and short term, feedback from patients and medical personnel has been positive. Patients have welcomed support with the demands of rehabilitation, and medical personnel have valued the more positive approach to rehabilitation that this has led to on patients' part. Nevertheless, without backing from government policy, it is unlikely that medical institutions will incorporate social work personnel in their staff and provide social work services on a regular basis, no matter how much they are recognised as needed.

Community-based health education

Community education is a local government priority in the interests of instilling a sense of social cohesion, especially in communities with high concentrations of migrant workers. However, in contrast to the government's approach to public education which tends to be formal and top-down, social work adopts a new, more person-centred, approach, much welcomed by service users. Health promotion initiatives among disadvantaged groups have incorporated a wide range of strategies, for example, distributing health-related information by means of a mobile van and small group health talks with themes like 'Know your legal rights', 'Understanding your own body', 'Leadership skills for volunteers'. Similar programmes have been undertaken by social work students in some factories. The factory workers' response has been enthusiastic, as these provide some stimulation in their mechanistic daily routine. Workplace-based social work has much to offer in helping workers acquire a positive attitude towards self-care and in preventing health hazards. However, employers may see such interventions as increasing production costs and may not be willing to share the financial commitment (Liu, 2006).

Social support and advocacy

As well as boosting knowledge and information concerning physical and psychological well-being, a primary aim of social work is to empower specific groups to enhance their social networks and ability to advocate for their own needs.

Traditionally, the family is the main source of social support in Chinese society. Migrant workers, away from home, have to rely on the support of their kin who have already migrated to the city. However, as the main source of information on accommodation and jobs, the migrants' own kin tend to form close-knit communities that are isolated from mainstream society. Encouraging them to participate more actively in the broader local community enhances the social resources available to them. The informal and personal nature of the interaction between social workers and service users also makes it easier for migrants to express their feelings and raise grievances. As social workers, the students are not handling complaints in an official capacity. Nevertheless, feedback on their interventions has provided examples of them managing to encourage migrants to be more assertive in seeking compensation from employers and medical services. They have also been able to raise the profile of social problems faced by poor migrants in the course of resettlement, as an issue in public debate in the local community. In this way they have begun to perform a bridging function in reflecting migrants' needs (Liu, 2006).

Conclusion

Because of its peripheral role in the overall Chinese welfare system, what social work can do in tackling health inequalities is at present rather limited. The fact that social work's values and its approach are not well understood by the government and general public is also a major limitation. Nevertheless, the pilot projects indicate that social work can be effective in empowering service recipients through education, and providing them with the skills to improve self-care and mental health. Augmenting social networks also provides a way to help poorer populations cope with social isolation and seek additional community resources in combating illness.

To eliminate discrimination and health inequalities, the Chinese government must be willing to take major steps in reforming the existing complex health care system: by redistributing resources, imposing greater scrutiny of public medical institutions and putting in place a universal medical insurance scheme that removes the urban–rural divide and caters for the specific needs of poorer people. For their part, social service personnel from government and NGOs, as well as academia, have to collaborate not only in promoting the provision of direct services, but also in developing research evaluations of health policies that aim to solve the unmet health needs of those living in poverty.

Notes

[1] Hukou, is a form of residence registration that signifies whether you belong to a rural or urban community, and is a basic determinant of an individual's welfare entitlement, including medical benefits.

[2] RMB7.8 = US$1 (2006).

[3] Decisions of the 6th meeting of the 16th General Assembly of the Chinese Communist Party.

10.2: All things equal? Social work and lesbian, gay and bisexual (LGB) global health inequalities

Julie Fish

Reconceptualising LGB health identities

The history of LGB identities being considered as individual pathologies in need of treatment has persisted until very recently. Homosexuality was only removed from the World Health Organization's International Classification of Diseases in 1992 and it was not until 1996 that the American Medical Association removed the recommendation of conversion to heterosexuality from its guidelines. LGB identities were associated with disease in the early terminology for HIV, initially known as Gay Related Immuno Deficiency (GRID), and in section 28 of the UK 1988 Local Government Act, where a specific link with disease was made. Moreover, despite increasing international recognition of a number of dimensions to social inequality – class, sexism and racism – as key mediating factors in inequality in health, research on health inequalities has tended to exclude the situation of LGB people (Fish, 2006; see, for exceptions, McNair, 2003; Scott et al, 2004).

Why sexual orientation should be considered as a health inequality

Bywaters (2006) contends that central to debates about health is an understanding of how everyday experiences of inequality may result in poor health outcomes. These 'pathways' are not clearly understood in relation to LGB people. Drawing on social domains highlighted by Staley et al (2001), and referring to international evidence, I provide a brief overview of the ways disadvantaged social positions may translate into ill-health for LGB people.

Cultural and citizenship inequalities

Homophobia and heterosexism have an impact on LGB people's everyday lives (Fish, 2007a). Heterosexism – a set of assumptions and practices which runs through public life – promotes heterosexuality as normal and natural. Institutionalised heterosexuality perpetuates heterosexual superiority in cultural values, public services, education, the media, language, religion and legislation (Fish, 2006). The UK, for example, had perhaps the most oppressive legislation in Europe for LGB people until the end of the 20th century (Fish, 2007b). A range of legislative penalties contributed to their unequal status: including the age of consent, the lack of recognition of homophobia as a hate crime and discrimination in public services. The early 21st century has seen a repeal of much of this legislation in the UK (Fish, 2007b). However, legal inequalities are a continuing global concern (Ottosson, 2007).

Socially constructed health inequalities

Social factors perceived by LGB people as adversely affecting their physical and psychological well-being include discriminatory laws, everyday discrimination and social exclusion (Rogers, 2007). They are more likely to report both daily and lifetime discrimination as victims of violence or abuse than their heterosexual counterparts (Stonewall, 1996). Homophobia and heterosexism, specifically experiences of discrimination and concealing sexual orientation, create a social environment that can lead to mental health problems (Meyer, 2003). International research suggests that discrimination has a negative impact on their health in terms of lifestyles, mental health and the ability to live open lives (NIMHE, 2007). In a systematic review of the world literature, LGB people were at higher risk than heterosexual people of mental disorder, substance misuse and dependence, suicide and deliberate self-harm (NIMHE, 2007). Studies have shown a higher incidence of suicide in lesbian and bisexual school girls, an increased lifetime risk of suicide attempts among gay and bisexual men and greater risk of eating disorders (Toro Alfonso, 2008), and an increased risk of suicide ideation in lesbian and bisexual women (NIMHE, 2007).

Health care inequalities

Studies suggest that LGB people also receive a lower standard of health care than heterosexual people. Some of the barriers to effective health care include the attitudes and behaviour of health professionals, the routine presumption of heterosexuality and staff's lack of knowledge and understanding of LGB health needs. A recent UK report found that up to 14% of LGB people expected worse hospital treatment if their sexual orientation was known (Hunt and Dick, 2008). Consequently, LGB people are often reluctant to come out because they anticipate an inappropriate response or have concerns about confidentiality. Heterosexual assumptions also form a barrier to disclosure (Fish, 2007a).

Research inequalities

Increasing attention to evidence-based practice (Regehr et al, 2007) may paradoxically further contribute to the exclusion of LGB people in health and social care. Policy and service improvements rely on research which demonstrates a known statistical health risk, evidence on which to base preventive measures, the number of people the risk relates to and effective monitoring (NIMHE, 2007). Yet LGB people are largely invisible in large-scale population-based studies and in statistical information on which governments make policy decisions about health (Plumb, 2001; Aspinall and Mitton, 2008). This absence of data has often been used to justify the exclusion of LGB people's health concerns from policy making. According to Rosenblum (1996), this invisibility is far from benign, but is itself a human rights violation.

LGB health inequality as a global human rights issue

In many countries, LGB people do not enjoy basic protection from the state, with profound consequences for their physical and psychological well-being. Although the United Nations (UN) has considered sexual orientation as a status protected from discrimination for almost a decade (Human Rights Watch, 2007), in 2008, 86 UN member states continue to criminalise consensual same-sex acts among adults. Seven countries impose the death penalty (Ottosson, 2007); one of the most shocking examples being the public hanging of two gay Iranian teenagers in 2005, whose state execution was widely reported in the world media. In 14 countries, men are imprisoned simply for being gay (Ottosson, 2007). A recent Human Rights Watch report documented the arrest, torture and imprisonment of gay men in Egypt and highlighted the legally enforced abuse of basic human rights such as the right to freedom from torture, arbitrary arrest and detention, and the right to a fair trial and to freedom of association (de Gruchy and Fish, 2004). The lack of human rights for LGB people as described here, also leads to the need to seek asylum in countries which have implemented sexual orientation equality legislation.

Conversely there has also been some progress in recognising the human rights of LGB people, with positive implications for health. In 1996, South Africa became the first country to include protection in its constitution leading to a number of legal decisions which advanced LGB people's interests (Reding, 2003). A number of countries have introduced laws prohibiting discrimination on the grounds of sexual orientation including Mexico, Ecuador and Venezuela (Ottosson, 2007). In the UK the Department of Health (DH) has begun to address LGB health requirements in the context of a programme of legal reform (Fish, 2007a; 2007b). One of the most high-profile developments has been the legal recognition of same-sex relationships which emanated from Article 12 of the 2000 Human Rights Act – the right to marriage and a family life. In 2001, the Netherlands became the first country to legalise marriage for same-sex partners; five countries have since followed this lead. Elsewhere, the registration of civil partnerships has been allowed. But the rights conferred by legal recognition differ between countries. In some countries, civil partnership confers more rights than afforded by same-sex marriage; however, there are continuing concerns that a two-tier system has been established with LGB people afforded second-class status (King and Bartlett, 2006). Although worldwide acknowledgement of relationship rights is a distant achievement, legal recognition may contribute to reducing health inequalities for same-sex couples. Marriage is said to confer health benefits for heterosexual relationships: similar benefits may be derived from same-sex civil unions (King and Bartlett, 2006).

LGB global health inequalities: a target for social work

Notwithstanding recent gains in LGB human rights, social conditions for LGB people worldwide remain problematic and adversely impact on their health. Nevertheless, LGB health inequalities increasingly feature on social work agendas internationally, and social work can contribute to reducing such health inequalities. There is growing documentation of heterosexism and LGB health requirements (Curzi, 2006; Hunt and Fish, 2008). Specifically, voluntary organisations have worked to improve social work services for young LGB homeless people (Maberley and Coffey, 2005; Ray, 2006). Non-governmental organisations (NGOs) have also provided documentary evidence of unequal LGB protection worldwide and have successfully lobbied their national governments by citing more tolerant asylum policy in other countries (Canning, 2008). The following two detailed examples of NGO initiatives illustrate how social work has begun to address LGB health inequalities. They concern issues with cross-national relevance – asylum and homelessness.

Providing a safe haven for LGB asylum seekers

It was not until 1999 that a UK House of Lords decision recognised LGB people as a group from whom claims for UK asylum could be made. Prior to this, the Home Office had resisted acknowledgement of sexual orientation as grounds for persecution. Claiming asylum on the grounds of sexual orientation still remains distinctive from other claims in several ways. First, LGB asylum seekers must make the decision to come out. Coming out to officials may be difficult when the person may have risked death for revealing their sexual orientation in their country of origin. People may also fear that someone from their home country will find out about their sexual orientation and target the family they have left behind. The lack of terminology in many languages for describing sexual orientation poses a further barrier to coming out. The UK Lesbian and Gay Immigration Group (UKLGIG) has both highlighted cases of extremes of physical and psychological injury among LGB asylum seekers, and has also identified injustices in the process of seeking asylum. Asylum seekers have had claims rejected on the grounds that they can conceal their sexual orientation, that is, 'you can go home, hide your true self, never live with your partner … force yourself to deny your whole identity' (UKLGIG, 2008, p 6). They are vulnerable to homophobic bullying from fellow detainees if held in detention centres. Cutbacks in legal aid provision also make it difficult to find legal representation (UKLGIG, 2008).

Recently, voluntary organisations have addressed such issues that have serious implications for physical and psychological health and well-being. They have, for example, lobbied for a moratorium by the UK government on all deportations involving gay and lesbian Iranians (Verkaik, 2008). UKLGIG is one NGO which offers personal support and legal advice for LGB asylum seekers in the UK. Internationally, similar organisations campaign for immigration equality and global human rights for LGB people (Ottoson, 2007).

Opening doors: homelessness among young LGB people

Homelessness is a cross-national issue affecting young LGB people: it undermines their opportunity to become healthy and independent adults, increasing their risks of mental health problems, substance abuse, risky sexual behaviour and victimisation (Maberley and Coffey, 2005). Young LGB people who 'come out' as gay risk rejection from their family: sometimes running away from home or being thrown out by their parents. Research in the US has found that when young LGB people leave home they are more likely than their heterosexual peers to live on the streets than in public care (Ray, 2006). Homophobic attitudes are also common in residential care and social workers have found there is a dearth of foster homes available for them. One such 16 year old, a runaway from a UK children's home, fell to his death trying to escape a car of 'queerbashers'. A voluntary project, set up in his name, has provided supported lodgings, mentoring and independent living skills to young, homeless LGB people for almost two decades (Albert Kennedy Trust, 2008). Similar projects have been set up in the US and Australia offering street outreach, residential and supported accommodation assistance programmes (Maberley and Coffey, 2005; Ray 2006).

Conclusion

As this chapter has shown, recognition of LGB health inequalities is uneven between countries. At one extreme, LGB identity and/or behaviour remains a capital offence, while in other countries LGB rights to health are included in national legislation. However, LGB health inequalities have begun to gain recognition internationally, including in social work discourse. As a result, they have begun to be targeted in social work practice through a range of initiatives concerning assembling evidence, lobbying and service provision. Nevertheless, the continuing challenge remains the achievement of equal protection of LGB people globally, to underwrite equal chances of health and well-being.

10.3: The role of advocacy assessment and action in resolving health-compromising stress in the lives of older African American homeless women

David Moxley and Olivia Washington

The global challenge of homelessness

Globally, homelessness is a serious and growing problem that does not simply coincide with poverty but reflects the growing inequities between rich and poor, both within the developing and developed world (The United States Conference of Mayors, 2004; Tipple and Speak, 2005). Becoming homeless not only represents the absence of housing, it also involves deprivation in its profoundest terms: the loss of basic resources for health and well-being, whether shelter, adequate nutrition, health care, opportunities for access to decent work, and regular and adequate income. That homelessness is a serious worldwide problem is an understatement: displacement is a product of socio-economic changes as well as climatic and environmental ones. Displacement can be the result of war and violence. Factors pushing people into homelessness are multiple and systemic: they emerge and escalate from fundamental changes in social structure, relationships among nations and the literal collapse of infrastructure within local communities (Springer, 2000).

Those who are most vulnerable to homelessness are those who are most sensitive to social and environmental change and include women, children, older people and particularly people of minority status. Those individuals and families who live closest to subsistence levels can easily tip into homelessness because even small changes in economic conditions, social benefits and social support can exacerbate existing vulnerabilities. Appreciating the full seriousness of homelessness involves what Springer (2000) refers to as houselessness: those for whom living on the streets, in makeshift shelters, in sub-standard housing or concealed and out of sight are realities of daily life. A single definition may also simply fail to capture just how many people are actually homeless in a given community and obscure the type of homelessness they experience (Tipple and Speak, 2005). And the dynamic nature of homelessness, in which people may move in and out of housing but over time do not achieve stability in their domiciliary arrangements, further reveals the complexity of this social issue (Minnery and Greenhalgh, 2007).

The Leaving Homelessness Intervention Research Project (LHIRP)

Within this international context, homelessness in the US is not simply most prevalent among the poor, it is a problem of poverty. Those who are poor and homeless share much in common with those who are poor but housed (Toro, 2007): the absence of universal health care benefits and adequate and flexible social welfare benefits can reduce the stability of housing arrangements. The instability of domiciliary arrangements among older African American women, as a serious social issue in Detroit, Michigan, first came to the authors' attention at the end of the 1990s. This was when the authors began the process of documenting homelessness among this so-called 'new homeless population' (Minnery and Greenhalgh, 2007) who became homeless through multiple avenues including health problems, marital disruption, household accidents or house fires, and job loss.

Employing narrative methods, the authors were able to examine more closely the experience of homelessness among older African American women who 'suddenly' became homeless, although well before the event, social forces had increased their vulnerability and risk of homelessness. Many of the over 500 women who have participated in some aspect of the Leaving Homelessness Intervention Research Project (LHIRP) (see Washington and Moxley, 2008a; forthcoming, for a more detailed discussion) experienced serious health issues before they were homeless. However, they also experienced the exacerbation of these problems (such as Lupus or Arthritis) after they had become homeless, or saw the emergence of new serious illnesses, such as cardiac or respiratory problems, as stress accumulated and undermined their health.

One of the principal operating assumptions of the research project was that the physical well-being of older African American homeless women was seriously compromised by multiple stressors that worked to overwhelm them physically, emotionally and cognitively. As Wilkinson (2006) has shown, stress formed through deprivation and constant exposure to anxiety-producing situations literally threatens safety, weakens physiological functioning and triggers somatic vulnerabilities. Inadequate health, social and housing services leave homeless women with few buffers that can protect their health (Keith, 2003). Any inherent somatic or emotional vulnerability is likely to be amplified under such conditions. Serious health issues emerge in the face of overwhelming stressors in a context in which suitable policy, programmes and practice fail to offer adequate support for women who are highly sensitive to social, economic and policy changes.

LHIRP has been in operation for seven years and incorporates policy and practice consistent with that advocated in relation to homelessness in Europe, the US and Australia, by Minnery and Greenhalgh (2007). The Project seeks to work in partnership with homeless individuals, not only by explicitly addressing housing issues, but also participants' physical and emotional health requirements and their need for social inclusion. LHIRP incorporates what the authors identify as a developmental action research strategy. Through the formation of strong partnerships with older African American homeless women, the Project identifies and tests practice that may foster the movement of participants out of homelessness, through increasing social and material resources, by means of solidarity, support and ultimately advocacy. The Project's staff members recognise that its scope lies in focusing on 'tertiary issues', that is, not on the origins, but on the consequences, of wider social issues that the participants experience personally. These consequences of homelessness take a serious psychological and motivational toll on participants, for example, in the form of depression (Washington and Moxley, 2008a). The social stress the women experience compromises their innate physical and emotional resources and capacity for adaptability, key aspects of good health.

Issues as foci of assessment

The development of a social work assessment protocol designed to identify and foreground women's own assessment of the nature and damaging effects of the issues they experience in their daily lives, stands as an important product of LHIRP. A central aim of the assessment is to help participants articulate the major issues they confront daily and identify how these issues compound the stress they experience. Entitled the Getting Out of Homelessness Interview (GOOHI), older African American female service users work closely with LHIRP staff members to identify stressful (or distressful) issues across many domains of daily life, including housing and household, mobility, health, social and dental services, children and family life, work and income, education, legal needs and credit, food and nutrition, clothing and footwear, and residual categories of a participant's own definition.

A staff member guides the participant through a given domain (for example, legal and credit), encourages her description of the issues she faces, and uses the participant's own language to describe an issue so her own words and phrases dominate the assessment. The participant then assigns priorities to the issues she faces and encodes her own assessment of their severity and the toll the issues take on her physical and psychological well-being. Continued assessment of each prioritised issue further reveals the physical and emotional toll the participant experiences, the hassles she faces in resolving prioritised issues, and the worry or anxiety these negative experiences induce. For example, a woman who faces damaged credit due to predatory lending practices and/or unpaid electric bills can accumulate constant worry and rumination, which in turn can exacerbate ill-health.

Seeking resolution of issues through advocacy

Research on the assessment process the Project has undertaken indicates that the participants find some measure of relief in simply identifying the issues they face, in explaining their situations to an attentive person and in identifying what they consider to be the most serious issues they face (Washington and Moxley, 2008b). While the assessment offers some psychological relief, the intent, however, is to proceed into the advocacy phase. In this, each woman receives staff support in the preparation of a general advocacy strategy (in which issues and barriers are clearly identified for resolution) and specific advocacy plans in which each prioritised issue is staged for resolution through elaboration of actual advocacy activities undertaken by:

- the participant herself with the support of a Project staff person;
- the Project staff person her/himself who engages in dedicated representation; or
- an 'expert' who has substantive knowledge of the life domain in which the participant is seeking the resolution of an issue (for example, health care access).

Advocacy is envisioned as either direct representation that strengthens the status of the participant and helps her address directly what she perceives as serious barriers to the resolution of her homelessness, or a personal support system. Resolution of prioritised issues is a Project strategy designed to reduce the overall burden of demands a woman experiences and facilitate her movement out of homelessness. It is also seen as a means of alleviating stress. Theoretically, issue resolution is viewed as associated with stress reduction (Lu, 2002; Brown, 2004), and as being able to accelerate further the movement out of homelessness, by supporting the woman's application of her own personal resources. The accumulation of numerous serious issues that the participant perceives as insurmountable or irresolvable is viewed as disrupting the woman's equanimity, wearing her down emotionally and thereby undermining her health. The corollary of this is that it becomes harder to negotiate great personal challenges. However, the resolution of issues and the stress associated with them can facilitate a woman's more active engagement in getting out of homelessness. The advocacy procedure recognises and seeks to address the interplay between social issues – inegalitarian income and poor housing policy – and their personal consequences, including the erosion of well-being and physical and emotional stamina.

Issues as products of poor policy

Examination of the issues the participants identify reveals the inadequacy of social policy in the US to prevent or even resolve homelessness in practical and expeditious ways. Older African American homeless women experience serious and multiple issues because of their diminished social status: they command few personal resources and may literally give up in the face of serious stressors when they surmise that 'good policy' is not working for them and 'good practice' is nowhere in sight. The issues women identify are serious and complex and they cannot resolve them on their own. Fixing damaged credit, for example, can require considerable expertise and, given the limited access of people in poverty to legal services, locating relevant help is not easy. Such issues may have further consequences such as when damaged credit exposes women to predatory lending arrangements to which they may succumb from desperation to get resources for housing, transportation or other necessities. The stigma and disadvantage involved here can follow the participants as they move from one housing arrangement to another – credit records in the US, for example, are easily retrievable by a range of institutions and businesses and hard to correct. Resolving such issues also means negotiations with complex bureaucracies, which demands fortitude and tenacity on the part of the participants, requiring energy they may not have because of the health issues they face. Moving from one office to another in search of a resolution can wear down even the most determined. Drawing on the experience of a participant in the Project: a woman living in poverty who has diabetes may simply not have the appropriate shoes to walk the streets and navigate stairs, in order to attend multiple meetings with case workers.

Since homeless individuals' unsupported efforts to resolve issues can be unproductive, leading to frustration and adding to distress, it is not surprising that the absence of successful outcomes is demoralising. This is especially problematic, given how even basic survival in a state of homelessness requires virtues of ingenuity, tenacity and adaptability. Facing a serious issue with limited social support and in isolation is daunting, and the lack of control a woman may exercise over the framing and content of the issue weakens the expectation of success. A policy system which integrated advocacy in support of homeless service users could actually strengthen the standing of a vulnerable person and foster productive effort and better solutions. In the absence of such a system, older African American women, like all homeless people, can experience the unmitigated impact of serious social forces, and, in turn, the emergence of serious health conditions. This means that the kind of advocacy LHIRP is testing in Detroit, is necessary to fill the gap.

One LHIRP participant, Ellen, captured this state of affairs when she emphasised in her account of her homelessness (Washington and Moxley, forthcoming) that she had 'three strikes' against her. She was referring to her race: African American; gender: female; and socio-economic situation: poor. This was a strong woman who became homeless after her sturdy but vulnerable house succumbed to a fire due to an electrical accident. Her odyssey out of homelessness stretched into years as she tried to make sense of the indignity she faced in the shelter care system, the lack of access to benefits she sought and the multiple jobs she held simultaneously, each of which failed to offer either adequate wages or benefits. The internalisation of the injustices she faced compromised her emotional well-being, but in spite of the discrimination she experienced, she persisted. However, in her uphill fight, without much relief, her dental and physical health decayed. Buffering people from overwhelming stressors is an important protective factor in any system of health. For Ellen, good health was not in reach since good policy and practice were simply absent. This account epitomises the conditions of homelessness among older African American women who have been participants in LHIRP.

Conclusion

In the face of shortcomings in housing and homelessness policy more generally, we have explored the case for a strategy for social work with homeless individuals that addresses the poor health outcomes of homelessness. LHIRP has orchestrated a broad range of social support for older African American women who are seeking to resolve their homelessness and avoid moving back into such a dire situation. Such a blend of advocacy and collective action represents a promising health intervention, but tends to be overlooked in the portfolio of social work tools (McLeod and Bywaters, 2007). Building personal and social resources through facilitated self-assessment and advocacy is to assist participants to activate pathways to help. Admittedly, advocacy cannot prevent the accumulation of further issues once a person moves on in their life. However, it is possible that advocacy nested within a supportive community of participants and staff can help those concerned face issues early on and work with others to resolve events that can fester, induce crisis and return them to the ranks of the homeless. The involvement of social workers in projects such as LHIRP should also be seen as a means of building local capacity for health promotion: through either reaching out to other older women who are vulnerable to homelessness, or offering assistance with their struggle to escape from homelessness. It is a logical, local, facilitated self-help strategy, with important implications for health when undermined by inequality and inadequate social welfare policy at the root of homelessness.

References

Albert Kennedy Trust (2008) *History of Albert Kennedy Trust*, London: Albert Kennedy Trust.

Aspinall, P.J. and Mitton, L. (2008) 'Kinds of people and equality monitoring in the UK', *Policy & Politics*, vol 36, pp 55–74.

Brown, D. (2004) 'Everyday life for black American adults: Stress, emotions, and blood pressure', *Western Journal of Nursing Research*, vol 26, no 5, pp 499–514.

Bywaters, P. (2006) 'Key issues for health inequalities research, UK and international comparisons', Paper presented at the ESRC Social Work and Health Inequalities Research seminar series, Birmingham University, Birmingham, 20 January.

Canning, P. (2008) 'A crack in the UK's asylum edifice', *PinkNews*, 22 May, www.pinknews.co.uk/news/articles/2005-7710.html

CSWER (Centre for Social Work Education and Research) (2007) *Social Work Education and Research Center, Five-year Report 2003–2007*, Guangzhou: Sun Yat-sen University.

Curzi, P. (2006) *Lesbian and Bisexual Women's Health: Common Concerns, Local Issues*, Brussels, Belgium: International Lesbian and Gay Organisation.

Dai, J.(2007) *The Social Development Report of China's Capital 2007*, China: Social Science Academic Press.

de Gruchy, J. and Fish, J. (2004) 'Doctors' involvement in human rights abuses of men who have sex with men in Egypt', *The Lancet*, vol 363, pp 1903.

Fang, L. (2007) 'Study of medical protection for people in city and rural areas', *Journal of Population* (Ren kou yue kan), vol 2, pp 48–53.

Fish, J. (2006) *Heterosexism in Health and Social Care*, Basingstoke: Palgrave.

Fish, J. (2007a) *Reducing Health Inequalities for LGBT People: Briefing Papers for Health and Social Care Staff*, London: Department of Health.

Fish, J. (2007b) 'Getting equal: The implications of new regulations to prohibit sexual orientation discrimination for health and social care', *Diversity in Health and Social Care*, vol 4, pp 221–8.

Han, J. and Lou, D. (2005) 'Report on health situation in Chinese rural areas', *Journal of China Development Observation*, vol 1, pp 12–22.

Human Rights Watch (2007) *International Jurisprudence on Sexual Orientation and Gender Identity*, New York: Human Rights Watch.

Hunt, R. and Dick, S. (2008) *Serves You Right: Lesbian and Gay People's Expectations of Discrimination*, London: Stonewall.

Hunt, R. and Fish, J. (2008) *Prescription for Change: Lesbian and Bisexual Women's Health Check*, London: Stonewall.

Keith, V.M. (2003) 'In and out of our right minds: Strengths, vulnerabilities, and the mental well-being of African American women', in D.R. Brown and V.M. Keith (eds) *In and Out of Our Right Minds: The Mental Health of African American Women*, New York: Columbia University Press, pp 277–92.

King, M. and Bartlett, A. (2006) 'What same-sex civil partnerships may mean for health', *Journal of Epidemiology and Community Health*, vol 60, pp 188–91.

Law, A. and Gu, J. (2008) 'Social work education in mainland China: Development and issues', *Asian Social Work and Policy Review*, vol 2, no 1, pp 1–12.

Li, Y. (2004) *A Study of Poverty and Social Assistance*, Beijing: Peking University Press.

Li, X., Zhang, X. and Tang, L. (2005) 'The situation of rural poverty in China', *Journal of China Agricultural University*, vol 4, pp 67–74.

Liang, S. (2006a) 'Poor in the city', *Human Resources*, vol 15, pp 10–12.

Liang, S. (2006b) 'Poor in the city', *Human Resources*, vol 17, pp 34–5.

Liu, Y. (2005) *Chinese New Urban Poverty and its Spatiality Under Market Transition*, Beijing: Science Press.

Liu, Y.L. (2006) 'Summary report on the service project for migrant female workers', unpublished report, Guangzhou: CSWER, Sun Yat-sen University.

Lu, Y. (2002) 'Effects of care-giving stress on functional capacity and health promoting behaviour in elderly caregivers', Paper presented at the Annual Meeting of the Gerontological Society of America, Boston, MA.

Maberley, E. and Coffey, P. (2005) *Opening the Door? Exploratory Research into LGBT Young People's Access to Supported Accommodation in Queensland*, Queensland: Youth Housing Coalition.

Man, L. (2005) 'Study on empowering social education model: Family life education for migrant workers in Yuancun', unpublished MA Thesis, Guangzhou: CSWER, Sun Yat-sen University.

McLeod, E. and Bywaters, P. (2007) 'Ill-health', in M. Davies (ed) *The Blackwell Companion to Social Work*, 3rd edn, Oxford: Blackwell Publishers, pp 43–9.

McNair, R.P. (2003) 'Lesbian health inequalities: A cultural minority issue for health professionals', *Medical Journal of Australia*, vol 178, pp 643–5.

Meyer, I.H. (2003) 'Prejudice, social stress, and mental health in lesbian, gay, and bisexual populations: Conceptual issues and research evidence', *Psychological Bulletin*, vol 129, no 5, pp 674–97.

Minnery, J. and Greenhalgh, E. (2007) 'Approaches to homelessness policy in Europe, the United States and Australia', *Journal of Social Issues*, vol 63, pp 641–55.

NIMHE (National Institute for Mental Health in England) (2007) *Mental Disorders, Suicide and Deliberate Self Harm in Lesbian, Gay and Bisexual People: A Systematic Review*, London: Care Services Improvement Partnership.

Ottosson, D. (2007) *State-Sponsored Homophobia: A World Survey of Laws Prohibiting Same-Sex Activity Between Consenting Adults*, Brussels, Belgium: International Lesbian and Gay Association.

Pan, N.Z. and Guo, R.J. (2007) 'Market economy and medical system reform', *Group Economy*, vol 223, March, pp 49–50.

Plumb, M. (2001) 'Undercounts and overstatements: Will the IOM report on lesbian health improve research?', *American Journal of Public Health*, vol 91, no 6, pp 873–5.

Ray, N. (2006) *Lesbian, Gay, Bisexual and Transgender Youth: An Epidemic of Homelessness*, New York: National Gay and Lesbian Task Force Policy Institute and the National Coalition for the Homeless.

Reding, A. (2003) *Sexual Orientation and Human Rights in the Americas*, New York: World Policy Institute.

Regehr, C., Stern, S. and Shlonsky, A. (2007) 'Operationalizing evidence-based practice: The development of an Institute for Evidence-Based Social Work', *Research on Social Work Practice*, vol 17, no 3, pp 408–16.

Rogers, G.D. (2007) 'Health priorities and perceived health determinants among South Australians attending GLBTI festival events', *Health Promotion Journal of Australia*, vol 18, pp 57–62.

Rosenblum, R. (ed) (1996) *Unspoken Rules: Sexual Orientation and Women's Human Rights*, London: Cassell.

Ru, X., Lu, X. and Li, P. (2006) *Analysis and Forecast on China's Social Development*, China: Social Science Academic Press.

Scott, S.D., Pringle, A. and Lumsdaine, C. (2004) *Sexual Exclusion: Homophobia and Health Inequalities: A Review of Health Inequalities and Social Exclusion Experienced by Lesbian, Gay and Bisexual People*, London: UK Gay Men's Health Network.

Shue, V. and Wong, C. (eds) (2007) *Paying for Progress in China: Public Finance, Human Welfare and Changing Patterns of Inequality*, London: Routledge.

Song, Y.D., Kong, F.S. and Li, J. (2005) 'Study of food safety control in large meeting', *Preventive Medicine*, vol 11, no 6, pp 28–30.

Springer, S. (2000) 'Homelessness: A proposal for a global definition and classification', *Habitat International*, vol 24, pp 475–84.

Staley, M., Hussey, W., Roe, K., Harcourt, J. and Roe, K. (2001) 'In the shadow of the rainbow: Identifying and addressing health disparities in the lesbian, gay, bisexual and transgender population: A research and practice challenge', *Health Promotion Practice*, vol 2, pp 207–11.

Stonewall (1996) *Queerbashing – A National Survey on Homophobic Violence and Harassment*, London: Stonewall.

Tipple, G. and Speak, S. (2005) 'Definitions of homelessness in developing countries', *Habitat International*, vol 29, pp 337–52.

Toro, P. (2007) 'Toward an international understanding of homelessness', *Journal of Social Issues*, vol 63, pp 461–81.

Toro Alfonso, J. (2008) 'Body image, masculinity, homonegativity and eating disorders in a sample of Latino gay men', Paper presented at the XXIX International Congress of Psychology, Berlin, Germany 22 July.

UKLGIG (UK Lesbian and Gay Immigration Group) (2008) *Annual Report*, London: UKLGIG.

United States Conference of Mayors (2004) *A Status Report on Hunger and Homelessness in American Cities, Hunger and Homelessness Survey*, Sodexho: United States Conference of Mayors.

Verkaik, R. (2008) 'Now Iranian who fled to Britain faces deportation', *The Independent*, 7 March, p 3.

Washington, O. and Moxley, D. (2008a) 'Telling my story: From narrative to exhibit in illuminating the lived experience of homelessness among older African American women', *Journal of Health Psychology*, vol 13, no 2, pp 154–65.

Washington, O. and Moxley, D. (2008b) 'Development of a multimodal assessment framework for helping older African American women transition out of homelessness', unpublished paper.

Washington, O. and Moxley, D. (forthcoming) '"I have three strikes against me": Narratives of plight and efficacy among older African American homeless women and their implications for engaged inquiry', in S. Evans (ed) *African Americans and Community Engagement in Higher Education*, New York: State University of New York Press.

Wei, C. (2007) *Survey on Chinese Farmer Workers*, Beijing: Law Press-China.

Wilkinson, R. (2006) 'Ourselves and others – For better or worse: Social vulnerability and inequality', in M. Marmot and R. Wilkinson (eds) *Social Determinants of Health*, 2nd edn, Oxford: Oxford University Press, pp 355–71.

Wu, L.B. (2006) 'Summary Report on the community project for migrant workers in Nanhai Lishui', unpublished report, Guanzhou: CSWER, Sun Yat-sen University.

11

Preventive social work intervention and health promotion

Introduction

One dimension of social work's contribution to tackling health inequalities is to focus on preventive interventions which both build and build on the resources of disadvantaged local communities to benefit their health. This chapter offers three contrasting examples of this kind of intervention drawn from very different social contexts in Australia, China and Hong Kong. These show how social workers, acting alongside public health and other professionals, can develop and support grassroots action for better health by members of geographical communities and communities of interest in the face of the rapid social, economic and environmental changes accelerated by globalisation.

Section 11.1 analyses the context in which Indigenous Australians experience an average life expectancy of some 17 years less than that of the majority population (CSDH, 2008). A substantial distrust of social workers and health professionals has resulted from their involvement in oppressive and discriminatory social policies including the removal of children. However, this analysis of a group work intervention based on a transdisciplinary, Family Wellbeing empowerment programme shows that social workers can help to strengthen Indigenous people's own sense of control and their capacity to take prominent roles in local public policy making with the aim of reducing health damage.

Section 11.2 discusses a joint Canadian–Chinese development programme, particularly focused on women's health, in rural Mongolia where one response to poverty has been a large-scale exodus of men to seek work in cities. Rooted in a training programme based on basic social work methods and values, this project recruited local women to be leaders in health education and promotion work with a number of expected and unexpected consequences. Trainers came to recognise the expertise of rural women in analysing and addressing the barriers they face to health, including the inadequacy of health care provision.

This has produced a shift in the approach of the All China Women's Federation to its task of nationwide health promotion.

Finally, Section 11.3 reports on an intervention to build health–related social capital in Hong Kong through the Community Investment and Inclusion Fund, with social work leaders. Although a strategic intervention led by the Fund's managers, the core principle of the model was the building of social capital through a fundamental change in welfare approach from service provision to participatory grassroots action. Operating on a large scale, the Fund worked in 176 local projects to enable recipients from a variety of vulnerable populations to become volunteers and partners working for better conditions and better health. In turn, this new approach required significant changes in social work roles and skills.

11.1: Empowerment as a social determinant of Indigenous Australian health: the case of the Family Wellbeing programme

Mary Whiteside, Komla Tsey and Yvonne Cadet-James

Introduction

Globalisation has brought new dimensions and depths to the inequalities which have always characterised human societies. For indigenous peoples across the world, globalisation has too often meant new invasions of traditionally-held land and the destruction of natural environments for deforestation, mining, agribusiness or other forms of exploitation, and has brought in its train the devastating effects of climate change. Meanwhile exclusion from majority societies' pathways to economic and social security through education and employment has exacerbated the inequalities that have long been experienced. One consequence, despite the best efforts of indigenous peoples themselves and their allies, has been acute inequalities in health outcomes (see Chapters 4 and 9, this volume, by Alston and Fawcett, respectively).

The people whose lives are most affected, and practitioners wanting to address the social and health rights of indigenous peoples, are at risk of feeling overwhelmed in the face of such powerful macro-level forces. The situation is compounded by the problematic history between professionals and indigenous peoples in countries like Australia where professionals have too often been implicated in oppressive practices. However, even in the face of such powerful and often destructive social and economic processes, there are examples of ordinary people making extraordinary personal changes and taking greater control of their health and well-being, on occasions with effective professional support. International research into the social determinants of health has demonstrated the significance of people's experience of 'control', a term described as being synonymous with empowerment as critical to health and well-being, irrespective of whether or not these changes ripple to effect wider social systems (Tsey et al, 2003). Despite this research, this important psychosocial factor, which resonates with

Indigenous Australians' desire to be self-determining in relation to the health and social services in their communities, has received little attention in research literature. This chapter analyses an attempt by a transdisciplinary team of social workers, public health practitioners and Indigenous academics and community partners to engage with international research addressing the social determinants of health, particularly the critical psychosocial factor of empowerment (Tsey et al, 2003). The Family Wellbeing empowerment programme (FWB), developed by and for Indigenous Australians, will provide a case study to illustrate the approach.

Background

The multiple impacts associated with colonisation, dispossession and social and economic marginalisation have been devastating for Indigenous Australians who experience significantly higher levels of illness and premature death compared with the rest of the Australian population. They are also more likely to be incarcerated, experience violence and abuse, have lower levels of education and employment, and suffer from excessive use of alcohol and other substances. Although the health improvement of other indigenous populations in comparable wealthy nations such as Canada and New Zealand has shown that concerted action can make a difference, in Australia there has been a lack of progress or even deterioration in some health indicators (Steering Committee for the Review of Government Service Provision, 2007).

Professionals across disciplines are grappling with how best to more effectively respond to this disturbing situation. Some disciplines have the added complication of needing to overcome the perception by those whom they are seeking to assist that their profession has been complicit in policies that led to the problems in the first place. Social work is one profession that struggles with this legacy (King, 2003; Briskman, 2007) and is seen to have played a role in the disempowerment of Indigenous Australians, as agents of policies that were devastating to Indigenous families and communities and, as a result, to individuals (Briskman, 2007). While such clearly discriminatory policy has changed, King (2003) argues that the nature of the relationship between the two groups remains problematic and that Indigenous people have played the role of the client and powerless almost exclusively in any contact between them. Health research and service provision has mirrored the relationship between social work and Indigenous Australians. For example, the National Health and Medical Research Council's

(NHMRC's) ethical guidelines for Aboriginal and Torres Strait Islander health research (NHMRC, 2003) state that Aboriginal and Torres Strait Islander people continue to express concerns about poor consultation, lack of communication and infringement of deeply held values arising from cross-cultural insensitivity, even where researchers have complied with the legal requirements of ethical guidelines. Given these experiences, it is not surprising that many Indigenous people remain sceptical about the value of research (Briskman, 2007) and resist becoming involved.

Despite this troubled background, there are many professionals across disciplines seeking to change relationships and more effectively address the needs of Indigenous Australians. There is increased attention being paid to, and a growing understanding of, the specific structural social determinants of Indigenous health, including history, land and place, racism, poverty and social class, social capital, education, employment, welfare, and housing (Carson et al, 2007). However, with so many of these social determinants related to factors outside the control of individual professionals, it can be hard to know where to start.

Researching empowerment through Family Wellbeing

There exists widespread international recognition of the health significance of empowerment (Tsey et al, 2003), defined as a multi-level construct that involves people assuming control and mastery over their lives in the context of their social and political environment (Wallerstein, 1992), to the extent that it has been defined as a social determinant of health. The relevance of this research for Indigenous health appears evident given the recognition that relative powerlessness has long been seen as a major factor shaping Indigenous health, however there remains a lack of tested and validated empowerment programmes in the Indigenous health literature. There are many examples across Australia of Indigenous people taking action to address their situation but without research evidence they rarely attract the recognition or support they deserve. Aware of the critical need for such research we, a team of researchers from James Cook University and the University of Queensland in North Queensland, designed a phased long-term research programme to explore the concept of empowerment and its relevance to Indigenous health.

Two key assumptions underpin the research programme. First, the importance of self-determination in research design. This involves looking at what people are doing, what strategies are already working, where the centres of energy are, and how researchers and practitioners can support these. As a result of this process the Family Wellbeing empowerment programme (FWB) became a central focus of the research. Second, that complex Indigenous health issues require transdisciplinary approaches, defined as a process moving beyond the concept of interdisciplinary partnerships to take into account Indigenous knowledge traditions (Christie, 2006), and intersectoral collaboration. In the case of this project the research team consists of Indigenous and non-Indigenous academics, health professionals, social workers, social scientists and community workers. Partnerships have been established with key Indigenous communities, as well as non-governmental and government organisations and partner universities.

The Family Wellbeing programme is a highly regarded personal empowerment programme developed by and for Indigenous Australians in mid-1993 by the Aboriginal Education Development Branch of the South Australian Department of Education. The programme initially took the form of a community support programme designed to help people, many of whom were survivors of the 'stolen generation', cope with grief and stress. The term 'stolen generation' refers to the thousands of Indigenous Australians that were forcibly removed by the state from their families to be raised in foster homes or institutions as part of Australian policy to assimilate Aboriginal children into mainstream Australian society (Briskman, 2007). As participants requested more skills to deal with the complexity of their own lives and those of their families and communities, FWB evolved into an accredited counselling training programme.

FWB seeks to provide safe, supportive learning environments for people to share stories and reflect on important phronetic questions for life such as 'Where am I going with my life?', 'What is working and what is not working so well?', 'Who is benefiting and who is losing out?', 'Is it fair?', 'What can I do to change the situation and with what consequences?' (Flyvbjerg, 2001). The course is structured into four stages. Each stage has 10 half-day sessions which translates into 30 programme hours. The topics covered include understanding our basic needs, exploring human qualities, understanding patterns in relationships, conflict resolution, managing crisis, analysing beliefs and attitudes and how these can constrain or allow us to move on in life, and address grief and loss, family violence and child abuse.

Central to the learning experience are participants' personal histories, stories and knowledge. Beyond this the programme draws from a range of theories and resources. This eclecticism is a clear example of self-determination as people take control of the decisions regarding what systems of knowledge are most useful to them. Meditation and creative visualisation techniques have been taken from psychosynthesis, a branch of transpersonal psychology which aims to enrich lives through direct spiritual experience (Clinebell, 1981). Concepts and techniques of building inner peace and linking this to broader processes for world peace were incorporated following a cross-cultural exchange with Tibetan monks from the Dalai Lama's Gyoto Tantric University. Strategies for dealing with the effects of childhood sexual abuse on adults were drawn from *The Courage to Heal* (Davis, 1990). Information about addressing family violence, child abuse and conflict have been taken from a range of government and non-government resources. FWB also encourages participants to learn outside the confines of the course, through their own reading, attendance at seminars or courses, joining support groups or seeking one-on-one professional help.

Outcomes

Since the FWB empowerment research programme commenced in 1998 over 400 adults and 150 school children have been exposed to FWB across towns and communities in Far North Queensland and Central Australia. The research accompanying the programme delivery has demonstrated profound benefits for programme participants and their communities and confirmed FWB's efficacy as an effective empowerment intervention, particularly at the level of personal empowerment, when analysed in relation to the attributes of empowerment identified in Table 11.1.1.

Participants, almost without exception, described an enhancement of their sense of self-worth, analytic skills, their ability to cope with the stresses of day to day life and their ability to help others to do the same. Many of the changes they reported in their life related directly to the social and health issues identified at the outset of this chapter. At an individual level people spoke of taking better care of themselves, reducing their alcohol intake, changing their diet, doing more physical exercise and in some cases losing weight. While changes were most marked at the individual level, many people went on to take a greater role in local organisational and political affairs. There was evidence of people organising to address community issues such as poor school attendance rates, critical housing shortages, endemic family violence, alcohol and drug misuse, higher levels of chronic disease and the over-representation of Indigenous men in the criminal justice system. Community empowerment was evident in the capacity of FWB participants to attract significant resources from government and

Table 11.1.1: A framework for multi-level empowerment

Levels of empowerment	Empowerment attributes
Personal empowerment	Improved perceptions of self-worth and mutability of social environment as evident by: • empathy and perceived ability to help others; • capacity to deal with change; • ability to analyse the root causes of problems; • belief in one's ability to exert control over life circumstances; • a sense of coherence about one's place in the world.
Organisational empowerment	Stronger social networks and community/organisation competence to collaborate and solve problems as evident by: • participation in organisational decision making; • perceptions of support, satisfaction and community connectedness; • ability to reach consensus on goals and strategies to achieve change.
Community empowerment	Actual improvements in environmental or health conditions as evident by: • changes in public policy; • systems level changes; • community's ability to acquire resources to create healthier environments.

Source: Adapted from Wallerstein (1992)

non-government agencies, for example, in one community, to take community control of state-run health services.

The research agenda of building an evidence base around an Indigenous-developed programme has led to mutual gains for participants and researchers alike. Participants are enthusiastic about being involved in a research programme which is directly linked to their priorities. The relevance of FWB to community issues is evident in the extent to which people are taking ownership of the programme and integrating it into local service development. Planning is under way to make FWB a central component of welfare reform strategies being implemented across Cape York communities, in Far North Queensland. Further, participants value the external support they receive from the research team and see the research outcomes leading to increased security of funding for local initiatives. For the research team the process of undertaking research that is owned and relevant to participants enables not only a greater likelihood that research goals will be achieved but also the satisfaction that the outcomes are useful and leading to sustained change. Few of the difficulties often cited by researchers undertaking research in Indigenous settings, for example the need to overcome scepticism and distrust of the research process, have been an issue with this approach.

Conclusion

The impacts of global forces have been overwhelming for Indigenous societies in Australia and internationally, yet this power is by no means absolute. There are countless examples throughout the world, at micro-levels, of individuals, groups and communities taking control of their affairs and working for a better life (Chino and DeBruyn, 2006), as is the case of FWB. The importance of empowerment or personal capacity as a critical social determinant of health is at risk of being underestimated. Empowerment needs to be recognised and addressed as a key element in local, national and international initiatives aimed at reducing socio-economic inequalities and promoting equity in health.

11.2: Social work in rural China: advancing women's health and well-being in the village

Tuula Heinonen, Yang Jiao, Lawrence Deane and Maria Cheung

Introduction

In poor rural areas of Inner Mongolia, like many developing areas in the world, rural health is connected to environmental, social and economic conditions. Diminishing economic opportunities, limited arable land, environmental degradation and urban migration of men for wage labour have forced women to become the mainstay, tending family farms with aging in-laws, while also managing household chores, raising domestic animals and caring for other family members. In rural China, we have observed how health promotion and illness prevention can be fostered through local social work efforts and education.

The China Women's University in Beijing, in partnership with the University of Manitoba, initiated a project for rural social work training in which county and township cadres of the All China Women's Federation and village-level women leaders are trained to provide social services for rural women and families. With support from the Canadian International Development Agency (CIDA) and newly-armed with gender-aware rural social work training provided by instructors from the China Women's University, trainees applied their learning to respond to rural women's needs. Built into the training were respect for rural women's knowledge, use of participatory methods (Chambers, 1998; Holland and Blackburn, 1998) and locally relevant activities.

Social work, a new profession in China, has emerged in many cities where a small number of new social workers educated in universities and colleges primarily practise in urban communities, hospitals and schools (Cheung and Liu, 2004; Tsang et al, 2004). Despite rapid introduction of social work in post-secondary education, rural China has remained largely untouched by the profession.

Framing rural women's health and well-being

Our project views rural women's health and well-being holistically. Connections are made between the health of poor rural women and factors such as livelihood activities, workload, environmental conditions, educational opportunities and remote location (Tinker, 1990; Anson and Sun, 2005).

In China, rural women's health and well-being are related to multiple factors in their daily lives including; material conditions and livelihood, entitlements and access to health care and other social welfare, geography and environment, gender and family relations, social support, and individual beliefs and behaviour (Xie, 2003; Li, 2004; Wu et al, 2004; Yen, 2007; Zhang et al, 2007). Their health status is also shaped by the chronological stages and circumstances of their lives as they age (Cheung et al, forthcoming). For example, a woman's reproductive stage is a time marked by greater health vulnerability, particularly in poor, rural areas where gynaecological problems are often left untreated (Xie, 2003; Li, 2004; Xia et al, 2004). Kaufman (2005) found that in such areas women seldom sought health care, not only due to poverty, but also because quality local care did not exist.

Figure 11.2.1 depicts determinants of rural women's health and well-being in Inner Mongolia. Local livelihoods, geographic and environmental characteristics such as sandy grasslands and seasonality and the cultural, political, collective and personal forms of capital are included.

Social networks and social support may be important for rural women's health and assistance during illness and when extra-familial help may be required. Stage of life may affect poor village women's health care as they grow old (Cheung et al, forthcoming). Household members may be unable or unwilling to expend resources for the care of older women in need when they are perceived as an economic burden. Stress and mental health problems of rural women can remain hidden because care is not available locally and would otherwise be a drain on the family's resources. The large number of suicides of reproductive age and older rural women (Phillips et al, 2002) attest to unaddressed psychological problems.

Finally, social structures play a role in women's well-being. Social equality of rural women with men tends to result in a greater value placed on women's contributions and rights in society which, in turn, affects the command women have over pooled household resources and household decision making (Kabeer, 1989). When women increase their ability to command resources, their status in the household and in the community tends to rise (Manderson and Mark, 1997; Kabeer, 2001).

Figure 11.2.1 illustrates the determinants that influence the conditions and circumstances of rural women's health and well-being. The three arrow shapes contain broad features which affect the more specific health determinants. To illustrate, viable local livelihoods affect the availability of material resources for women because they enable them to earn income and pay for goods and services to enhance social welfare and quality of life. Women's well-being is also shaped by their collective capital, fostering the social networks and social support that operate as resources.

Figure 11.2.1: Health determinants affecting women in rural Inner Mongolia

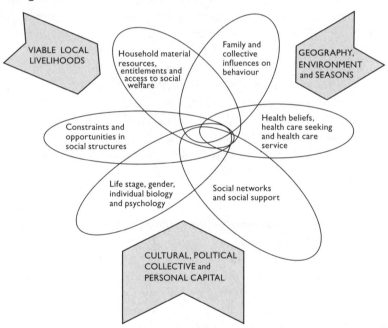

Note: Diagram template designed by Seija Veneskoski.

Rural women's health

During research in our project sites (Heinonen, 2006), village women provided information about their life conditions and how these affected their health and well-being. For example, women in poor Inner Mongolian villages explained that a lack of water for washing contributed to their reproductive health problems and that due to poverty, they delayed seeking or did not seek health care for themselves. They reported being unable to bathe in cold water, particularly in winter, because, to them, cold water washing was unacceptable. Village women said that they experienced gynaecological problems because they could not wash adequately and were overworked. A Women's Federation official later stated that among poor village women, between 70% to 80% experienced gynaecological problems.

Although rural women worried about health problems and felt they lacked knowledge, they did not often seek help due to high costs of health visits and medications. Further, clinics and hospitals were located far away in the county, requiring additional expenditures for transportation. Poor households tended to prioritise expenditures and health care costs for men, who were seen as primary workers, rather than women whose work was secondary and home-based.

Research in Inner Mongolia (Heinonen, 2006) found that not only were specific symptoms and illnesses a concern, but so too was the burden of physical labour and household responsibilities that fell on women's shoulders as a result of increased migration of men for work in urban areas. In one village, it was estimated that 80% of men had taken up work in urban areas. Women were left to perform heavy agricultural work in the village home with help from in-laws and any children old enough. Due to the short growing season and limited arable land, agriculture no longer supported the family adequately. As the women stated, their heavy work and lengthy work days added additional physical and emotional stress to their lives and, for some, made it difficult for them to meet their own and their family's basic needs. Older women said they worried that their adult children would have no resources to support them in old age because poverty affected them all.

Project activities promoting women's health and well-being

Through participatory methods (Cornwall and Pratt, 1999) integrated into their training, the Women's Federation workers' capacities have been enhanced so they can mobilise rural women to learn about their own needs, including health and well-being. These workers thus acquire knowledge about using participatory methods, such as in group discussions and role plays, to help rural women articulate their needs. For example, education about breast cancer and gynaecological health were organised for rural women and small groups were formed during slack farming seasons so that women could obtain health-related information.

Health promotional activities have also been organised using methods that are culturally indigenous, such as locally-developed plays and songs, and pamphlets, calendars and displays of health-related information (for example, the prevention of violence against women) designed by rural women. A community approach has also been used to mobilise medical professionals to provide regular health screening and free consultations for village women who might not otherwise have access to such services. Such activities have contributed to greater knowledge about health and well-being among rural women and men.

Women are now more aware of their health and, importantly, the Women's Federation workers, through practical engagement with the village women, have learned to pay attention to rural women's ideas and respect their need to make decisions on their own. Training in social work values and on women's strengths has given trainees new skills and understandings of rural women's issues. This is significant because the common practice in the Women's Federation was directing and advising rural women about what to do to solve problems. It was believed that because of their positions, Women's Federation workers knew best. These workers increasingly see themselves as service providers and facilitators who help rural women realise their own potential. The village women engaging with newly-trained Women's Federation workers reported increased self-confidence (Women's Federation, Chifeng, Inner Mongolia, 2007).

Policy implications

In many areas of the world, there has been a growing recognition of the importance of participation as an element of community work, a realisation that promotion of health must be understood holistically, and that increasing market delivery of health care leads to problems of inequitable access and the need to develop new forms of collective provision of medical care. In the context of community, these factors tend to be interdependent.

Both trainers and trainees have highlighted the importance of community participation in the delivery of rural social work. This is innovative for China. Women's Federation workers, like other party representatives and government officials, are used to working in a centralised system where plans and directives originate far from the local context. Women's Federation cadres in our project increasingly recognised that appropriate community intervention must incorporate an intricate knowledge of local social, historical and cultural characteristics related to communities and residents with whom they work. Such knowledge applied to intervention with rural women creates a sense of efficacy, personal competence, learning and social support that contributes directly to improved health for participants (Wong et al, 1995; Hendrickson et al, 2002).

Empowerment approaches must often be consciously learned by those who work in rural communities. Professionals worldwide are challenged to learn greater respect for local capabilities and to incorporate local understandings of need more fully into development planning.

Once considered a leader in public health and primary health care, China is now struggling to address a growing problem of unequal access to medical treatment and a resurgence of public health problems (Zhang et al, 2006; Drummer and Cook, 2007). The Chinese government has introduced a system of modest subsidies for the purchase of prepaid health care in rural areas and western provinces (Zhang et al, 2006). Although this is an important step, there are challenges in inducing primarily poor farmers to join the plans. However, participation by low-income farmers increased when they had had a say in the management and monitoring of local plans (Zhang et al, 2006). This experience again emphasises the significant implications for greater equality in health of community building and local participation, but also emphasises the role of equitable social policy at higher levels.

11.3: Social capital and health outcomes: implications for social work practice

Grace Fung-Mo Ng[1] and Raymond W. Pong

Introduction

Hong Kong enjoys high living standards and health status, with an infant mortality rate among the lowest and life expectancy among the highest in the world.[2] However, rapid and unprecedented changes that accompany globalisation also bring about fear, uncertainty and doubt that may affect social health and increase health inequality. Social work educators and practitioners are being challenged to stay ahead as agents of social change.

In his 2001 Policy Address, the Chief Executive of the Government of the Hong Kong Special Administrative Region (HKSARG) announced the establishment of the Community Investment and Inclusion Fund (CIIF) as a new policy initiative. CIIF is a seed fund with an initial injection of HK$300 million (US$38.4 million) to support bottom–up initiatives that build capacity, develop mutual–help networks, increase community participation and enhance social capital development.

Social capital and health outcomes

This chapter is an examination of the link between social capital and health – a link that has yet to be convincingly established – and the role for social work in promoting health equity by means of social capital enhancement. The view that social capital has an impact on health reflects a major shift from health being regarded as the outcome of medical interventions to the realisation that the health of the population is determined by a multitude of factors, a reconceptualisation in health policy which can be dated back to the Canadian Lalonde Report (1974). In the context of population health and its determinants (Wilkinson and Marmot, 2003), social capital has attracted considerable research and policy attention.

Social capital has been variously defined. Some see it as the manifestation of interpersonal trust between citizens, norms of reciprocity and density of civic associations (Kawachi et al, 1999).

Robert Putnam (1995; 2000; 2002), who has popularised the notion of social capital, sees it mostly in terms of social trust, participation and connectivity. Some regard it as similar to social networks (Johnson et al, 2003), and it is sometimes used interchangeably with social cohesion, social support and civic engagement.

In a document of the World Health Organization Commission on the Social Determinants of Health (www.who.int/social_determinants/en/), Wilkinson and Marmot (2003) assert that social cohesion helps to protect people and their health. Johnson et al (2003) have cited studies which show that people with rich social capital appear to suffer less illness and live longer, with improved mental health and reduced anxiety and depression.

This chapter further examines the relationship between social capital and health for three reasons: (a) because not all research on social capital has shown definitive positive impact on health, there is considerable interest in understanding how it affects individuals, communities and institutions; (b) because the mechanism by which social capital influences health is also not well understood (Macinko and Starfield, 2001; Leung et al, 2007), but it is a mechanism of interest to social work educators and practitioners, particularly in relation to whether stronger communities and social networks can be deliberately created; and (c) because CIIF has generated a substantial body of empirical and evaluative data on social capital (see the CIIF Evaluation Consortium Reports at www.ciif.gov.hk/en/evaluation/index_e.html).

Operationalising a social capital framework: the CIIF experience

CIIF has adopted a social capital development framework that integrates various interpretations of social capital into a coherent framework. First, it makes a deliberate link between concepts and policy with practice. The framework, see Figure 11.3.1, serves as a process to promote paradigm shifts, especially among the welfare sector, local stakeholders and business partners, in how new social problems and realities are to be understood and addressed.

The components of social capital are based on key definitions formulated by the World Bank and social researchers: 'social norms' (individual attitudes and social values), 'networks' and 'institutions'. The strategies used in social capital development include: encouraging role and value transformation that changes attitudes and social values at the 'cognitive' level; building 'social trust' through cross-strata networks involved in the 'relational' dimension; and horizontal 'bridging' across heterogeneous groups as well as vertical 'linking' across power hierarchies in the institutional and 'structural' dimensions.

Figure 11.3.1: CIIF social capital framework

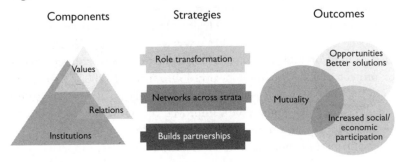

Second, CIIF is clearly positioned. The 80–20 figures in Figure 11.3.2 illustrate the intent of CIIF to shift resources and emphasis on supporting bottom-up social capital initiatives that are more developmental and preventive in nature, relative to social welfare services that are more remedial in nature.

Figure 11.3.2: Social capital initiatives and social welfare services

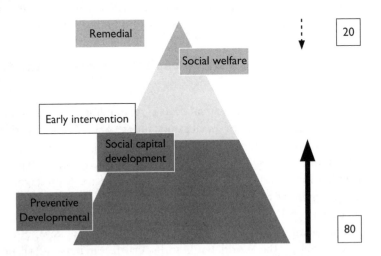

Third, CIIF has generated some unique case studies. Social capital-building strategies have been systematically applied to CIIF-supported initiatives. As of March 2008, CIIF has supported 176 social capital-initiatives distributed in all districts of Hong Kong, involving

3,000 tripartite partners, transforming 20,000 help-recipients into contributing volunteers and establishing over 340 networks with over 300,000 participants.

CIIF project participants include older people, at-risk youth, new arrivals, middle-aged unemployed, ethnic groups, ex-psychiatric patients, single-parent families and low-income working parents on Comprehensive Social Security Assistance (CSSA). Projects mostly take place in rapidly growing new towns or redeveloped housing estates where residents tend to be socially disconnected from their relatives, friends and neighbours, or in old communities that are losing population, relationships and jobs.

CIIF collects quarterly performance data on social capital outcomes achieved from each funded project. The overall effectiveness and impact of these initiatives have been systematically evaluated by an independent Evaluation Consortium of seven research teams from five universities. Evaluation activities took place between December 2004 and March 2006 and covered 56 social capital initiatives funded by CIIF at that time.

The 2006 evaluation outcomes were largely positive, showing increased social engagement and participation, and reporting positive outcomes with respect to the health and well-being of people, families and communities often considered vulnerable or marginalised. However, these findings are not conclusive because most of the 56 initiatives were only in the first two years of implementation, as of 2006.

Social capital strategies that work[3]

Role transformation

Hong Kong surpasses its neighbours in terms of GDP and per capita income, yet the rate of elder suicide in Hong Kong is among the highest in the region. Loss of purpose, value, respect and meaningful roles in the family or community is probably a contributing factor. Transformation of social roles is one of the strategies promoted by CIIF to build capacity, establish new relationships, create new opportunities and generate hope.

Elders who used to be passive participants in a social centre for older people became part-owners and part-operators of an Elder Shop supported by CIIF. This Elder Shop changed the roles of these older people completely. They operated the Elder Shop as a traditional corner store cum community hub starting with serving the much-valued Chinese traditional soup. The older people became well in tune with their community and responded promptly and flexibly to the needs of the community by offering an increasing range of services such as after-school care, cleaning and home repairs. A fee was charged for those who could afford to pay and free services were offered to those who could not.

The Elder Shop earned almost HK$2 million in three years to support their operations post–CIIF funding. Ranging in age from their 60s to their 80s, the older people are busily engaged in their community, such as becoming 'adopted grannies' to children from families in need. They reported improved health and feeling younger and happier. This illustrates the efficacy of role transformation strategies to achieve positive, active and healthy aging.

Bridging across generations and social strata through mentoring

Social disengagement, dropping out from mainstream society and preoccupation with video games are often precursors to social disconnection, poor health behaviours, drug abuse and low motivation among youth. Social capital enhancing strategies in the form of cross-generation and cross-strata mentoring were used in several CIIF projects such as the Red Apprentices. At-risk youths were matched with volunteer mentors from such fields as modern dance, sports, music and property management.

Apart from teaching job-related skills, the volunteer mentors helped the young people by building confidence, instilling life values, raising motivation and encouraging them to search for new directions through special one-to-one or small group mentoring relationships. Over a two-year period, an over-80% success rate (as measured by changes in lifestyle, return to study or gainful employment) was achieved for over 250 young people involved, with some even becoming self-employed.

In another project, the child-rearing experience of a group of middle-aged unemployed women with limited education and no formal employment experience were mentored by a group of health care professionals to become post-natal carers. They provided practical assistance, emotional support and infant care advice to first-time parents. After two years, 70 of these post-natal carers became financially independent, each earning over HK$8,000 a month, and contributing to assisting first-time mothers, reducing the risks of post-natal depression while more importantly building up a sense of community belonging among the participants and building up social networks among families from different social strata.

Weaving safety nets

According to an old Chinese saying, close neighbours are more indispensable than distant relatives. But as a result of dwindling family size, migration and urbanisation, community relationships and family connections are dissipating. Most Hong Kong families now live in 30- or 40-storey high-rise buildings, where neighbours no longer know each other despite close proximity. Home-alone children or living-alone elders are symptomatic of such urban disconnection.

CIIF encourages weaving of new social safety nets in these 'vertical' communities, to foster trust, build relationships, recreate support networks in situ among families and engender a sense of community. Project teams encouraged families and people from diverse backgrounds to be involved, including new arrivals from Mainland China, ethnic communities, former psychiatric patients and corporate volunteers.

Neighbourhood support models were adopted, such as a system of 'floor mentors' and 'estate leaders' who learned to self-manage these semi-formal networks of support established among their neighbours. Modern-day cooperatives were formed to provide services such as after-school care, affordable home-cooked meals, escort to medical appointments, home maintenance, computer repair, personal care or beauty services and so forth. These floor mentors, estate leaders and neighbourhood cooperatives served multiple functions. First, they made practical assistance available to residents. Second, new work opportunities including part-time, paid and unpaid work were created. Increased social and work participation helped build confidence, capacity and pathways for gainful employment. Third, the networks provided social and emotional support to individuals and families. The networks fostered a sense of community belonging especially in the new housing estates. There was anecdotal evidence of increased mutual help, enhanced well-being and reduced child/elder neglect, relative to comparison communities. Fourth, such community networks facilitated civic engagement at the neighbourhood level and formed the basis of more resilient, safer, more caring and healthier communities, as well as producing local leaders. An example is Tung Chung, a newly-built community near the new Hong Kong international airport, which has been acknowledged as a healthy community by the World Health Organization in 2006.

Implications for social work practice

These CIIF projects show that stronger social networks bring about economic and social benefits for individuals, families and communities. They can increase personal competence, cushion the impact of adversities, increase social and economic participation and facilitate social inclusion. The four basic tenets of the CIIF projects, empowerment through role transformation, social connectivity through mentoring relationships, building safe neighbourhoods through cross-generation and cross-strata networks, and the creation of new opportunities through intersectoral collaboration, have created health-enhancing conditions.

The social capital development strategies outlined above present new challenges and opportunities for the social work profession:

- the first challenge is for social workers to take on different roles; they must have sufficient trust in and work systematically to build the capacity of the participants to assume more active roles, enabling them to take increasing responsibility and control;
- the second is the development of active engagement strategies that would enable the participants to gain confidence and have sustained motivation to take on further responsibilities;
- the third is a shift from the perspective of providing help to the vulnerable to one of identifying, developing and maximising their strengths as the main problem solvers;
- the fourth is to extend the horizon of traditional service recipients by bridging them with people from different backgrounds or with complementary strengths so that they can forge more lasting mutual-help relationships;
- the fifth requires social workers to supplement centre-based programmes with community-based work; and
- finally, social workers need to have competencies to work across sectors, create new opportunities or develop conditions for greater social inclusion.

Overall, social capital development strategies require a shift from professional-led service provision to community initiation, engagement, empowerment, self-management and shared ownership, which could result in stronger social networks and social connectivity. Since many CIIF projects have now lasted more than three years, a second round of research and evaluation is being planned, which will focus on social capital outcome measurements; identifying linkages, if any, between changed social roles and increased social networks; and assessing reductions in health inequalities.

Notes

[1] In this article, Ng presents her independent views as a social work professional, and is not representing those of the HKSARG.

[2] Hong Kong Food and Health Bureau statistics covering years up to 2005 (www.fhb.gov.hk/statistics/en/statistics.htm), based on OECD health data, show Hong Kong as having lower infant mortality rates and higher life expectancy than almost any developed country.

[3] Six of the seven evaluation studies included in the first CIIF Evaluation Consortium Studies (2006; with all summary and full reports posted on the CIIF website: www.ciif.gov.hk) assessed the effectiveness of various change strategies, for example for building up social trust, changing intergenerational, cross-ethnic and cross-strata relationships.

References

Anson, O. and Sun, S. (2005) *Health Care in Rural China: Lessons from Hebei Province*, Aldershot: Ashgate.

Briskman, L. (2007) *Social Work with Indigenous Communities*, Leichardt, NSW: The Federation Press.

Carson, B., Dunbar, T., Chanhall, R. and Bailie, R. (eds) (2007) *Social Determinants of Indigenous Health*, Crows Nest, NSW: Allen and Unwin.

Chambers, R. (1998) 'Beyond "Whose reality counts?"': New methods we now need', *Cultures, Organisations and Societies*, vol 4, pp 279–301.

Cheung, M. and Liu, M. (2004) 'Self-concept of Chinese women and the indigenization of social work in China', *International Social Work*, vol 47, no 1, pp 109–27.

Cheung, M., Heinonen, T. and Liu, M. (forthcoming) 'Gender analysis of Chinese rural women's marginalization over the life span after economic reform', *International Journal of Social Development Issues*.

Chino, M. and DeBruyn, L. (2006) 'Building true capacity: Indigenous models for indigenous communities', *American Journal of Public Health*, vol 96, no 4, pp 596–9.

Christie, M. (2006) 'Transdisciplinary research and Aborginal knowledge', The Australian Journal of Indigenous Education. vol 35, pp 78–89.

CIIF (Community Investment and Inclusion Fund) (2006) 'Evaluation Consortium Reports, 2006, to the Legislative Council Welfare Services Panel', HKSARG, available from CIIF website www.ciif.gov.hk

Clinebell, H.J. (1981) 'Growth resources in psychosynthesis', in H.J. Clinebell (ed) *Contemporary Growth Therapies*, Nashville: Abingdon Press.

Cornwall, A. and Pratt, G. (eds) (1999) *Pathways to Participation: Reflections on PRA*, London: ITDG Publishing.

CSDH (Commission on the Social Determinants of Health) (2008) *Closing the Gap in a Generation: Health Equity through Action on the Social Determinants of Health*, Geneva: World Health Organization.

Davis, L. (1990) *The Courage to Heal Workbook: For Women and Men Survivors of Child Sexual Abuse*, New York: Perennial Library.

Drummer, T.J.B. and Cook, I.G. (2007) 'Exploring China's rural health crisis: Processes and policy implications', *Health Policy*, vol 83, pp 1–16.

Flyvberg, B. (2001) *Making Social Science Matter: Why Social Inquiry Fails and How it can Succeed Again*, Cambridge: Cambridge University Press.

Heinonen, T. (2006) 'Gender roles and health determinants in the lives of rural women in China', in *International Conference on Social Work in Health and Mental Health Conference Proceedings*, Hong Kong: University of Hong Kong.

Hendrickson, J., Dearden, K., Pachon, H., Hoi An, N., Schroeder, D. and Marsh, D.R. (2002) 'Empowerment in rural Vietnam: Exploring changes in mothers and health volunteers in the context of an integrated nutrition project', *Food and Nutrition Bulletin*, vol 23, no 4 (Supplement), pp 83–91.

Holland, J. and Blackburn, J. (1998) *Whose Voice? Participatory Research and Policy Change*, London: Intermediate Technology Publications.

Johnson, D., Headey, B. and Jensen, B. (2003) *Communities, Social Capital and Public Policy: Literature Review*, Melbourne: Melbourne Institute Working Paper no. 26/03, Melbourne Institute of Applied Economic and Social Research, University of Melbourne.

Kabeer, N. (1989) *Monitoring Poverty as if Gender Mattered: A Methodology for Rural Bangladesh*, IDS Discussion Paper 255, Brighton: Institute of Development Studies.

Kabeer, N. (2001) 'Conflicts over credit: Re-evaluating the empowerment potential of loans to women in rural Bangladesh', *World Development*, vol 29, no 1, pp 63–84.

Kaufman, J. (2005) 'China: The intersections between poverty, health inequity, reproductive health and HIV/AIDS', *Development*, vol 48, no 4, pp 113–19.

Kawachi, I., Kennedy, B.P. and Glass, R. (1999) 'Social capital and self-rated health: A contextual analysis', *American Journal of Public Health*, vol 89, no 8, pp 1187–93.

King, C. (2003) 'Indigenous issues and social justice from an Indigenous social work framework', www.aasw.asn.au/adobe/papers/paper_christine_king.pdf

Lalonde, M. (1974) *A New Perspective on the Health of Canadians*, Ottawa: Canadian Department of National Health and Welfare.

Leung, K.K., Chan, W.C., Cheung, C.K. and Ng, S.H. (2007) 'How recent migrants from the Chinese Mainland acculturate in Hong Kong: Success factors and policy implications', Paper presented to the Asian Association of Social Psychology Conference, July 2007.

Li, J. (2004) 'Gender inequality, family planning, and maternal and child care in a rural Chinese county', *Social Science and Medicine*, vol 59, no 4, pp 695–708.

Macinko, J. and Starfield, B. (2001) 'The utility of social capital in research on health determinants', *The Milbank Quarterly*, vol 79, no 3, pp 387–421.

Manderson, L. and Mark, T. (1997) 'Empowering women: Participatory approaches in women's health and development projects', *Health Care for Women International*, vol 18, no 1, pp 17–31.

NHMRC (National Health and Medical Research Council) (2003) *Values and Ethics: Guidelines for Ethical Conduct in Aboriginal and Torres Strait Islander Research*, Canberra: Australian Commonwealth Government.

Phillips, M., Li, S. and Zhang, Y. (2002) 'Suicide rates in China, 1995–99', *Lancet*, vol 359 (9309), pp 835–40.

Putnam, R.D. (1995) 'Bowling alone: America's declining social capital', *The Journal of Democracy*, vol 6, no 1, pp 65–78.

Putnam, R.D. (2000) *Bowling Alone. The Collapse and Revival of American Community*, New York: Simon and Schuster.

Putnam, R.D. (2002) *Democracies in Flux: The Evolution of Social Capital in Contemporary Society*, New York: Oxford University Press.

Steering Committee for the Review of Government Service Provision (2007) 'Overcoming indigenous disadvantage: key indicators 2007', Canberra Productivity Commission, www.pc.gov.au/gsp/reports/indigenous/keyindicators2007

Tinker, I. (ed) (1990) *Persistent Inequalities: Women and World Development*, New York: Oxford University Press.

Tsang, A.K.T., Yan, M.C. and Shera, W. (eds) (2004) *Social Work in China: A Snapshot of Critical Issues and Emerging Ideas: Proceedings of the International Colloquium in Beijing in 2000*, Toronto, ON: Faculty of Social Work, University of Toronto.

Tsey, K., Whiteside, M., Deemal, A. and Gibson, T. (2003) 'Social determinants of health, the "control factor" and the Family Wellbeing empowerment program', *Australasian Psychiatry*, vol 2, Supplement, pp S34–9.

Wallerstein, N. (1992) 'Powerlessness, empowerment and health: Implications for health promotion programs', *American Journal of Health Promotion*, vol 6, pp 197–205.

Wilkinson, R. and Marmot, M. (eds) (2003) *Social Determinants of Health: The Solid Facts*, Copenhagen, Denmark: World Health Organization.

Women's Federation, Chifeng, Inner Mongolia (2007) 'Annual report of building human capacity: Social work for rural women in China', unpublished report, Ottawa, Ontario: Canadian International Development Agency.

Wong, G., Li, V.C., Burris, M.A. and Xiang, Y. (1995) 'Seeking women's voices: Setting the context for women's health interventions in two rural counties in Yunnan', *Social Science and Medicine*, vol 41, no 8, pp 1147–57.

Wu, J., Liu, Y., Rao, K., Sun, Q., Qian, J. and Li, Z. (2004) 'Education-related gender differences in health in rural China', *American Journal of Public Health*, vol 94, no 10, pp 1713–16.

Xia, D.Y., Liao, S.S., He, Q.Y., Choi, K.H. and Mandel, J. (2004) 'Self-reported symptoms of reproductive tract infections among rural women in Hainan, China: Prevalence rates and risk factors', *Sexually Transmitted Diseases*, vol 31, no 11, pp 643–9.

Xie, L. (2003) 'Women's reproductive health – A lifelong health', *Women of China*, March, pp 9–11.

Yen, F.T. (2007) 'The impact of gender and hierarchy on women's reproductive health in a Kam village, Guizhou Province, China', *Culture, Health and Sexuality*, vol 9, no 1, pp 55–68.

Zhang, L., Wang, H., Wang, L. and Xiao, W. (2006) 'Social capital and farmers' willingness-to-join a new established community-based health insurance in rural China', *Health Policy*, vol 76, pp 233–42.

Zhang, T., Liu, X., Bromley, H. and Tang, S. (2007) 'Perceptions of tuberculosis and health seeking behaviour in rural Inner Mongolia, China', *Health Policy*, vol 81, nos 2–3, pp 155–65.

Developing new forms of service design and delivery

Introduction

There are many reasons why people entitled to use health and social work services do not use them. Service design may preclude even those with the most complex and greatest needs. Some may be excluded because services are not acceptable, adequate or appropriate. Others may place themselves out of the reach of services, for instance because of the stigma attached to their illness. This chapter shows how social work can be a prime mover in reviewing and reshaping health and social work service provision.

Section 12.1 describes an action research project conducted in Glasgow, Scotland, with black and minority ethnic populations whose reluctance to use mental health services has been compounded by their ongoing experience of racism and isolation. Willingness to disclose illness required changes in beliefs and attitudes within communities and changes to the ways that providers approached planning and delivery processes. The authors describe the 'community conversations' that acted as the crucial vehicle for creating greater acceptance of mental distress and more appropriate services.

The setting for the changes described in Section 12.2 is an oncology social work service of a large metropolitan hospital in Melbourne, Australia. Social workers were traditionally assigned to treatment units rather than disease streams, resulting in unequal access to services, insufficient continuity of care and inadequate identification of and responsiveness to patients in greatest personal and social distress. The authors outline the changes they instituted to provide universal access to basic services, improve continuity of care and introduce a screening model to identify those most at risk of distress, while addressing the demand for evidence-based practice and the limits of resource constraints.

These accounts demonstrate how alliances with like-minded colleagues and organisations, and in partnership with potential users of services are essential for effecting change towards greater equality.

12.1: Addressing mental health inequalities in Scotland through community conversation

Neil Quinn and Lee Knifton

Introduction

Mental health problems are increasingly recognised as a global health issue. The associated stigma and discrimination result in social exclusion and inhibit help-seeking and recovery (WHO, 2002). Stigma involves a combination of ignorance, stigmatising attitudes and discriminatory behaviour, and operates at the level of self, family, community and society. Biomedical perspectives that are often used to understand and frame mental health issues offer little evidence about what works in addressing stigma and discrimination. We argue that other approaches, including community development, campaigning, structural change and service user empowerment, offer more promise and must have a mainstream role in addressing mental health inequalities. The challenge is to harness these different perspectives in practice.

To address mental health inequalities, Scotland has developed a 'community of practice' that draws on rights-based perspectives to inform research, policy and practice. The importance of this approach is brought into sharp focus when working with those who often experience multiple discriminations, such as members of black and minority ethnic communities. This chapter illustrates the potential of this approach and its challenges in addressing mental health inequalities and stigma.

The social construction of mental health problems

Approaches to understanding and addressing mental health problems have been dominated by positivism and psychiatric explanatory frameworks (Double, 2002). Within the context of globalisation, this results in standardised ideas, policies and practices in mental health (Fawcett and Karban, 2005). Attempts to address mental health inequalities mean that top-down, uniform public education approaches often follow. For instance, they are reflected in the Scottish Government's Mental Health First Aid programme, which provides information to the general public from a biomedical perspective. Positivist approaches are reductionist; they fail to capture the complexity of mental health and illness, whereby psychiatric diagnostic categories are contingent. For example, views of homosexuality vary across cultures over time. Protagonists of critical perspectives associate psychiatry with a cycle of progressive infirmity (Gergen, 1994) and argue that mental illness is used by those with power as a means of social control (Szasz, 1972; Pilgrim, 2005). Feminist writers have often viewed diagnostic categories as created by psychiatry to control women (Busfield, 1996). Similarly, people from black and minority ethnic communities have argued that these categories ignore the cultural dimensions of many communities (Fernando, 2002).

Significantly, biomedicine fails to address inequalities in mental health: certain population groups are at higher risk of developing mental health problems, based on gender, ethnicity and sexual orientation (Scottish Executive, 2005), and relative deprivation is more prevalent in unequal societies (Wilkinson and Pickett, 2007). Consequently, a constructivist approach (Pilgrim and Rogers, 1999) that incorporates multiple perspectives on mental health offers a more appropriate framework for addressing inequalities. A constructivist approach, which acknowledges multiple perspectives, validates the views of a range of stakeholders, including practitioners, policy makers and academics and acknowledges the realities of those experiencing inequalities. It validates the personal narratives of people with mental health problems within their cultural and social context (Faulkner and Thomas, 2002), narratives that have informed the emergence of the recovery movement and service user research.

Black and minority ethnic communities in Scotland

While Scotland has a long history of migration, black and minority ethnic communities comprise only 2% of the settled population. The majority of this population lives in Greater Glasgow, Scotland's largest industrial centre, representing about 5% of the region's population. The largest three communities are from Pakistan, India and more recently China (Scottish Executive, 2001). These communities encompass diverse religious, cultural and economic groups. Second and third generations, who are born in Scotland, report stronger identification with their ethnic background and are less likely to identify being Scottish than first generations. Communities report significant racism and greater isolation than the wider population (NHS Greater Glasgow, 2006). A number of studies suggest an under-representation in the use of mental health services (National Resource Centre for Ethnic Minority Mental Health, 2005), together with examples of increased prevalence of mental health problems and evidence of particular forms of stigma and discrimination towards people with mental health problems from black and minority ethnic communities (Scottish Executive, 2005).

Developing an anti-stigma partnership

Within Scotland we have created a partnership that combines local, regional and national partners. It brings together over a hundred diverse organisations, including health and social care agencies, universities, arts institutions, community organisations, mental health groups and private sector business. This 'community of practice' (Wenger, 1998) uses constructivist principles, such as valuing community knowledge and service user narratives, in both the framing of inequalities and the evaluation of the success of the initiatives. An ambitious mental health inequalities programme was negotiated between partners. The process required an acknowledgement of issues of power and a willingness to debate contested ideas about the nature of mental health and how inequalities could be tackled. Partner organisations were expected to make an active contribution to the creation of knowledge through research and to the development of subsequent interventions. In most cases this led to the use of community development approaches in tackling mental health inequalities. Particular consideration was given to groups that experience marginalisation. A major initiative of the partnership was to work with black and minority ethnic communities to tackle mental health stigma and discrimination, and to illustrate some of the promising practices, along with the challenges, that emerge from this approach.

Stigma and discrimination within black and minority ethnic communities

Major studies have found that mental health problems attract particular forms of stigma, including dangerousness, social distance, blame, poor prognosis and recovery pessimism (Corrigan and Penn, 1999). However, as there are varied explanatory models of mental health and illness across cultures and communities, it can be difficult to both understand and address stigma. This is further complicated for black and minority ethnic communities, who may experience multiple forms of stigma, including racism and disempowerment. Gary (2005) uses the term 'double stigma' to describe structural discrimination, which can heighten and sustain individual and community stigma towards people with mental health problems.

The partners undertook a piece of research to explore stigma with the major minority ethnic communities that have migrated to Scotland from India, Pakistan and China. The first stage of the process was to conduct a global literature review. This identified different patterns of stigma, which may be attributable to a set of factors including community and family structure, beliefs about mental illness and experiences of racism and migration. Key themes include shame, concern about marriage prospects and family reputation (Tabassum et al, 2000; Yeung, 2004; Lee et al, 2005; Wynaden et al, 2005). The studies suggest that stigmatising attitudes and beliefs and discriminatory behaviour are prevalent within the communities. However, there is significant heterogeneity within and between communities linked to generation, wealth and gender, suggesting any initiative to tackle stigma and change attitudes should be developed in partnership with these communities, acknowledging diverse concepts and beliefs.

Approaches that have been recommended in the literature to address stigma with these three communities include exploring perceptions about shame and recovery in community venues, targeting appropriate media used by the communities, working with family members and conducting workshops with practitioners to understand the range of mental health beliefs (Weiss et al, 2001; Phillips et al, 2002; Wynaden et al, 2005). There is evidence that national mental health programmes are often inappropriate (Tilbury et al, 2004) and would benefit from culturally appropriate materials, media campaigns and community development approaches.

Developing a community conversation

This review of the literature was followed by an action research project, whereby universities, public organisations and community groups collaborated to explore patterns of stigma in a local context (Glasgow Anti-Stigma Partnership, 2007). Experienced researchers trained and supported members of black and minority ethnic communities to design, implement and evaluate focus group research. This approach helped to build capacity within communities to understand mental health inequalities and to promote cultural awareness among academic researchers. The research was an iterative process in which the research partners continuously reviewed findings and conclusions drawn from the findings. A key theme that emerged was shame, resulting in concealment of mental health issues due to profound concerns about its impact on marriage prospects. Issues around perceived dangerousness and concerns about low educational achievement emerged in some groups. There was also a strong belief that mental health problems are incurable. This had serious implications: people were reluctant to seek help. In some cases mental health was seen as a punishment from God or caused by black magic, spirits or jinn. This might be accompanied by avoidance of individuals and families linked to notions of contagion.

The findings varied in nature and extent across communities and by generation but highlighted stigma within these communities just as significant as is found within the wider indigenous population. This local research identifies the value of community development approaches, which engage with people, and are designed and delivered by community organisations and work within cultural understandings of mental health.

In response to this community research, the existing partners continued to work together to develop an intervention that used community development approaches to address stigma and discrimination, entitled 'community conversation'. This aimed to explore mental health and stigma in safe, supportive workshops. Community organisations led the design and evaluation of the workshops, to ensure the process was culturally sensitive in terms of language, process and content. A continuous process of learning and development was undertaken to inform the development of the programme. The evaluation aimed to measure changes in the knowledge, attitudes and behavioural intent of the participants as well as participants' views on the workshop. In order to evaluate impact, pre- and post-questionnaires were administered in conjunction with qualitative feedback. Workshops were delivered to over 250 participants from Chinese, Indian and Pakistani minority ethnic communities. The baseline results reinforced findings from the previous community research, which indicated that significant levels of stigma exist within these communities as they do in the wider population. Areas of concern include perceptions of dangerousness, social distance, capability, secrecy and shame, but there were positive findings in relation to recovery optimism.

The evaluation of change in attitudes and perceptions as a consequence of the workshops is promising. There was a significant positive impact on attitudes towards mental health problems among participants. In particular we see a greater recognition that mental health issues are common, alongside a willingness to tell someone when you are experiencing a mental health problem. There is possibly a reduction in secrecy and shame, accompanied by a reduction in desire for social distance, an increased willingness to talk to someone and a willingness to allow someone to marry into the family, an area of particular concern. We see a reduction in perceived blame of the person for their condition and also greater recovery optimism. Overall, the workshops had a similar impact on participant attitudes according to age, gender and ethnicity. However, sufficient variation between and within communities indicates that intervention models need to be developed by and not for communities, if we are to respond adequately to diversity within them.

Policy implications

The findings of the study suggest that a community conversation approach that effectively engages black and minority ethnic populations has a strong positive impact in terms of reducing mental health stigma among participants. The acceptability and impact of this approach provide strong support for community development approaches that construct shared understandings. The approach, which began with black and minority ethnic communities, has been used to tackle mental health inequalities within the wider population. It has led to a range of policy and practice initiatives in Scotland, in different areas of public policy, including the development of a mental health curriculum for schools; workplace campaigns and equality workshops; a national mental health arts and film festival; peer-educators for mental health in later life; and action research initiatives with asylum seekers and refugees. In addition, it has led to a greater interest in validating the use of narratives and community action research in government mental health policy. We would argue that while initiatives such as these should form only one aspect of an overall approach to addressing stigma, since structural discrimination must also be addressed, the principles of this approach can make a valuable contribution to developing approaches to addressing global mental health inequalities.

Acknowledgements
The authors would like to acknowledge the wide range of organisations and individuals who have contributed to the work of the Anti-Stigma Partnership, particularly Nuzhat Mirza.

12.2 Improving psychosocial care for cancer patients

Carrie Lethborg and Sonia Posenelli

Introduction

In an era of health care driven by fiscal policy, social work in the hospital setting is challenged to direct limited resources effectively towards areas of most need. This challenge is heightened by the profession's desire to provide services that are evidence based. In this chapter we discuss one example of how social work can offer leadership in cancer care by focusing on health inequalities as the motivation for service delivery planning.

Recent Australian evidence highlights deficiencies in the psychosocial care of cancer patients (Barton et al, 2003; Kefford et al, 2003; NBCC and NCCI, 2003). Lack of continuity of care and limited identification of psychosocial distress were specific concerns. While psychosocial care improves quality of life in the cancer population, it is suggested that 60% do not have access to such interventions (Fawzy et al, 1990). This gap is partly due to inadequate funding but also to inadequate methods of identifying high-risk patients. Consequently, much of the psychosocial support available to this group is crisis-oriented. Zabora et al suggest it occurs 'well after the initial crisis of diagnosis, usually when [patients] begin to manifest inappropriate behaviour that the staff find difficult to manage' (1990, p 195).

Social Work at St Vincent's Hospital (St V's) in Melbourne sought to translate evidence about best practice into the practice setting, in spite of the constraints of limited resources and organisational structures. The challenge was to influence policy from the clinical practice setting in order to improve patient care in ways that are sustainable, cost neutral and in keeping with social work values. Social work brings to the translation of practice guidelines a unique ability to consider micro- and macro-issues involving the client base as well as the wider organisational structure, community context and policy conditions.

This chapter illustrates how it is possible within existing resources to address the gap between evidence and practice in relation to the psychosocial needs of people diagnosed with cancer, by providing a minimum standard of psychosocial care.

Background

Cancer is one of the leading causes of death and an increasingly important factor in the burden of disease (WHO, 2008). The prevalence of psychosocial distress in the adult cancer population ranges from 15%–40% (Zabora et al, 2001). Those patients at increased risk one month after diagnosis can remain at increased risk of psychosocial morbidity one year later (Ganz et al, 1993). However, the literature reveals a poor correlation between health professionals and patients themselves in identifying levels of distress (Cull et al, 1995).

It is incumbent on social work to seek to improve the quality of cancer survivorship and end of life care by identifying and addressing social, psychological and environmental factors with a view to reducing inequalities in care. Services for this population need to be planned around patient needs, guarding against haphazard and fragmented service provision.

The Australian guidelines for the psychosocial care of adults with cancer (NBCC and NCCI, 2003) summarise best practice aims pertinent to cancer-based social work. These include the acknowledgement that optimal psychosocial care of a person with cancer begins from the time of initial diagnosis through treatment, recovery and survival, or through the move from curative to non-curative aims of treatment, initiation of palliative care, death and bereavement. Throughout this journey, the guidelines suggest that all patients should be able to identify a key health professional responsible for the continuity of their care. In order to ensure this, referral pathways for psychosocial staff should be established and known to the care team.

StV's is a large metropolitan hospital where the Oncology department sees 1,500 new patients a year, while the hospital overall treats over 3,000 cancer patients annually. Prior to our own policy changes, cancer social work services were largely oncology focused.

Identifying inequalities

It was clear that social work services to cancer patients were not equally available and did not provide adequate continuity of care. Historically we assigned social workers to specific treating units rather than disease streams. A patient with lung cancer might pass through three medical units, see three social workers and not be seen in Oncology, thus missing out on specific oncology-based psychosocial services. As well as failing to provide continuity of care, social work was not providing a comparable service to all patients with cancer. Of particular concern was the likelihood that we were not identifying all cancer patients experiencing or at risk of psychosocial distress. Policy and structural changes within social work were required.

We developed a service delivery model that reflected a basic standard of care. The model, which was influenced by the work of Fitch (2000) and Piggott et al (2004), was evidence based and addressed the differing levels of psychosocial needs of adult cancer patients (see Figure 12.2.1). Here all cancer patients are presented as requiring information, screening for distress, orientation to the health care setting and continuity of care (Level 1); many cancer patients also require referral to appropriate services and resources (Level 2); some require targeted psychosocial

Figure 12.2.1: Service delivery model

All cancer patients require information, screening for distress, orientation to the health care setting and continuity of care

Many will also require referral to appropriate services and resources

Some will also require targeted psychosocial interventions to assist in managing specific difficulties at specific points in their cancer experience

A few will also require targeted intensive or longer-term psychosocial interventions

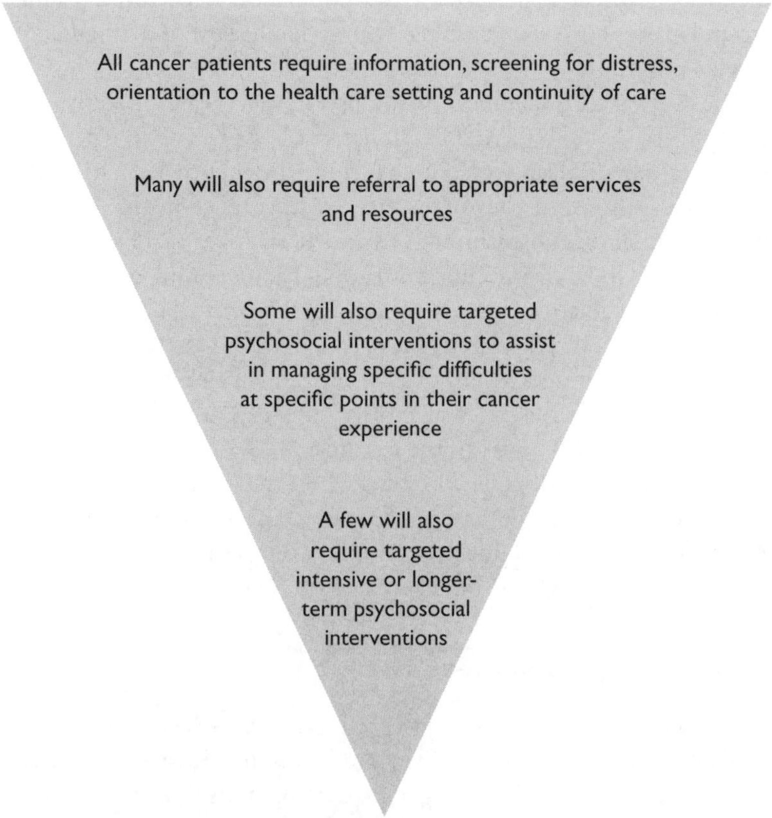

Source: Adapted from Fitch (2000) and Piggott et al (2004)

interventions to assist in managing specific difficulties at specific points in their cancer experience (Level 3); and a few require targeted intensive or longer-term psychosocial interventions (Level 4).

In order to achieve the first level of baseline care in this model, we restructured the method of social work allocation of patients and developed a standardised assessment protocol for all new patients with cancer.

The development of a Cancer Social Work Team (CSWT)

First, we assigned social workers to tumour streams rather than treatment units in order to ensure a continuous relationship with each patient throughout their journey. The model also aimed to provide earlier intervention and assistance in navigating the hospital system, regardless of the availability of streamed clinical care pathways. We trialled the new model for three months and then evaluated client satisfaction, impact on the multidisciplinary team and social work job satisfaction. Results showed little disruption to the team or negative impact on job satisfaction. The CSWT model increased continuity and ease of access to social work care for cancer patients. We also streamlined and enhanced communication on social work care plans and outcomes successfully. This ensured the maintenance of knowledge about patients and families through consistency of care provision.

The trial showed that continuity of care could be improved, while not disrupting the ongoing and pre-existing systems in place. It could be achieved with no new funding, only a reconfiguration of workloads. This model of social work service delivery has been adopted by St V's for most cancer patients, with some additional work required to develop systems of early referral and identification in some treating units.

The development of an Orientation and Distress Screening Model

Despite the assignment of social workers to tumour streams, we still lacked resources to provide full and ongoing assessments of each new patient (a common issue in cancer care worldwide). While psychosocial assessment of all patients with cancer by trained clinicians remains the gold standard, directing limited resources to those with most need was essential. The next step was to develop a strategy for systematic provision of minimum information and risk assessment of distress. The assessment of psychosocial needs by screening is considered widely in the cancer literature as a means to identify and target individuals and subgroups of patients with higher levels of need (Montgomery et al, 1999; Sanson-Fisher et al, 2000).

We developed the Orientation and Distress Screening (ODS) Model. The three components are systematic provision of information, screening of risk of distress using standardised measures and dissemination of information about psychosocial needs to members of the multidisciplinary team.

Information and orientation

In the diagnosis phase of cancer, information needs are cited as the most common unmet psychosocial need (Coreil and Ravish, 1999). Patients commonly request information about prognosis and treatment, and strategies to manage the impact of cancer on life, relationships and work (Mills and Sullivan, 1999; Harper Chelf et al, 2001). However, information needs are highly individualised and it is suggested that strategies be tailored to the person concerned (Mills and Sullivan, 1999). Based on this evidence, we developed a package of standardised information with individualised modules that could be added depending on patient need. Additionally, we developed an orientation package related to the hospital and the cancer experience, including information flow charts for procedures, information about parking and directions for services.

Psychosocial screening for distress and unmet needs

The use of screening to assess psychosocial needs has been considered widely in the literature as a means to identify and target individuals and subgroups of patients with higher levels of need (Montgomery et al, 1999; Sanson-Fisher et al, 2000). We considered distress in two broad ways. First we used the Australian *Clinical Practice Guidelines for the Psychosocial Care of Adults with Cancer* (NBCC and NCCI, 2003) for a summary of the characteristics of individuals, disease and treatment associated with an increased risk of such distress. These include demographic factors such as social isolation, younger age and economic adversity and diagnostic information such as poor prognosis and chronic pain. Using this list at various multidisciplinary meetings illustrated the complexity involved in identifying patients at risk, given the limited risk factor information available in the clinical setting. Processes were needed to flag pertinent information for clinicians. A variety of methods was used to achieve this such as the development of a data collection tool and the inclusion of a psychosocial section to St V's cancer database.

Second, we focused on psychosocial distress screening and identification, selecting a brief and validated distress measure so that we could consider a multi-focus response. The Distress Thermometer (Roth et al, 1998) includes a visual analogue scale for distress in cancer patients and incorporates a problem checklist, where patients can identify their specific areas of personal distress. Uniquely, we linked this problem checklist to our individualised information packages. For example, if a patient noted concerns about their children as a source of distress, a module of information was provided about 'Parenting when you have cancer' in addition to the standardised information about cancer.

We developed a 'psychosocial profile' of each patient, including a distress score, its meaning, problems identified and information provided, and disseminated this via email to key members of the multidisciplinary team, to increase team focus on psychosocial issues. The time required to access, screen, orientate, provide information then summarise and send it out to team members takes approximately 40 minutes per patient. The measures identified risk of distress on a par with larger studies undertaken worldwide (30% of newly diagnosed patients are found to be at risk of distress).

Drawing only small amounts of funding to trial each step of this process (for administration and evaluation), we extended social work services to all cancer patients in the hospital, provided the majority of these with continuity of care and implemented protocols to identify new patients at most risk of psychosocial distress.

Discussion

Space limitations have not allowed for an adequate description of each of the steps involved in the process. Rather we have discussed a social work response to unmet needs in light of evidence-based guidelines. Our experience illustrates the complexity involved in translating evidence into practice. Such translation requires a mindful meeting of organisational realities and gold standard aims. While busy clinicians aim to follow guidelines for best practice, the reality of implementing these can require substantial time and effort, collaboration and a realignment of organisational resources and processes. The entire process took four years of work but was achieved with minimal funding. Certainly, without specific funding to consider these translational issues, it is difficult to resource trials such as the ones reported. However, through innovative practices and a quality approach focusing on those with most need, it is possible to target limited resources for greatest effect. In this example a pre-emptive response to policy imperatives enabled social work to deliver results for patients with cancer, for the organisation and for the profession. Each initiative has been successful and interventions have been developed for under-served patient populations so as to reduce inequalities that impede the delivery of quality psychosocial care.

References

Barton, M., Frommer, M., Olver, I., Cox, C., Crowe, P., Wall, B., Jenkin, R. and Gabriel, G. (2003) *A Cancer Services Framework for Victoria and Future Directions for the Peter MacCallum Cancer Institute*, Sydney: Collaboration for Cancer Outcomes Research and Evaluation.

Busfield, J. (1996) *Men, Women and Madness: Understanding Gender and Mental Disorder*, Basingstoke: Macmillan.

Coreil, J. and Ravish, B. (1999) 'Man to man prostate cancer support groups', *Cancer Practice*, vol 7, no 3, pp 122–9.

Corrigan, P. and Penn, D. (1999) 'Lessons from social psychology on discrediting psychiatric stigma', *American Psychologist*, vol 54, no 9, pp 765–76.

Cull, A., Stewart, M. and Altman, D. (1995) 'Assessment of and intervention for psychosocial problems in routine oncology practice', *British Journal of Cancer*, vol 72, no 1, pp 229–35.

Double, D. (2002) 'The limits of psychiatry', *British Medical Journal*, vol 324, pp 900–4.

Faulkner, A. and Thomas, P. (2002) 'User-led research and evidence based medicine', *British Journal of Psychiatry*, vol 180, pp 1–3.

Fawcett, B. and Karban, K. (2005) *Contemporary Mental Health: Theory and Practice*, London: Routledge.

Fawzy, F., Cousins, N., Fawzy, N., Kemeny, M., Elashoff, R. and Morton, D. (1990) 'A structured psychiatric intervention for cancer patients, I. Changes over time in methods of coping and affective disturbance', *Archives of General Psychiatry*, vol 47, pp 720–5.

Fernando, S. (2002) *Cultural Diversity, Mental Health and Psychiatry: The Struggle Against Racism*, London: Routledge.

Fitch, M. (2000) 'Supportive care for cancer patients', *Hospital Quarterly*, Summer, pp 39–46.

Ganz, P., Hirji, K., Sim, M.-S., Coscarelli Schag, C., Fred, C. and Polinskiy, M. (1993) 'Predicting psychosocial risk in patients with breast cancer', *Medical Care*, vol 5, pp 419–31.

Gary, F. (2005) 'Stigma: Barrier to mental health care among ethnic minorities', *Issues in Mental Health Nursing*, vol 26, no 10, pp 979–99.

Gergen, K. (1994) *Realities and Relationships*, Cambridge: Harvard University Press.

Glasgow Anti-Stigma Partnership (2007) 'Mosaics of meaning: Exploring stigma and discrimination towards mental health problems with black and minority ethnic communities in Glasgow', www.healthscotland.com

Harper Chelf, J., Agre, P., Axelrod, A., Cheney, L., Cole, D., Conrad, K., Hooper, S., Liu, I., Mercurio, A., Stepan, K., Villejo, L. and Weaver, C. (2001) 'Cancer-related patient education: An overview of the last decade of evaluation and research', *Oncology Nursing Forum*, vol 28, no 7, pp 1139–47.

Kefford, R., Chesterman, C. and Boyages, J. (2003) 'Review of cancer services at St Vincent's Health Melbourne', unpublished.

Lee, S., Lee, M., Chiu, M. and Kleinman, A. (2005) 'Experience of social stigma by people with schizophrenia in Hong Kong', *British Journal of Psychiatry*, vol 186, pp 153–7.

Mills, M. and Sullivan, K. (1999) 'The importance of information giving for patients newly diagnosed with cancer: A review of the literature', *Journal of Clinical Nursing*, vol 8, no 6, pp 631–42.

Montgomery, C., Lyndon, A. and Lloyd, K. (1999) 'Psychological distress among cancer patients and informed consent', *Journal of Psychosomatic Research*, vol 46, no 3, pp 241–5.

National Resource Centre for Ethnic Minority Mental Health (2005) Equal Services – Report of Race Equality Assessment in Health Boards in Scotland, Edinburgh: NHS Health Scotland.

NBCC and NCCI (National Breast Cancer Centre and National Cancer Control Initiative) (2003) *Clinical Practice Guidelines for the Psychosocial Care of Adults with Cancer*, Camperdown, NSW: National Breast Cancer Centre.

NHS Greater Glasgow (2006) *Black and Minority Ethnic Health in Glasgow: A Comparative Report on the Health and Well-Being of African & Caribbean, Chinese, Indian and Pakistani People and the General Population*, http://library.nhsggc.org.uk/mediaAssets/library/nhsgg_report_bme_health_and_wellbeing_summary.pdf

Phillips, M., Pearson, V., Li, F., Xu, M. and Yang, L. (2002) 'Stigma and expressed emotion: A study of people with schizophrenia and their family members in China', *British Journal of Psychiatry*, vol 181, pp 488–93.

Piggot, C., Aranda, S. and Pollard, A. (2004) 'Developments in supportive care: Implications for nursing', *Cancer Forum*, vol 28, no 3, pp 120–3.

Pilgrim, D. (2005) *Key Concepts in Mental Health*, London: Sage.

Pilgrim, D. and Rogers, A. (1999) *A Sociology of Mental Health and Illness*, 2nd edn, Buckingham: Open University Press.

Roth, A., Kornblith, A., Batel-Copel, L., Peabody, E., Scher, H. and Holland, J. (1998) 'Rapid screening for psychological distress in men with prostate carcinoma: A pilot study', *Cancer*, vol 82, no 10, pp 1904–8.

Sanson-Fisher, R., Girgis, A., Boyes, A., Bonevski, B., Burton, L. and Cook, P. (2000) 'The unmet supportive care needs of patients with cancer', *Cancer*, vol 88, no 1, pp 226–37.

Scottish Executive (2001) *Census of Population for Scotland 2001*, Edinburgh: Scottish Executive.

Scottish Executive (2005) *Equal Minds: Addressing Mental Health Inequalities in Scotland*, Edinburgh: Scottish Executive.

Szasz, T. (1972) *The Myth of Mental Illness: Foundations of a Theory of Personal Conduct*, London: Paladin.

Tabassum, R., Macaskill, A. and Ahmad, I. (2000) 'Attitudes towards mental health in an urban Pakistani community in the United Kingdom', *International Journal of Social Psychiatry*, vol 46, no 3, pp 170–81.

Tilbury, F., Slee, R., Clark, S., O'Ferrall, I., Rapley, M. and Kokanovic, R. (2004) 'Listening to diverse voices: Understandings and experiences of and interventions for depression among East African migrants', www.mmha.org.au/mmha-products/synergy/2004_No2

Weiss, M., Jadhav, S., Raguram, R. and Littlewood, R. (2001) 'Psychiatric stigma across cultures: Local validation in Bangalore and London', *Anthropology and Medicine*, vol 8, no 1, pp 71–87.

Wenger, E. (1998) *Communities of Practice: Learning, Meaning and Identity*, New York: Cambridge University Press.

WHO (World Health Organization) (2002) *Nations for Mental Health*, www.who.int/mental_health/media/en/400.pdf

WHO (2008) *Fact Sheet No. 297: Cancer*, www.who.int/mediacentre/factsheets/fs297/en/index.html

Wilkinson, R. and Pickett, K. (2007) 'The problems of relative deprivation: Why some societies do better than others', *Social Science and Medicine*, vol 65, no 9, pp 1965–78.

Wynaden, D., Chapman, R., Orb, A., McGowan, S., Zeeman, Z. and Yeak, S. (2005) 'Factors that influence Asian communities' access to mental health care', *International Journal of Mental Health Nursing*, vol 14, no 2, pp 88–95.

Yeung, E. (2004) *Endurance: Improving Accessibility to Mental Health Services for Chinese People. Training Manual/Resources Pack*, 2nd edn, Liverpool: Merseyside Health Action Zone.

Zabora, J., Smith-Wilson, R., Fetting, J. and Enterline, J. (1990) 'An efficient method for psychosocial screening of cancer patients', *Psychosomatics*, vol 31, no 2, pp 192–6.

Zabora, J., Brintzenhofeszoc, K., Jacobsen, P., Curbow, B., Piantadosi, S., Hooker, C., Owens, A. and Derogatis, L. (2001) 'A new psychosocial screening instrument for use with cancer patients', *Psychosomatics*, vol 42, no 3, pp 241–6.

13

Developing the evidence base for practice and policy

Introduction

In this chapter, authors from Ireland, Australia and Hong Kong illustrate how social workers can use research not only to build evidence about health inequalities but as a form of intervention. A variety of models of research enable researchers to make links between policy makers and the experiences of people who are both excluded from direct access to policy-making processes and unequally treated in social and health care provision. A key consequence of employing a research-based approach is a shift in perception by social workers from the individual case to the population as the focus for analysis and intervention.

In Section 13.1, Quin and Clarke, lecturers in social work and nursing, describe a multidimensional national study of the experiences of families with children who have life-limiting conditions. Social workers participated in the study as respondents and by making it possible for the researchers to access families facing this situation. This revealed the need for social workers to effectively challenge the status quo in order to secure adequate services and equality of provision for families in different situations, including across a rural–urban divide. This research informed the national government strategy document, but changes in practice will be the real test of success.

Section 13.2 describes the research approach known as 'data-mining', in which existing documentary sources, such as social work records, are analysed to explore a key practice issue, in this case the engagement of hospital emergency department social workers in the human consequences of crimes of violence. While social workers are widely aware of their involvement with victims of crime such as domestic violence and child abuse, an initial trawl of records, backed by national evidence, found that the largest group presenting with injuries from assaults were young men, including men in prison. These men did not fit the profile of 'victims' and so remained hidden as a population requiring a strategic service response until revealed through research.

In Section 13.3, the case study again focuses on a minority ethnic population which is liable to be excluded from mainstream provision. The Pakistani population in Hong Kong is a small group which has been adversely affected by the reversion of the former British colony to Chinese control, because of their lack of social status and resources and enhanced language barriers. It is a minority with poor comparative health and reduced access to health care. This study, which focuses on women and children, provides clear evidence both about the consequences of barriers to good health and the mechanisms through which a mixed private–public health care market exacerbates inequalities.

13.1: From research to policy: advocacy for families caring for children with life-limiting conditions

Suzanne Quin and Jean Clarke

Introduction

'Social workers practice at the intersection of private troubles and public issues' (Miley and DuBois, 2007, p 31). In Abramovitz's (1998, p 512) view, the profession of social work has the potential both 'to meet individual needs and to engage in social change'. Miley and DuBois (2007, p 32) argue that 'when social workers only focus on "the clinical" without regard to ensuring a just or caring society, they abandon a core social work purpose'.

Whether or not this dual mandate is fulfilled in practice is raised by Haynes (1998, p 501) who expresses concern that social work may have 'lost sight of the public social services and the public arena as a legitimate place for social work intervention'. Taking it beyond the realm of individual professional practice, she contends that, as a profession, social work would be stronger 'if we truly believed that to do social work and to be a social worker requires commitment both to the goals of social justice as well as to the goal of healing individual pain' (p 509). Hence, advocacy at both a micro- and macro-level can be regarded as a core task of social work practice in health care (Badawi and Biamonti, 1990; Smale et al, 2000; Thompson, 2000). The purpose of advocacy as a process of empowerment is to ensure that the voices of those who are marginalised are heard and incorporated in the policy process.

Within health care, one group with wide-ranging and immediate needs are children with life-limiting conditions and their families (Spencer and Battye, 2001). Drawing on the findings of a national study of paediatric palliative care carried out by the authors, the focus in this chapter will be on the contribution of the social work respondents to the identification of the psychosocial needs of such children, the evaluation of the adequacy of current services taking account of possible socio–economic, diagnostic and geographical inequalities, and the social workers' views of the implications of any identified inadequacies for policy developments in this field in Ireland (Quin et al, 2005).

The study design

The study was carried out by a team whose professional background was in social work and in public health nursing. It involved a wide range of stakeholders, incorporating service users, service providers (in the public and voluntary sectors) and policy planners. It sought to ensure that the experiences of the families, and those of the service providers who had intimate knowledge of the issues based on contact with such families, were heard and responded to in the government strategy document which would direct the future planning of services to meet identified needs.

The definition 'life-limiting' used in the study incorporated four categories of conditions likely to result in death before adulthood (ACT/RCPCH, 2003). This broad-based definition succeeded in including children and their families whose needs would not always be taken into consideration in the identification of paediatric palliative care needs.

Both quantitative and qualitative methodologies were used to maximise service user and service provider participation. Over 1,200 questionnaires were sent to a range of statutory and voluntary service providers throughout the country. These were followed by individual interviews and focus groups with professional service providers, service users and policy planners. Seminars were then held in regional locations throughout the country to which all survey participants (including social workers) were invited. The purpose of the seminars was for respondents to hear the preliminary study findings and to contribute to policy recommendations arising from them.

Social work responses

The initial questionnaires for social workers were sent to the social work teams in the three major children's hospitals and every general hospital in the country with a paediatric unit (16 in total). Social workers also participated in the focus groups for professional service providers. Service participants were recruited via service providers (including social workers) in both community and institutional settings. Fourteen teams returned questionnaires indicating that they had provided services for children in at least one of the categories of children with life-limiting conditions. In most cases, they had actually provided services for a number of children and their families in more than one category within the given time period. Not surprisingly, psychosocial support, help with practical support needs (for example, equipment) and meeting the information needs of both child and family were the key services directly provided by the respondents. It was also evident that the social workers played an important role as referral agents to other hospital and community-based professionals and to national, regional and local support services. In relation to their referral role, all of the social work teams were very conversant with what was available locally, regionally and nationally.

The responses were remarkably consistent on what the social workers regarded as the strengths and weaknesses of current support provision. On the positive side, there was the significant role played by key statutory services and not-for-profit agencies (in particular those providing information and support for a particular condition or those meeting specific needs of dying children and their families, such as 24-hour specialist nursing). On the negative side was lack of specific supports for those with unusual/rare syndromes, geographical variation in the range and quantity of services and differences in provision for children with the same objective needs but having different diagnoses. The social workers' experiences were that children with cancer had more ready access to a better range of services than did other children with similar needs. Overall, the social workers considered home support services to be very inadequate to meet needs and not always provided in ways that were 'in the best interest of the child'. This was related in particular to the provision of respite care whereby the only relief for many families was temporary residential/institutional care, often in less than ideal conditions. In such circumstances, social workers found an unnecessarily large portion of their time was taken up with individual referral and advocacy in trying to access an essential service for a family.

Location of death is a specific issue for children with life-limiting conditions. While home is the preferred place of death (Goldman, 1998), the reality was that the majority of such children died away from home in acute hospital settings or in extended care with variation by diagnostic category (Department of Health and Children, 2005). The social workers cited lack of 24-hour community-based nursing and medical support, limited practical and financial resources and the overall lack of a specialist home-based multidisciplinary palliative care service for dying children throughout the country to explain the difference between preferred and actual place of death.

The social workers regarded the lack of service provision in general, the geographical and diagnostic category inequities and the lack of choice for families with children who were dying as all serving to add to the burden of care on families. In addition, increasing workloads and bureaucratisation of the social work role had, in their view, diminished the already inadequate level of social work services they could provide at all stages of their work with families, particularly at the post-bereavement phase. These limitations were a repeated theme of the focus groups with professional service providers. The continuous effort on behalf of families to access much-needed services by pleading 'special cases' with funding authorities and trying a variety of ways to 'get around the system' resulted in a sense of frustration and poor use of their time.

A related theme was the sense of helplessness that the front-line professionals such as social workers felt in 'bearing witness' to the struggles of families to cope in the context of inadequate and unevenly distributed service provision. Furthermore, there were situations where social workers were part of the decision-making process about the deployment of limited resources such as respite care. Such experiences were reported to result in a sense of powerlessness on the part of social workers to ease the circumstances of the family's burden of care.

Implications of the study findings

The study findings showed that the number of children dying from life-limiting conditions per year in Ireland is relatively small, which is in keeping with similar figures from other economically developed societies (Hynson and Sawyer, 2001). In less economically developed countries, death in childhood is all too common and service provision to meet the needs of so many dying children only rudimentary at best (WHO, 2005a). The death of a child is every parent's ultimate nightmare and has profound effects on the family both during the dying trajectory and post-bereavement (Goldman, 1998; Goodenough et al, 2004). Given the small numbers and the sense of tragedy surrounding the death of a child in Ireland, it could be expected that the range of services on offer to this group of children and their families would be extensive. However, the responses from the medical social workers, as experts in this field, indicate that this is not the case in reality.

The inadequacy of service provision for children with life-limiting conditions and their parents is not unique to Ireland (Stephenson, 2000). Spencer and Battye (2001) remarked that the area of home support was particularly limited and that access to key services such as social work varied considerably, both geographically and according to diagnostic category. The rural–urban divide is one aspect of inequality of provision that was highlighted in our study that holds true for service provision globally (WHO, 2005a). Socio-economic inequalities are also of major import in that families with better-off parents can augment inadequate state provision by accessing private support services in the context of the mixed economy of welfare. The trend towards the increasing private sector in health care internationally, will further exacerbate inequality of access to services between those who can afford to pay, either directly or through private insurance schemes, and those who must rely on the state sector only.

The importance of social workers having a holistic view of client need and not accepting the status quo was evident in our study. The challenge is to translate this value into the social policy arena. Smale et al (2000) argue that social workers may need to challenge those who have traditionally controlled resources, often managers within organisations, whose value systems may have a different basis from those of the worker or service users and carers. Badawi and Biamonti (1990, p 193) also highlight the importance of social workers not accepting 'wholesale the values of their workplace', values which can include an acceptance of scarce resources as a fact of life to be disputed on a case by case basis but not by challenging collectively.

Thompson (2000) argues that a core task of social work is to increase, where possible, the range of options available to their clients. Ensuring that the voice of service users is included in service planning is a core task of social work which can be neglected in the context of having to deal with the immediate needs of clients. This devalues the potential social work role as, 'the absence of social workers from social policy practice is damaging to the identity of the profession and to the clients whose interests they should represent and defend' (Figueira-McDonough, 1993, p 180). The International Federation of Social Workers and International Association of Schools of Social Work (IFSW/IASSW, 2004) code of ethics clearly identifies the dual mandate of social workers to operate at the level of both policy and practice.

The findings of our study show social workers' expertise, based on knowledge and practice, in relation to the practical and emotional support needs of dying children and their families. Yet this expertise is not always acknowledged (McGrath, 2001) and accessed for service planning. Pecukonis et al (2003, p 14) argue that social work's 'ethical principles of service, social justice, dignity and self-determination within the matrix of human relatedness are central to the health care debate'. The high response rate from the social work teams demonstrated willingness to engage in research and policy development in spite of the many conflicting demands on their time.

The study findings and the resultant policy recommendations, as agreed at the outset of the research tendering process, informed the subsequent strategy document which sets out a blueprint for the development of a national children's palliative care service, based on the core principles of inclusiveness, partnership, comprehensiveness and flexibility (Department of Health and Children, 2005). In this way, the social workers contributed to the development of policy as a first step to redressing the issues of scarcity and inequity in the distribution of resources for children with life-limiting conditions and their families. However, a policy document is only the beginning and the real challenge is to ensure that services are developed to match the aspirations. This is where the key challenge lies for social workers in the policy process – to keep engaged on an ongoing basis to ensure that service users' and carers' needs are met in practice as well as in theory.

13.2: Data-mining 'victim of crime' presentations in hospital emergency departments: a research tool with wider significance

Rosalie Pockett

Introduction

Social workers in hospital emergency departments play an important role in the provision of services to victims of crime – usually crimes of violence – and their referral to appropriate services in the community. While social workers provide services to individuals who are victims of crime, at the same time, they may also be involved with those who are 'affected' by crime. This may include not only individual victims but also offenders and communities (Moore, 2005).

Such is the complex nature of social work practice, that social workers providing services to victims of assault or other violent crime may, at the same time, be mindful of the 'bigger picture' of crime and violence as manifestations of broader social issues. Both may be consequences of social inequalities that perpetuate cycles of generational disadvantage. In a study of the distribution of disadvantage in Australia, the rates of criminal convictions and prison admissions supported the conclusion 'that the bulk of crimes are committed by people from low [sic] socio-economic background with limited formal education suggesting some form of association between disadvantage and crime' (Vinson, 2007, p 18).

The data-mining study outlined here, researching an area of everyday practice, demonstrates how practitioners can both contribute to the improvement of the health and well-being of the individual, and also to the social and public policy debates around broader issues that address inequalities.

Global trends

During the late 1980s and 1990s neoliberalism provided broad ideological challenges for contemporary social policy debates. Terms such as 'economic rationalism' (Australia), 'new managerialism' (UK) and 'neo-conservatism' (US) were expressions of neoliberalism that underpinned contemporary public policy (Ife, 1997).

Another trend during this period was the emergence of the victims' rights movement. From a human rights and social justice perspective, victims gained social and legal legitimacy, that is, victims of crime were defined, charters of victims' rights were developed and victim impact statements became part of criminal court proceedings (Strang, 2001, cited in Moore, 2005). Community-based victim support agencies and self-help groups for victims of crime also began to be established, for example the Homicide Victims Support Group (HVSG) in Australia, Support after Murder and Manslaughter – Merseyside (SAMM) in the UK and the National Organization for Victim Assistance (NOVA) in the US.

These global trends provided the context for this Australian study, which aimed to investigate the effectiveness of current services, from a managerialist perspective, and the responsiveness of health services, from a social justice perspective, to victims of crime.

Rationale and setting for the clinical data-mining project

The study was undertaken by a small group of social workers, led by the author, at a principal referral and university teaching hospital in Sydney. The social work department provided services to all areas of the hospital including two after-hours on-call services. The availability of social work services 24 hours a day was based on the principle that those requiring the social work service would have immediate access to it. A number of government initiatives had been put in place for victims of crime and social workers were curious to find out more about those patients who presented to the emergency department (ED) who fell into this category and whether they were referred to the social work service (NSW Health, 1995; 1997; NSW Government, 1996).

Project design

Clinical data-mining, or using available clinical information in practice-based research, was identified as a method that would lend itself to this type of review for a number of reasons. These included the availability of an existing information system, that is, the patients' medical records; the ability to divide the inquiry into manageable tasks; the ability of social work practitioners to participate in the study; and finally, and most importantly, the proven track record of this approach to support reflective practice (Epstein and Blumenfield, 2001). The approach can also provide results that challenge existing perceptions and help identify new areas of inquiry that can be pursued using other types of research methods. The medical audit design was compatible with the guidelines set down by the hospital's Human Research Ethics Committee that enabled the project to be undertaken with the objective of reviewing service delivery rather than as a research project investigating the experience of individual participants (Western Sydney Area Health Service, 2003).

Parameters for the project included all patients who had presented to the emergency department where completed coding of the medical record classified the presentation using an Assault Code (X85–Y09) from the International Classification of Diseases – Australian Modified Version (ICD-10 AM) (NCCH, 2002). The date range selected was for the 12-month period from 1 July 2001 to 30 June 2002 and sexual assault and child abuse cases were excluded. The four assault codes used are described in the following Table.

Table 13.2.1: Assault codes and descriptions

Assault code	Examples	Resulting Injuries
Bodily force (n 72)	Kicked and punched	Fractures, open wounds, loss of consciousness, facial, hand, eye, abdominal injuries
Blunt object (n 54)	Hammers, baseball bats, bar stools, bottles, iron bars, capsicum spray	As above
Sharp object (n 53)	Knives, scissors, glass, tools	Stab wounds to all parts of the body
Unspecified means (n 63)	Assault by others, self-harm	As above, head injuries

A total of 242 medical records meeting the inclusion criteria were returned and a random sample from each group was selected for review. An audit tool was developed for data extraction from the medical records with a number of specific but de-identified categories of information. These included: an allocated file number (linked to a master list of medical record numbers kept by the researcher); age; presenting medical problem; ICD-10 AM Principal Diagnosis; and the Assault Code. A number of other categories described the presentation, the pathways of treatment and the involvement of a social worker.

Results

Of the 90 files reviewed, the majority of presentations were young males aged between 20 and 30 years old. The numbers of presentations for each of the four Assault Codes was fairly evenly spread.

Figure 13.2.1: Assault presentations by age and gender

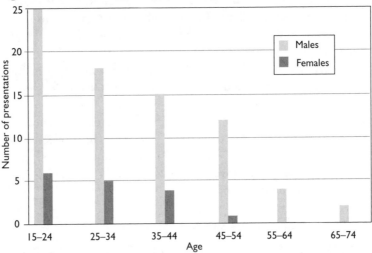

These results are consistent with trends reported by the Australian Bureau of Statistics (2003; 2006) and the NSW Bureau of Crime Statistics and Research (2004), where males are more likely to be victims of personal crime than females, with younger males having the highest rates reported. A further review of the files indicated that young males presenting to the ED included assault presentations from the prison population treated in the emergency department. The results prompted a further review of the records to try and explain the low referral rates of all presentations to social workers and the unexpected finding of presentations of young males that were a result of assaults in prison. The expected and unexpected outcomes of the study are presented in Table 13.2.2.

Limitations of the study

The study aimed to review the medical records of patients presenting at the emergency department with a classification of injury as 'assault'. Although victims of crime policies and procedures had been developed for implementation there was no separate code for victims of crime in any patient classification system. When assault victims are brought to a hospital it is often unclear whether they are victims or perpetrators in

Table 13.2.2: Study outcomes

Expected outcome: service delivery information	Unexpected outcome: local variants
■ Presentation of these four categories of assault victims are most likely after hours	■ The hospital was a nominated treatment centre for prisons in the local area
■ Social workers were more likely to be called 'in hours' than 'after hours' for this type of presentation	■ Social workers would not be called to assault victim presentations from prison
■ Social workers were more likely to receive referrals for assault victims if they were admitted	■ In the same 12-month period, social workers registered an equivalent number of total cases with domestic violence as an identified problem using a profession specific database. These cases were more likely to be women
■ The majority of cases were treated in ED and discharged within 24 hours, usually from ED	

the incident and anecdotal evidence would suggest that staff are unclear about whether it is their role to undertake this level of investigation.

The use of existing databases, in this case, medical records, presents a number of challenges (Epstein, 2001, p 19). In this study, familiarity with hospital language was helpful as documentation can reflect the jargon of various systems, for example the triage notes may state, 'Patient brought to ED following an "alleged assault"'. This is the language of the police (who may have accompanied the person to the emergency department). The paucity of information is also a problem. For example another entry read: '22 y o female BIBA [brought in by ambulance] – presenting medical problem – assault by unknown man with hammer'. The ICD-10 AM Principal Diagnosis of 'open wound to scalp' and the treatment summary, 'treated and discharged from Emergency Department. LoS [Length of Stay] 1 day', provide little further information. Thus databases such as medical records are often unfinished stories about patients' circumstances. The binary situation that has been created by the construction of the term 'victim of crime' places others who may have been involved in an oppositional position. This was demonstrated in medical records where it was noted that the patient had 'absconded' from the emergency department before further medical treatment or the social worker could be called. Some patients presenting with assault injuries did not wish to be identified as victims of crime particularly if they were involved in an illegal activity when the assault occurred.

This small study highlighted the differences that exist between statistical collections, the differences in definitions and classifications and the difficulties that this creates in 'whole of government approaches' when an evaluation of effectiveness is required. Victims of crime statistics tend to be composites of data collections across a number of government departments. The limitations of the information systems in this area are another iteration of systemic failures that hide or obfuscate inequalities that better data management would illustrate.

Study outcomes, practice implications and health inequalities

The expected outcome of the exercise was to gain information about how services were being delivered and identify ways in which they might be improved. As a result of the study a number of new initiatives were put in place such as providing training for emergency department staff and developing information packages that are easily accessible to patients who may be victims of crime but who are not referred to social workers.

The unexpected outcome involved the identification of local variants that had a significant impact on the implementation of policy, and which represented broader health inequalities. The study investigated 'victims of crime' where victims have been constructed in a way that places them in a binary position to the person who has assaulted them. The incidence of violence among young males in the prison population does not have such a dominant construction of the relationship. Had the study investigated patients whose ED attendance resulted from violence then different data may have emerged. The results of the study lead on to other questions about the levels of violence in the young male population generally, and more specifically in young males in lower socio-economic groups who are more likely to be imprisoned (Connell, 1987; 2000; 2005; Hanlon, 2008). Those male patients with assault injuries which did not occur in prison were most likely to have sustained the injuries as a result of assaults in public places such as hotels, restaurants and in the street. In two instances the males were described as 'homeless' and several other triage reports mentioned alcohol and/or substance abuse. The study results raise questions about the access to, and engagement with, social work services by this group of patients.

The significance of the study can be identified in three areas. First, it represents a small, local study undertaken by health practitioners to inform their practice using a methodology that is 'practitioner friendly' and which can lead on to more rigorous research inquiry. It reflects the importance of a social epidemiological perspective which moves from individual cases to populations as a focus of practice.

Second, it demonstrates the imperative of understanding policy implementation tensions in service delivery systems, that is, there must be an ability to critically analyse the dominant discourses around how service recipients and 'problems' are identified and constructed. The ability to critique the implementation process in terms of policy successes and failures as features of the differences between contextual, theoretical and ideological perspectives is vitally important for professional practice.

Third, the study illustrates the importance of case finding and assessment by skilled practitioners. The findings suggest that the group most affected by crime were not identified as victims of crime within the health system. Initiatives targeting victims of crime and violence have been located within a contemporary discourse of human rights and a neoliberal policy context that has influenced policy implementation. Contemporary responses have been based on the notion of empowerment over oppression and regaining control of the personal within the political/public discourse (Thompson, 2001). However these responses have still been located within the dominant construction of who is a victim of crime.

Effective professional practice must include critical evaluation of the knowledge claims, context and construction of prevailing social policies to facilitate the recognition and naming of inequalities that may otherwise be silent as a result of competing discourses. The ability to practise within multiple and ambiguous contexts and meanings, using critical reflection and reflexivity, enables social workers to appropriately identify the needs of clients, and the wider context by which they are defined. The prevailing tensions between these approaches challenge professionals to ensure that health inequalities are recognised and acted on.

Acknowledgements
The author would like to acknowledge the assistance of Sarah Smith, Jo Harvey and the Social Work Department, Westmead Hospital, Sydney, in the completion of this project.

13.3: Promoting health equality through evidence-based study: health care access for Pakistani women and their children in Hong Kong

Amy Po Ying Ho

Introduction and background

Since the 19th century, social workers, together with other health care professionals, have played an important role in disease prevention, health care and the promotion of health equality through case management, psychosocial services and advocacy for vulnerable groups in the community (Siefert, 1983; Bracht, 1987; Dhooper, 1997; McLeod and Bywaters, 2000). Ill-health that is a consequence of inequality is a concern for social workers because of its socially constructed nature and its tremendous impact on people's welfare (McLeod and Bywaters, 2000). A disproportionate burden of ill-health is borne by those disadvantaged due to gender, ethnicity, education, income or geographical location (US Department of Health and Human Services, 1991; Shi and Stevens, 2005).

In the 1800s, small groups from India, Pakistan and later Nepal came to Hong Kong (HK) to work as civil servants in the colonial British administration. They subsequently settled and established the roots of the South Asian communities in Hong Kong today (HK Poverty Web, 2004). According to the HK Population Census of 2006, minority ethnic groups, including Filipinos, Indonesians, Indians and Pakistanis from south-east Asia, account for approximately 5% of the total population. The Pakistani community is the fourth largest of these groups. In 2006, there were approximately 11,100 Pakistanis in Hong Kong.

In the predominantly Chinese society of Hong Kong, the health care concerns of racial minorities have gained little public attention. Ku et al (2003) report that 29% of Pakistanis regard lack of medical care as the most serious problem they face in Hong Kong. A government study found that Pakistanis had a higher prevalence of chronic illnesses and were more likely to be obese than the rest of the Hong Kong population. It also concluded that the hygiene practices of Pakistanis were inadequate and that Pakistani women were more physically inactive than women of other ethnicities (Department of Health, 2006). Many Pakistanis in Hong Kong are also financially disadvantaged: they have difficulty finding jobs due to prejudice and discrimination (Ku et al, 2003; 2006). These findings suggest that Pakistanis find it difficult to lead a healthy life in Hong Kong.

Pakistani women are doubly disadvantaged – by race and gender. In a study of women belonging to ethnic minorities conducted by the South Asian Support Alliance (2007), one half of the respondents stated that difficulties in communicating with health care professionals had significantly hindered their access to services. A study conducted by the Department of Health (2006) reported that Pakistani women found it extremely uncomfortable, if not entirely unacceptable, to be touched by male doctors during medical consultations.

Objectives and methodology

This chapter is based on a study, undertaken jointly by the Hong Kong Polytechnic University and the Hong Kong S.K.H. Lady MacLehose Centre in 2006. The study examined health care access for Pakistani women and their children in Hong Kong. The specific objectives of the study were to identify the respondents' health care needs, to examine their use of health care services, to explore the factors affecting health care access and to evaluate the role played by non-governmental organisations (NGOs) in facilitating health care access.

The study used both quantitative and qualitative methods. Focus group interviews were conducted, followed by structured interviews and five in-depth interviews. Two focus groups, attended by 19 Pakistani women, were conducted in English with Urdu translation provided by Pakistani social workers. During the focus group interviews, the researchers encouraged the women to discuss their experiences in seeking medical advice and their health care needs.

On the basis of the findings from the focus group interviews, a structured questionnaire was developed with 28 core and 13 demographic questions. The core questions were categorised under four headings: health status, health care services utilisation, determinants of health care access and the role of NGOs in health care access. Representing approximately one per cent of the total Pakistani population in Hong Kong, 109 Pakistani women took part in the study. They were recruited through targeted and snowball sampling: the selection criteria specified Pakistani women aged 18 to 59, who were residents of the Kwai Tsing district of Hong Kong and had children under age 12. The respondents were interviewed at home by Pakistani social workers. To develop a comprehensive picture of health care access, in-depth interviews were also conducted (Yin, 2002). Five Pakistani women were interviewed with the assistance of a translator fluent in Urdu. The questions focused on their experiences when using health care services and the difficulties they encountered.

This study was limited by its small sample size and the absence of a comparison group. It focused on health care access for Pakistani women, and therefore our results cannot be generalised to include Pakistani men and other minority ethnic groups in Hong Kong.

Key findings and discussion

The socio-economic background of the Pakistani women in this study resembles that of participants in other local studies of Pakistani women in Hong Kong. The majority (61%) were full-time housewives between 24 and 35. Most were born in Pakistan, and over half (53%) had not completed secondary school. Over half had lived in Hong Kong for more than 10 years. Only 25% could speak English, and just 9% were Cantonese speakers. Approximately 21% received government subsidies, and in the case of almost all the women (94%), their family income was lower than the median family income in Hong Kong.

The questionnaires revealed that, regardless of the severity of illness, Pakistani women in this study mainly rely on Hong Kong's public health services. Almost half of them (41%) used health services on a regular basis: 43% found these services 'quite difficult' to use, and only 29% found their use 'quite easy'. Due to limited family income, over 90% of the Pakistani women reported the accident and emergency department (A&E) of public hospitals as the most frequently visited health care settings since they are open all hours, and patients enjoy a full-range of services at very affordable prices. Only about 17% visited doctors in private practice (see Table 13.3.1).

When asked to identify barriers to public health services, more than 72.4% stated that 'long queuing hours' were the primary problem, followed by 'language problems' (41.4%) and 'low income' (22.4%) (see Table 13.3.2). Among those who found private health services difficult to access, 86.1% claimed that 'low income' was the main barrier, followed by 'language problems' (47.2%). One of the clear indications of these findings is that the translation services in the Hong Kong health care system are inadequate. Findings from the focus groups and the in-depth interviews showed that since interpretation services are not

Table 13.3.1: Health care settings and providers: frequency of use

	Frequency *	Per cent of responses (n =186)	Per cent of cases (n = 109)
A&E in public hospitals	101	54.3	92.7
Private doctors	33	17.7	30.3
Private hospitals	30	16.1	27.5
Government clinics	15	8.1	13.8
Traditional healers	6	3.2	5.5
Pharmacists	1	0.5	0.9
Total	186	100.0	

* Respondents were able to choose more than one answer

Table 13.3.2: Difficulties in accessing public health services

	Frequency*	Per cent of responses (n = 89)	Per cent of cases (n = 57)
Long queuing hours	42	47.2	72.4
Language problems	24	27.0	41.4
Low income	13	14.6	22.4
Lack of escort services	4	4.5	6.9
Transportation problems	3	3.4	5.2
Lack of access to female doctor	2	2.2	3.4
Lack of health insurance	1	1.1	1.7
Total	89	100.0	

* Respondents were able to choose more than one answer

available, some Pakistani women are compelled to pay for translators, who are not medically trained.

Given the government's limited budget for health care, long waiting times for medical consultations are a problem faced by most citizens in Hong Kong (Leung and Bacon-Shone, 2006). For Pakistani women, however, access to alternative private health services is further limited by financial difficulties, since Pakistanis are four times more likely to be welfare recipients than local Chinese. Moreover, both patients and doctors often face difficulties in communication due to language barriers, which affect the quality of health care. The cost of hiring a lay interpreter creates another financial hardship for low-income Pakistani women. In Hong Kong, it is not illegal for hospitals to provide diagnoses and explanations in Chinese only. This inequitable legislation further entrenches the language barrier that racial minorities face.

Our findings also show that most Pakistanis (85%) receive health-related information from the mass media, while 57% receive such information from family and friends. Very few actually search the Internet (8%) or consult a health professional (6%). Information obtained from friends and family is often misleading. Television and radio programmes in Urdu or Pakistani could be used to convey accurate health care information to Pakistani households.

We found that a vast majority of the respondents (93.6%) would prefer a female doctor for physical check-ups, and some would further specify a Pakistani or Indian female doctor. Our focus group participants were almost unanimous in stating that they were unwilling to expose their bodies or to be touched by male doctors. Some even cancelled medical appointments when no female doctor was available.

Some participants also claimed that racial discrimination, either overt or subtle, is a major barrier to access to equitable medical treatment. This finding points to a lack of cultural sensitivity in the current health care system in Hong Kong. No special training in cultural attitudes is provided for health care professionals in public hospitals.

Many Pakistani families require help from social welfare agencies to access health services. Since there is no government aid, a small number of these agencies bridge the service gaps by providing basic physical check-ups, health screening, dental services and health education. With the help of Pakistani staff and volunteers, they also provide limited escort and translation services for Pakistanis who have medical appointments in public hospitals.

Implications of the study for social work practice

The promotion of health and well-being among Pakistani women and children must address the following obstacles to their health: poor living conditions, language barriers, cultural beliefs and lack of health information. Given the unique cultural traditions of Pakistani families, the strategies suggested by the Ottawa Charter (WHO, 1986), which include initiatives to develop personal skills through education and strengthen community organisations, would contribute to health promotion. It is necessary to develop unprejudiced attitudes towards health care, and an awareness of the social and economic factors that contribute to the poor health status of racial minorities (WHO, 2001). Hence, anti-discriminatory health-promotion strategies should be developed within the wider context of equal opportunities (Shi and Stevens, 2005).

Pakistani families in Hong Kong settle in certain districts and maintain close personal networks. A community-based empowerment approach to health promotion would be well-adapted to their situation. Social welfare agencies have strong local networks and geographically-based service delivery systems, which can promptly identify the health care needs of Pakistani women and their children, and encourage their active participation in maintaining their health. This bottom-up approach enables local Pakistani communities to identify their own health care needs, set priorities and participate in individual and community activities to achieve better health. This approach also reflects the aim of the Bangkok Charter (WHO, 2005b): to achieve sustainable health through capacity building among social welfare agencies, patients and their communities.

Health promotion also requires continuous access to health information. The aim of health education is to assist individuals, families and communities to make informed decisions on matters that affect the achievement and maintenance of health. This sometimes entails modifying their beliefs, attitudes and behaviours. Many major illnesses among ethnic minorities are preventable through education, preferably in native languages. The removal of language barriers is a prerequisite to improved health care access for racial minorities in Hong Kong.

The situation of Pakistani women in Hong Kong supports the view that vulnerability in health is very closely related to a host of social determinants, including socio-economic status, ethnicity, education, and social networks and interactions (Institute of Medicine, 2001). Over the past few years, social work educators and NGOs in Hong Kong have sought social equality for Pakistani families through policy advocacy using evidence-based studies (Ku et al, 2003; South Asian Support Alliance, 2007). The collaboration of local Pakistani communities, non-governmental organisations and social work educators towards this goal deserves to receive the encouragement it needs to succeed.

Acknowledgement

I would like to express my gratitude to the Hong Kong S.K.H. Lady MacLehose Centre and all the Pakistani women who participated in this study. This research could not have been undertaken without their participation.

References

Abramovitz, M. (1998) 'Social work and social reform: An arena of struggle', *Social Work*, vol 43, no 6, pp 512–26.

ACT/RCPCH (Association for Children with Life-Threatening or Terminal Conditions and their Families/Royal College of Paediatrics and Child Health) (2003) *A Guide to the Development of Children's Palliative Care Services*, 2nd edn, Bristol: Orchard Press.

Australian Bureau of Statistics (2003) *Recorded Crime, Australia 2002 (4510.0)*, Canberra: Australian Government Publishing Service.

Australian Bureau of Statistics (2006) *Crime and Safety, Australia, April 2005 (4509.0)*, Canberra: Australian Government Publishing Service.

Badawi, M. and Biamonti, M. (1990) *Social Work Practice in Health Care*, New York: Woodhead-Faulkner.

Bracht, N. (1987) 'Preventive health care and wellness', in A. Minahan (ed) *Encyclopedia of Social Work,* 18th edn, Silver Spring, MD: National Association of Social Workers, pp 315–20.

Connell, R.W. (1987) *Gender and Power: Society, the Person and Sexual Politics*, Sydney: Allen and Unwin.

Connell, R.W. (2000) *The Men and the Boys*, St Leonards: Allen and Unwin.

Connell, R.W. (2005) *Masculinities*, 2nd edn, Berkeley: University of California Press.

Department of Health (2006) *Community Development Project for Ethnic Minority Groups*, Hong Kong: HKSAR Government.

Department of Health and Children (2005) *A Palliative Care Needs Assessment for Children*, Dublin: Stationery Office.

Dhooper, S.S. (1997) *Social Work in Health Care in the 21st Century*, California: Sage.

Epstein, I. (2001) 'Using available clinical information in practice-based research: Mining for silver while dreaming of gold', in I. Epstein and S. Blumenfield (eds) *Clinical Data-Mining in Practice-Based Research: Social Work in Hospital Settings*, New York: Haworth Press, pp 15–32.

Epstein, I. and Blumenfield, S. (2001) *Clinical Data-Mining in Practice-Based Research: Social Work in Hospital Settings*, New York: Haworth Press.

Figueira-McDonough, J. (1993) 'Policy practice: The neglected side of social work intervention', *Social Work*, vol 38, no 2, pp 179–88.

Goldman, A. (1998) 'ABC of palliative care: Special problems of children', *British Medical Journal*, vol 316, pp 49–52.

Goodenough, B., Drew, D., Higgins, S. and Trethewie, S. (2004) 'Bereavement outcomes for parents who lose a child to cancer: Are place of death and sex of parent associated with differences in psychological functioning?', *Psycho-Oncology*, vol 13, pp 779–91.

Hanlon, M. (2008) 'Men and violence', in B. Fawcett and F. Waugh (eds) *Addressing Violence, Abuse and Oppression: Debates and Challenges*, London: Routledge, pp 17–24.

Haynes, K.S. (1998) 'The one hundred-year debate: Social reform versus individual treatment', *Social Work*, vol 43, no 6, pp 501–9.

HK Poverty Web (2004) 'Ethnic minority and social exclusion', hkpoverty.oxfam.org.hk/issue3/index_e_eng.htm

Hynson, J.L. and Sawyer, S.M. (2001) 'Paediatric palliative care: Communicating with the patient and family', *Acta Oncologica*, vol 39, no 8, pp 905–10.

Ife, J. (1997) *Rethinking Social Work: Towards Critical Practice*, South Melbourne: Longman Cheshire.

IFSW (International Federation of Social Workers)/IASSW (International Association of Schools of Social Work) (2004) *Ethics in Social Work, Statement of Principles*, Berne, Switzerland, www.ifsw.org/en/p38000324.html

Institute of Medicine (2001) *Health and Behavior: The Interplay of Biological, Behavioral, and Social Influences*, Washington: National Academy Press.

Ku, H.B., Chan, K.W., Chan, W.L. and Lee, W.Y. (2003) *A Research Report on the Life Experience of Pakistani in Hong Kong. Research Report Series No. 7*, Hong Kong: the Hong Kong Polytechnic University and S.K.H. Lady MacLehose Centre.

Ku, H.B., Chan, K.W. and Sandhu, K.K. (2006) *A Research Report on the Employment of South Asian Ethnic Minority Groups in Hong Kong. Research Report Series No. 12*, Hong Kong: the Hong Kong Polytechnic University.

Leung, G.M. and Bacon-Shone, J. (eds) (2006) *Hong Kong's Health System – Reflections, Perspectives and Visions*, Hong Kong: The Hong Kong University Press.

McGrath, P. (2001) 'Identifying support issues of parents of children with leukaemia', *Cancer Practice*, vol 9, no 4, pp 198–205.

McLeod, E. and Bywaters, P. (2000) *Social Work, Health and Equality*, London and New York: Routledge.

Miley, K. and DuBois, B. (2007) 'Ethical preferences for the clinical practice of empowerment social work', *Social Work in Health Care*, vol 44, nos 1–2, pp 29–44.

Moore, E. (2005) 'Criminal justice – Extending the social work focus', in M. Alston and J. McKinnon (eds) *Social Work Fields of Practice*, South Melbourne: Oxford University Press, pp 207–21.

NCCH (National Centre for Classification in Health) (2002) *International Classification of Diseases – Version 10 – AM*, Canberra: AGPS.

NSW Bureau Crime Statistics and Research (2004) *Rates of Personal Crime Victimisation by Age and Gender*, Sydney: NSW Bureau Crime Statistics and Research.

NSW Government (1996) *Victims Rights Act 1996*, Sydney: NSW Government Publisher.

NSW Health (1995) *Victims of Crime Policy*, Sydney: NSW Department of Health.

NSW Health (1997) *Victims Rights Act and Charter of Victims Rights*, Sydney: NSW Department of Health, NSW Health Circular 97/114.

Pecukonis, E.V., Cornelius, L. and Parrish, M. (2003) 'The future of health social work', *Social Work in Health Care*, vol 37, no 3, pp 1–15.

Quin, S., Clarke, J. and Murphy-Lawless, J. (2005) *Report on a Research Study of the Palliative Care Needs of Children in Ireland*, Dublin: Department of Health and Children and the Irish Hospice Foundation.

Shi, L. and Stevens, G.D. (2005) *Vulnerable Populations in the United States*, San Francisco: Jossey-Bass.

Siefert, K. (1983) 'An exemplar of primary prevention in social work: The Sheppard-Towner Act of 1921', *Social Work in Health Care*, vol 9, no 1, pp 87–103.

Smale, G., Tuson, G. and Statham, D. (2000) *Social Work and Social Problems: Working Towards Social Inclusion and Social Change*, New York: Palgrave.

South Asian Support Alliance (2007) *A Research Report on the Social Situations of Ethnic Minority Women in Hong Kong*, Hong Kong: the Hong Kong Polytechnic University and Hong Kong Christian Service Project.

Spencer, L. and Battye, L. (2001) 'Palliative care in the community for children with cancer in South East England', *European Journal of Oncology Nursing*, vol 5, no 3, pp 190–7.

Stephenson, J. (2000) 'Palliative and hospice care needed for children with life-threatening conditions', *Journal of American Medical Association*, vol 284, no 19, pp 2437–8.

Thompson, N. (2000) *Understanding Social Work – Preparing for Practice*, London: MacMillan.

Thompson, N. (2001) *Anti-Discriminatory Practice*, Basingstoke: Palgrave Macmillan.

US Department of Health and Human Services (1991) *Healthy People 2000: National Health Promotion and Disease Prevention Objectives*, Washington DC: US Government Printing Office.

Vinson, T. (2007) *Dropping Off the Edge: The Distribution of Disadvantage in Australia*, Canberra and Melbourne: Jesuit Social Services and Catholic Social Services Australia.

Western Sydney Area Health Service (2003) *Human Research Ethics Committee: Guidelines for Completion of Applications: Quality Assurance / Audit Study Checklist*, Westmead: WSAHS.

WHO (World Health Organization) (1986) *The Ottawa Charter for Health Promotion*, Geneva: WHO.

WHO (2001) 'WHO's contribution to the world conference against racism, racial discrimination, xenophobia and related intolerance: health and freedom from discrimination', www.who.int/hhr/ activities/q_and_a/en/Health_and_Freedom_from_Discrimination_ English_699KB.pdf

WHO (2005a) *The World Health Report 2005 – Make Every Child and Mother Count*, Geneva: World Health Organization.

WHO (2005b) *The Bangkok Charter for Health Promotion in a Globalized World*, Geneva: WHO.

Yin, R.K. (2002) *Case Study Research. Design and Methods. Applied Social Research Method Series Volume 5*, California: Sage Publications.

14

Social work education for
awareness and practice

Introduction

This chapter demonstrates the need for social workers to gain understanding of the social character of health in all its dimensions – physical, mental, emotional and social. It illustrates why social workers must understand social work in its historical and political context. And it shows how educators of student social workers must prepare graduates to work with the pressing health inequalities and priorities of the day.

One of these priorities is HIV/AIDS, identified in Section 14.1 as an epidemic in India, where effective prevention and management of a 'looming catastrophe' is threatened by ignorance, stigma and the difficulty of reaching people with information. The argument that social work can provide educational leadership by marrying strong vision with community and professional education which exploits new communication technologies, is forcefully put and backed up with evidence.

A no less significant priority is to prepare students to work with communities that carry unequal burdens of illness and suffering, made more complex when social work carries a legacy of being implicated in creating and sustaining this burden. Section 14.2 is an account of the early stages of a research project in Australian social work education, aimed at exploring social work practices with indigenous communities and, in turn, changing social work education. Achieving partnership between indigenous and non-indigenous collaborators is an essential step towards preparing social work students more effectively to tackle the gross health inequalities which exist.

At the University of Pretoria, South Africa, the priorities of the health social work curriculum match those officially identified for attention in national health care policy. These include people with HIV/AIDS, women, children, and old and disabled people. Section 14.3 describes the political and social context of health and health services – the health consequences of poverty and violence, the paucity of services and the overwhelming workloads carried by professionals – which frames the curriculum design process. It is argued that the extensive knowledge, diverse skills and fortitude that graduates require to practise in situations of profound social and health inequalities, demand specialist qualifications.

14.1: HIV/AIDS education and awareness campaign: reaching the unreached through distance learning

Gracious Thomas

Introduction

When HIV was first detected in India in 1986, there were only 10 cases in the country (Veeraraghavan and Singh, 1999). Recent conventions, estimates by UNAIDS and the epidemiological data released by the National AIDS Control Organisation (NACO), India's official Government agency on HIV/AIDS, indicate that during the past two decades, this epidemic has spread with unprecedented rapidity and has infected hundreds of thousands (NACO, 2007). The country now has over 2.5 million people living with HIV. The tragedy of HIV/AIDS in the worst-affected countries of sub-Saharan Africa is likely to repeat itself in India during the early part of the new millennium unless appropriate measures are taken in time to counter it. While offering curative care to those infected seems to be a distant reality in the absence of a vaccine for prevention and affordable drugs for treatment, evolving culturally relevant, academically sound and socially acceptable programmes and strategies for the prevention and control of the unabated spread of this pandemic is desirable and possible (Thomas, 2006). For this to materialise, immediate and effective responses from professional social work educators and practitioners are required. It is in this context that the initiatives of the Faculty of Social Work at Indira Gandhi National Open University (IGNOU), in launching a massive awareness campaign and formal programmes of study on HIV/AIDS through distance learning, assume importance.

Extent and nature of HIV/AIDS in India

The potentially vulnerable populations, to be targeted for any effective HIV/AIDS intervention programme involving social workers in India, include the millions of migratory labourers and their wives, truck drivers and their wives, street children and youth, sex workers, professional blood donors and people injecting drugs (CBCI Commission for Health Care, 2005), eunuchs, sperm donors, health care professionals and patients with thalassaemia and haemophilia. Hundreds of thousands of prisoners and institutionalised persons including orphans, beggars and those who are differently-abled swell the numbers who are vulnerable to infection. Given this complexity, it is an extremely difficult task for social workers to make effective interventions in a country where social work is yet to be recognised as a profession by the national government. However, social work practitioners and educators are providing much-needed services. These range from counselling services, awareness programmes, education on HIV/AIDS and related topics, training of trainers, research, advocacy, extension services and policy formulation on HIV/AIDS.

In India, the HIV/AIDS epidemic is now two decades old. During this period it has emerged as one of the most serious public health problems in the country. The initial cases of HIV/AIDS were reported among commercial sex workers in Mumbai and Chennai and among injecting drug users in the north-eastern states of Manipur and Nagaland. Even though the officially reported cases of HIV infections and full-blown AIDS cases are between 2.5 to 3 million only, it is assumed that 'there is a wide gap between the reported and estimated figures because of the absence of accurate epidemiological data from across the country' (NACO, 1999, p 1). The overall prevalence in the country is still, however, very low, a rate much lower than many other countries in the Asia Pacific region.

The national sentinel surveillance data, released by NACO annually, confirms that HIV infection is prevalent in all parts of the country. In recent years, it has spread from urban to rural and from individuals practising high-risk behaviours to the general population.

The NACO (2007) report indicates that 85.35% of the infection occurs sexually, through both heterosexual and homosexual routes; 3.80% pre-natally from mother to child; 2.05% through blood and blood products; 2.34% through injecting drug users; and 6.46% through unspecified routes. Almost 90% of the reported cases are occurring in the sexually active and economically productive age groups of 15 to 49. The attributable factors for such rapid spread of the epidemic across the country include labour migration (both within the country and abroad), mobility in search of employment from economically underdeveloped to more advanced regions, low literacy levels leading to low awareness among potentially high-risk groups, gender disparity, sexually transmitted infections and reproductive tract infections.

Extent of stigma and discrimination

Stigma and discrimination have compounded the misery of the infected and the affected in this country, where much emphasis is laid on traditional, cultural, social and moral values. This is so particularly among the rural masses that comprise more than two thirds of its population. This shows that at present India is a society at war with its own beliefs and traditions (Ravindran, 2004). Cases of refusal of admission and treatment of people infected with HIV/AIDS in both government and private sector hospitals and nursing homes are a regular feature (NACO, 1999). Instances of children being refused admission to schools, refusal and loss of employment on account of HIV infection, discrimination at places of worship and by village communities are common phenomena across the country.

Scope for social work intervention

The HIV/AIDS pandemic is a sickness that affects many different aspects of human life. It makes the role of social workers in various settings very challenging. It is a sickness which turns young and vibrant persons into living skeletons walking to an early grave. HIV/AIDS leaves families and communities with a legacy of infected babies and orphans to be cared for by grannies and strangers. It distorts human identity and cultural notions of the truth, as people pretend that there is no illness, refusing to identify its presence among them (Bate, 2003). The scope for social work intervention on various aspects pertaining to HIV/AIDS is much greater than one may imagine.

There is an urgent need to initiate well-defined and needs-based research studies, both at micro- and macro-levels of the social, economic, cultural, religious and moral aspects pertaining to HIV/AIDS and to the infected and the affected. Research into the extent and level of awareness among people belonging to various strata of society, into care and support initiatives, into responses of the community to stigma and discrimination are imperative, as is research into the roles of national and international bodies, donor agencies and school and higher educational institutions. The roles of the health care sector, agencies in government departments responsible for planning, financing and implementing programmes as well as the roles of faith-based organisations and the corporate sector require examination.

IGNOU: a role model

The Indira Gandhi National Open University (IGNOU) was established in 1985 by an Act of Indian Parliament. Within the short span of two decades, it has become the largest university on the globe in terms of enrolment and networking. As of July 2007, the university has about 1.8 million students with an annual enrolment of over 500,000 in its 130 programmes and 40 overseas study centres established (IGNOU, 2007).

One ray of hope for the functionaries in the social welfare and development sectors in the country is the establishment in 2007 of the first and only School of Social Work under the Open and Distant Learning (ODL) system. The interventions initiated by me before the establishment of the School of Social Work are categorised under two segments: awareness programmes and formal courses and programmes of study. These have made history in the higher education system of the world's largest democracy.

Awareness programmes on HIV/AIDS

Raising awareness and providing information is crucial. Since 1999, a folder providing basic facts about the what, why and how of HIV/AIDS, titled 'HIV/AIDS prevention guide for students', has been mailed to all the fresh students of IGNOU along with their study materials. The annual readership of this HIV/AIDS awareness package is over one million.

Over two-dozen educational video films and audio programmes on HIV/AIDS and related topics are telecast on the channels Gyandharshan and Doordarshan (DD) and broadcast on All India Radio (AIR). They reach out regularly to several million people across the country. HIV/AIDS, family life education, adolescence education and substance abuse are some of the topics of popular interest that capture the attention of the listeners of IGNOU's interactive radio counselling programme. Interactive Teleconferencing Sessions (ITS) is another unique programme of reaching the unreached through the 2,000 downlink stations and the Direct-to-Home (DTH) channels, being viewed by about six million families.

Every year several regional-level seminars and an Annual National Seminar on Social Work Response to HIV/AIDS are organised to sensitise academics, NGO functionaries, school teachers and those interested in the subject.

Programmes of study in social work and HIV/AIDS

The claim to professional authority, legitimating social work's capacity to work in this field, has been strengthened. During the first National Seminar held in 2004, participants unanimously decided to form the National Association of Professional Social Workers in India (NAPSWI). Within one year of its registration and concomitant legal status, the life membership of NAPSWI has crossed the 1,000 mark. NAPSWI is now drafting a bill to be presented to the Indian Parliament to achieve a council on professional social work in India.

Catholic Bishops' Conference of India Chair

The Catholic Church in India, which comprises about 1.51% of the population (Keenan et al, 2001), owns about 22% of all health care facilities in the country. On 29 February 2000, the Catholic Bishops' Conference of India (CBCI) signed a Memorandum of Understanding (MOU) and established the CBCI Chair (CBCI Commission for Health Care, 2005). I was assigned its coordinatorship. As Chair, I am charged with the development of several programmes of study and the organisation of an Annual Mother Teresa Memorial Lecture. Here I describe very briefly the range of programmes already developed.

Certificate and Diploma in HIV/AIDS and Family Education

The first ever university certificate programmes on HIV/AIDS and Family Education (CAFÉ) in India were launched by IGNOU in 2002 and 2003, respectively. In 2004 and 2008, respectively, IGNOU launched the Bachelor Degree Programme in Social Work (BSW) and the Master of Social Work programme (MSW). These are the only programmes in India offered through the ODL system which have compulsory courses on HIV/AIDS, sexual health, family life education and substance abuse. This initiative has actualised the need for indigenously developed learning materials (print, audio and video) on social work for the first time. As well, three courses on HIV/AIDS, substance abuse and sexual health education are being offered as optional papers in the BA, BSc and BCommerce programmes with effect from July 2008. These will benefit over a hundred thousand students. From 2008, the teacher education programme (BEd) incorporated two compulsory courses, HIV/AIDS and Adolescence and Family Education.

IGNOU has admitted the first batch of students to its research programme in social work leading to the Master of Philosophy and

Doctor of Philosophy through ODL. This is expected to motivate practitioners to undertake research programmes particularly on health-related issues including HIV/AIDS.

Impact

While the awareness campaign is found to have significant impact in terms of imparting accurate information on HIV/AIDS and motivating young people to volunteer themselves for blood donation, it is too early to comment on the outcome of various programmes of study. Some of the early feedback includes the following: the challenging by a Diploma in HIV and Family Education (DAFE) student of the negative contents in the HIV/AIDS awareness package of the State Government of Andhra Pradesh in the High Court, which paved the way for the Chief Minister and other elected representatives to volunteer for HIV/AIDS tests in the State Legislative Assembly; a couple who was involved in the course preparation team volunteering to adopt an unborn child whose parents wished to seek an abortion; a female student who decided to stop the use of alcohol and initiated social action against the use of alcohol in her neighbourhood community; and the adoption of CAFÉ/DAFE programmes by Kenyata Open University, Kenya, and the launching of these programmes in Nepal on public demand.

Policy implications

The positive aspects of IGNOU initiatives include the development of culturally specific, academically sound and socially acceptable awareness packages and programmes of study pertaining to HIV/AIDS and related topics and indigenously developed textbooks on social work in the context of the 21st-century issues in a developing country. These initiatives have helped in the formation of NAPSWI, an annual national seminar which provides a forum for both social work practitioners and educators to meet, share and learn from each other and bring about uniformity in the social work curriculum at undergraduate and postgraduate levels across the country. Use of satellite communication networks for social work education, establishment of the first school of social work in the ODL system, the opportunity for social work educators to take up refresher programmes and have involvement in making academic contributions through publications are all now available. Above all, social work education with an adequate health-related curriculum is being taken to the doorsteps of numerous people in unreached and far-flung areas of the country. This is bound to bring about much-needed improvement in the social and development sectors of the world's largest democracy.

The impact on policy formulation in both the educational and health care sectors will also be significant. At the national level, policy makers have to examine the proposal for the establishment of a National Council on Social Work, to accord professional status to social work in India and to ensure quality and standards in social work education. There is also a need for recognition by the national government about the involvement of social workers in various social and development sectors in the country. These initiatives are expected to provide new direction in the area of social work education and training as well as provide job opportunities to social work graduates. Eventually the country will be able to address one of the major problems in the health care sector, namely, the dearth of social workers, particularly counsellors. These initiatives are bound to have great impact in neighbouring countries in Asia as well as the African continent where India has major collaborations in the educational sector.

14.2: Social work education and indigenous health

John Douglass Whyte, Lou Harms and Angela Clarke

Overview

The social and health inequalities between Australian Indigenous and non-Indigenous communities are well documented both nationally and internationally. While social work as a profession has the ethical mandate to address these inequalities, it has a complex history of working with indigenous populations, one which has often led to a sense of mutual alienation. More recent critiques of the persistent personal and social impacts of colonialism challenge previously held perceptions of what constitutes ethical practice in indigenous contexts. The opportunity is ripe and long overdue for social work educators to raise cultural awareness and develop culturally sensitive and relevant skills in current and future social workers.

This chapter explores these themes and focuses on an international Australian Research Council-funded Linkage Project, 'From colonisation to conciliation: A collaborative examination of social work practice with Indigenous populations'. As members of the research team we are gathering information about social work practice with Indigenous communities from Indigenous community members, Indigenous and non-Indigenous social work practitioners, and Indigenous and non-Indigenous social work academics. The aims are to gain collaborative understanding of what works best in practice and in so doing to contribute to better social and health outcomes for Indigenous Australians.

Dimensions of indigenous disadvantage

Indigenous populations are the most disadvantaged of all Australians, with significantly poorer opportunities and outcomes across the breadth of measures of health, citizenship and well-being than non-Indigenous Australians (Jones, 1996; Bauert et al, 2003; AIHW, 2006; Sanson-Fisher et al, 2006). The fact that this reflects conditions experienced by the estimated 300 million indigenous peoples around the globe does not diminish this source of national embarrassment or shame. It points instead to the complexity of the underlying issues and to the importance of effectively identifying and addressing the myriad dimensions of disadvantage (Bourne, 2003; Bristow, 2003; Coates, 2004).

These dimensions of disadvantage and inequality are interconnected and inseparable. One example of the connections between social and health inequalities is that Indigenous Australians are twice as likely as non-Indigenous Australians to leave school before completing year 10 and only half as likely to complete the final year of secondary schooling (ABS, 2003). This educational disadvantage translates to significantly poorer rates of employment and income and is also associated with significantly poorer health indicators, including endocrine, nutritional and metabolic disorders. These in turn contribute to the nearly 20-year disparity in Indigenous Australian life expectancy compared to that of the total Australian population (Anderson et al, 2006).

In Australia, this disadvantage is long-standing. It has existed from colonisation (1788) to the present. It extends from a history of dispossession, exclusion and control to which Indigenous Australians have been subjected, and from attitudes that at best can be characterised as 'patronising and paternalist, at worst ... harsh, moralist, unsympathetic and condemning' (Wearing and Berreen, 1994, pp 27).

The formal and informal policies framing these practices have existed at governmental, organisational and professional levels. The race clauses that were part of the Australian Constitution from the 1901 Federation to the 1967 referendum explicitly excluded Indigenous Australians from public health policies and services afforded to all other Australians. They created a structure for racial rationing of health services. Even after their removal in 1967, attempts to develop a national Aboriginal health programme have lacked the necessary development of institutional links with national health financing and policy structures (Anderson and Whyte, 2006). The reports of both *Deaths in Custody in Australia* (McCall, 2004) and *Bringing them Home* (National Inquiry into the Separation of Aboriginal and Torres Strait Islander Children from their Families, 1997) reflect this history of colonisation of Indigenous Australians by the wider community, governments and social workers.

Poor collaboration and coordination between levels of government and government departments is ongoing. This results in social and health issues, including employment, education, housing, welfare and health being regarded as separate issues, rather than as interconnected and integral to a more holistic understanding of health and well-being (Eckermann et al, 1992).

These dynamics have also played out within social work. It has been particularly difficult to implement successive changes in policies and approaches while conflicting underlying assumptions and agendas have remained unexamined. As described next, these have served to obscure, and sometimes impede, social work's potential for influencing the very policies it serves to implement.

The changing landscape of social work

Social work was founded on 19th-century Western European notions of morality and professional ethics, historically reinforced through the profession's reliance on Western scientific disciplines. Until the latter half of the 20th century, social work was practised within a more intra-societal, and therefore assumed homogeneous, context of 'acceptable' means and 'preferred' outcomes. This context reinforced the profession's prevailing notions of the correctness of its own ethics.

Since the latter half of the 20th century, however, three intersecting theoretical and professional developments have challenged the assumptions underlying social work education and practice. First, the development of critiques of the impact and implications of colonialism enhances understandings of indigenous experiences. Potentially, more effective health policies and practices will follow. Second, the global expansion of the profession from European-derived Western to wider international contexts demands an appreciation of practice contexts that span both differences in cultural characteristics and in 'world views'. Third, the increased demand for evidence-based social work practice requires demonstrated relevance of efforts, within and beyond the profession. It is essential to review social work education in the light of these developments.

Dilemmas and opportunities in social work education

Social work is uniquely situated to respond to the issues influencing indigenous well-being. Its practitioners are engaged across the entire range of human service organisations, in both policy making and direct practice roles. Given this, competent and effective cross-paradigm understandings are essential. Their absence can result in a cascade of misunderstandings, wasted human service resources and further client disadvantage and suffering. The first step towards assuring such effective understanding is to change the academic preparation.

In Australia, 25 tertiary institutions offer formal social work educational programmes, at bachelors and/or masters levels. Each year, approximately 700 students graduate from these programmes, and are eligible for membership of the Australian Association of Social Workers (AASW). The AASW accredits social work programmes, rather than individual graduates. While all programmes are required to incorporate some explicit indigenous content into the curriculum, they vary in the extent to which it is covered and in how it is taught.

Codes of ethics for professional social workers, including the Australian Code, require the competent, ethical practitioner to actively seek to redress 'problematic relationships' (AASW, 2002), a term that describes relationships between Indigenous Australians and social workers succinctly. This process of redress must involve both an examination of the profession's practice methods and of professional education. The long-standing social work tenet of 'starting where the client is' addresses only half of the dynamic. Efforts must also be made to understand where the profession is.

Yet arguments of how to redress these 'problematic relationships' are still actively debated within Australian social work. In 2002, McMahon noted in the national social work journal, *Australian Social Work*, that only 1.71% of the 934 articles published over the past 50 years addressed indigenous issues in any way. He asked, 'Why, then, is there so little analysis of the practice that undoubtedly takes place?' (McMahon, 2002, p 178). Indigenous issues continue to struggle to be given voice within both social work practice and education, despite the plea that 'Indigenous practice needs to be positioned as core social work knowledge and accepted as transferable across cultures and not marginalised' (Bennett and Zubrzycki, 2003, p 69).

It is not surprising, then, to find that not only are many emerging practitioners often ill-prepared to respond to indigenous issues that arise across the breadth of professional practice (Quinn, 2000), but that Indigenous students are under-represented in Australian social work degree programmes, especially in the southern States (Commonwealth Department of Education, Science and Training, 2002).

Many social work educators are aware of the need to tackle these critical issues. Two related reports provide significant motivation for better understanding, the *Committee of Deans of Australian Medical Schools' Indigenous Health Curriculum Framework* (Phillips, 2004) and *Teaching Koori Issues to Health Professionals and Health Students*, produced by the Victorian Aboriginal Community Controlled Health Organization in collaboration with VicHealth's Koori Health Research and Community Development Unit (VACCHO, 2001). These, and other reports examining the practices of the health service professions with indigenous populations (Anderson et al, 2004; Genat, 2004; 2006) highlight that there are unique guiding principles, subject areas, modes of delivery, assessment and resource issues to address to engender indigenous perspectives into emerging professional practice.

In view of the history of Australia's Indigenous populations, a contextually specific, broadly geographic and fully participatory understanding of what social workers need to know for effective practice is vital. Unfortunately, no formal review to establish this understanding has been undertaken to date (Weeks, 1997). Such an effort must reflect and practise the awareness and understandings described earlier, since failure to do so risks perpetuating past professional misconceptions, stereotypes and ineffectiveness. It also risks blinding the profession to its own potential to more effectively inform political and practice policy, not just follow it.

Researching social work practice

In 2005, funding for a three-year project was granted by the Australian Research Council to explore social work practice within Indigenous communities. It is intended that the findings will inform the better educational preparation of social work students for working with Indigenous clients. The project brings together Indigenous community members and Indigenous and non-Indigenous social work academics and practitioners in an exploration of social work practices and the implications for social work education.

From its inception, the project has been shaped and guided by the sensitivities to post-colonial theoretical understandings, to the implications of social work's increasing globalisation and to the growing cross-disciplinary emphasis on evidence-based research described earlier. Collaboration and consultation are considered the key to any successful changes and underpin the establishment of research and Indigenous practice networks. These provide for the involvement of key Indigenous community representatives and elders in each of the States and Territories where social work programmes are offered; practitioners from practice sites across Australia; and representatives from the 25 Australian social work programmes. They facilitate the understanding of the current context of social work practice in Australia as experienced by all key stakeholders. Given the diversity across Australia of Indigenous experiences and issues, the inclusion of a range of stakeholders within Indigenous community, university and practice settings is essential.

Examination of the findings from these consultative processes and of international best practice in contemporary tertiary indigenous pedagogy will lead to the development of recommendations for the AASW and Australian schools of social work for social work practice.

One of the goals of this project is that its findings will, in turn, support new understandings in social work education and practice outside of Australia and, in that way, support further conciliation between indigenous and non-indigenous peoples beyond Australia. In very real ways, the project aims to foster and support the idea that the global can be understood as a framework for the local and the local does, indeed, inform the global.

Acknowledgement

The authors would like to thank the Australian Research Council for the Linkage Project funding. The members of the project research team and the reference committee are listed at the project website, www.c2c.unimelb.edu.au

14.3: The challenges of training social workers for health care in South Africa

Charlene Laurence Carbonatto

Introduction

The challenges facing tertiary education in South Africa are formidable. The postgraduate training of social workers specialising in health care is no exception. Students must be trained for unique circumstances: developed and developing world health and illness patterns, Western and indigenous African treatment paradigms, and diverse cultural and religious beliefs and practices. In this chapter, I describe the approach taken to preparing students to work in situations characterised by multiple, interlocking dimensions of health inequalities by the only university offering specialised postgraduate training in social work in health care in South Africa.

Training social workers in health care in South Africa

The Department of Social Work and Criminology at the University of Pretoria has remained dedicated to offering this specialised training in social work in health care since 1982, when the provincial health authority requested the university to provide specialised training for social workers practising in the provincial state hospitals. Health Care is one of four Masters coursework programmes offered by the Department, together with Research Masters and Doctoral programmes. Coursework programmes are two-year programmes, with coursework modules and fieldwork in the first year, followed by research and mini-dissertation in the second year. Staff capacity allows for admission of 10 students per programme per year. Students are qualified social workers with practice experience in South Africa, Southern Africa and more recently Central Africa.

Most graduates will work in interdisciplinary teams in one of the 400 public sector hospitals throughout the country, either small community or district hospitals, or one of the 10 larger, regional advanced training hospitals. Some will work in one of the 4,100 public sector primary health care or HIV antiretroviral (ARV) clinics, or for the Departments of Health or Social Development, for private sector hospitals or private practice.

The policy practice context

Graduates of our programme enter a health service that has clear aims and priorities, insufficient resources and personnel stretched to their limits. Prior to 1994, health services were fragmented, inequitable and inaccessible. The main focus was curative; primary services were not available to the majority of the population. The Ministry of Health (1997) and National Health Act (2003) acknowledged the legacy of socio-economic injustices. Both recognised the need to heal past divisions and establish a society based on democratic values, social justice and fundamental human rights. Now, the official goals are the promotion of all people's health and the provision of caring, accessible and high-quality services through a primary health care approach. Tackling service fragmentation, reducing inequalities, increasing access and integrating services through mobilising the support of partners in the private, non-government and community sectors are basic aims (Ministry of Welfare and Population Development, 1997).

The then Minister for Health, Dr Tshabalala-Msimang, stated in the 2007 Health Budget Speech: 'Since the dawn of our democracy in 1994 we committed to work together towards attainment of our collective goal – a better health for all.' How to achieve this is complex. The government's mission is 'to improve health status through the prevention of illnesses and promotion of healthy lifestyles and to consistently improve the health care delivery system by focussing on access, equity, efficiency, quality, and sustainability' (Department of Health, 2006, p 5).

Health services must respond to both 'diseases of life' and 'diseases of civilisation' according to Van Rensburg (2004), who argues that the health profile of South Africa is a mixture of a developed, developing and under-developed country and a mixture of chronic-degenerative and acute infectious diseases. 'Lifestyle' contributes to the growing burden of disease (Tshabalala-Msimang, 2007). But a primary health care approach is crucial: it aims to ensure provision of basic health resources – education, food, safe water and sanitation; prevention, control and treatment of local endemic diseases; and essential medicine and services to mothers and children (Dennill et al, 1999).

The official priorities identified for both health and social welfare are:

- HIV/AIDS and sexually transmitted diseases;
- maternal, child and women's health;
- nutrition;
- communicable diseases;
- chronic diseases, disability and gerontology; and
- mental health and substance abuse (Ministry of Health, 1997; Ministry of Welfare and Population Development, 1997).

Graduates of the social work programme must be able to address these priorities, the causes of which are underpinned by poverty and violence.

The social distribution of health

Students in our programme focus on the health inequalities that health care must address. There are stark differences in health status between:

- white, coloured (a term with which some South African people continue to identify), Indian and black people;
- people in urban and rural areas; and
- people in transitional circumstances.

The spectrum of needs is complex.

South Africa has made progress in attaining its espoused aims. As As Dr Tshabalala-Msimang (2007) pointed out, by 2007 there were significant advances, including:

- overall immunisation coverage in South Africa reaching 83%;
- South Africa being declared polio-free;
- improvement in infant mortality rates to around 45/1,000 live births;
- expansion of the prevention of HIV Mother to Child Transmission programme to 90% of public health facilities;
- distribution of more than 439 million male and more than 3 million female condoms in the HIV preventions programme;
- support of the home- and community-based programmes to 60% of sub-districts;
- more than 282,836 patients initiated on antiretroviral treatments (ARVs) in accredited facilities by the end of March 2007 since

the inception of the ARV component of the Comprehensive Plan; and
- strides made with respect to the Traditional Health Practitioners Act (2004).

These indicators of progress must be considered alongside the facts that:

- Poverty is a major problem in South Africa. For many poverty-stricken children, malnutrition follows. People simply cannot afford sufficient healthy, balanced nutrition. Emphasis is being put on Nutritional Programmes (Department of Health, 2006). Although school feeding schemes and food parcels are available for the poor, corruption or lack of manpower often prevents them from reaching the schools.
- While literacy rates are improving, many older people are still illiterate.
- Safe water and sanitation are still not available to all communities, especially in rural areas.
- Endemic diseases such as cholera still occur, because many people are drinking unsafe water from polluted rivers.
- Women, children and the elderly are very vulnerable: there are high rates of rape, assault and violence.

We focus on these identified areas in the curriculum. In South Africa, as in Africa as a whole, poverty, malnutrition, HIV/AIDS, women and children, and violence must remain the key focus for social work. The programme aims to strengthen students' capacity to work in demanding circumstances.

Inadequate health services

While the private sector health facilities and hospitals of the cities are modern, efficient and well maintained, they are very expensive and serve only the approximately 7 million people with medical aid. The public sector serves 40 million people, 80% of the population. Although many hospitals are in a poor state of maintenance, the Hospital Revitalization Plan is under way upgrading and re-equipping these hospitals (Department of Health, 2006). Emergency services are inundated, due to violence, rape and traumas. Lack of staff exacerbates long waiting times.

The Department of Health (2006) confirms 4,100 primary health care clinics nationally, and still many are needed in rural areas, where only mobile clinics operate. The stream of refugees, constantly crossing the borders illegally into South Africa from Zimbabwe and Mozambique, has an added impact on health services and resources.

Social workers working in district hospitals work in both the hospital and the surrounding community, with an unbearable workload. The infrastructure in many rural areas is inadequate. In one province visited, a rural clinic built with donor funds had all the state of the art facilities, but had no electricity or water and simply could not function as proposed. The district had no ambulance; in the case of an emergency, patients could not be transported from the clinic to the hospital. Roads were in a poor state, affecting accessibility. Such clinics often do not have essential medicines or appropriate storage facilities and lack medication for chronic diseases, affecting adherence.

The impact of high crime rates and violence adds even further to the unbearable workloads. Many health professionals are emigrating, mainly due to better working conditions and incentives abroad. Those left behind carry heavy workloads, suffer stress and burnout and eventually are unable to deliver effective services. Practice realities such as these are used as scenarios in classroom discussions, in order to debate ways of dealing with them in a team context.

The social work in health care programme

To be able to intervene in any of these circumstances, students require an education that is broad. The material must be locally relevant, but also enable graduates to be internationally competitive. Gaining knowledge and understanding of health policy, service structures and priorities underpin the curriculum. A holistic knowledge of diverse cultures, religions and health-related beliefs and rituals, is essential.

Students must be prepared for functioning as team members, so that within the African context the needs of the patient, family and community can be addressed. Teams include professional medical practitioners and other health-related professionals, alternative care providers and persons from sectors other than health, when it comes to primary health care services, such as provision of safe water and sanitation. Sometimes the indigenous health care provider also has to be taken into consideration.

Students gain knowledge of the whole array of diseases including HIV and AIDS, cancer, diabetes, malnutrition, psychiatric conditions and trauma-related conditions. They gain knowledge and skills to intervene with vulnerable groups, particularly women, children, elderly persons and people with disabilities.

Case examples, scenarios, videos and DVDs are used to stimulate class discussion and plan and simulate interventions. Reflection journals kept by students on media coverage of health issues in South Africa inform class discussion on health trends and social policy. Research methodology is of utmost importance in preparing them for the research and writing of the mini-dissertation.

Capacity to work with the complexities of HIV/AIDS

Our graduates must be able to work with people living with HIV/AIDS. The number of persons living with HIV is the highest in Africa, sub-Saharan Africa and specifically Southern Africa (UNAIDS and WHO, 2007; Department of Health, 2008). An estimated 22.5 million people are living with HIV in Southern Africa, 5.27 million of whom live in South Africa. Prevalence rates of HIV estimates by age of attendees of state antenatal clinics is 28% of 20–24 year olds; 37.9% of 25–29 year olds; and 40.2% of 30–34 year olds. Nationally the prevalence rate among women attending antenatal clinics is 28%, with KwaZulu-Natal and Free State provinces having the highest figures – 37.4% and 33.5%, respectively. Similar rates are found in neighbouring countries: Swaziland, Botswana and Zimbabwe. Factors contributing to high transmission rates of HIV/AIDS in Africa and specifically Southern Africa are very complex and can be linked to traditional cultural practices and gender issues.

Social workers are trained to think holistically, to understand how gender, cultural and traditional practices complicate the spread of this disease and why educating people regarding behaviour change is essential. This is a huge challenge.

Capacity to work with knowledge of African indigenous cultures

Social workers have to take the indigenous, cultural and religious beliefs and practices related to health into consideration when working in any country. Pervan et al (1995) explain that African indigenous culture focuses on the following with regard to health and illness:

- beliefs about the special significance of religious elements like dreams, evil spirits and ancestors in the causes and treatment of illness;
- differences between Western and traditional indigenous approaches to treatment;

- sorcery and the use of medicine to harm someone;
- the role of ancestors or death in the transition into the spiritual world;
- the responsibility of indigenous traditional healers for diagnosis, healing, protection of the individual and supply of herbal medicines;
- the differential role of different types of traditional healers: diviners, herbalists, faith healers and prophets.

There are approximately 25,000 registered medical practitioners and 350,000 traditional healers registered at Traditional Healers' Associations. These healers are in the communities, accessible to the people, trusted by the people and if recognised by the health sector could be incorporated as health service providers into the health system. With some additional appropriate training they can play a complementary role in rendering certain health services in South Africa, such as DOTS (directly observed treatment), monitoring adherence of tuberculosis sufferers and diabetics.

Students are trained to consider alternative and indigenous health care providers as integral to the holistic health care team. Video clips of these different health care providers are used to initiate wide-ranging controversial discussions.

Capacity to work with diversity

Diversity is an important dimension of health care. Students themselves are diverse in terms of culture, religion and ethnic origin. So too are patients. In practice our graduates have to be able to assess, understand and intervene with people from diverse cultural and ethnic backgrounds, holding diverse religious beliefs, living in diverse socio-economic circumstances and at different educational levels. Each has her/his own unique understanding, interpretation, experience, reactions and rituals regarding health and illness. Being responsive to diversity is key.

Conclusions

In South Africa, the sources of pain and suffering are so clearly associated with social, economic, political and cultural factors. Social workers need the support and strength that specialised training opportunities can provide. Our view is that postgraduate training should be a prerequisite to health and health care practice, as the knowledge and skills required are so extensive. Capacity for practising both developmentally and therapeutically is necessary. Having a thorough knowledge of HIV and AIDS is crucial. The South African Council for Social Service Professions (SACSSP), with whom social workers register in South Africa in order to practise, is currently finalising the process of registering social work in health care as a specialised field of practice. Establishing an International Association for Social Work in Health and Mental Health Care could support practitioners and help develop training standards and protect social work interests.

References

AASW (Australian Association of Social Workers) (2002) *Code of Ethics*, Canberra: AASW.

ABS (Australian Bureau of Statistics) (2003) *Population Characteristics: Aboriginal and Torres Strait Islander Australians 2001*, Canberra: Commonwealth of Australia.

AIHW (Australian Institute of Health and Welfare) (2006) *Australia's Health, No 10*, Canberra: Australian Institute of Health and Welfare.

Anderson, I. and Whyte, J.D. (2006) *Australian Federalism and Aboriginal Health: Australian Aboriginal Studies*, Canberra: Aboriginal Studies Press.

Anderson, I., Brabham, W., Genat, W., Keleher, H., Jessen, J., Fitzgerald, D. and Marshall, B. (2004) *National Indigenous Public Health Curriculum Audit and Workshop Project Report*, VKHRCDU Discussion Paper, No. 11, VKHRCDU, Melbourne: University of Melbourne.

Anderson, I., Crengle, S., Kamaka, M.L., Chen, T.H., Palafox, N. and Jackson-Pulver, L. (2006) 'Indigenous health in Australia, New Zealand, and the Pacific', *The Lancet*, vol 367, pp 1775–7.

Bate, S. (ed) (2003) *Responsibility in Times of AIDS, A Pastoral Response by Catholic Theologians and AIDS Activists in Southern Africa*, Pretoria: SACBC AIDS Office.

Bauert, P., McMaugh, E., Martin, C.M. and Smylie, J.K. (2003) 'Indigenous health: Chronically inadequate responses to damning statistics', *Medical Journal of Australia*, vol 178, no 5, p 246.

Bennett, B. and Zubrzycki, J. (2003) 'Hearing the stories of Australian Aboriginal and Torres Strait Islander social workers: Challenging and educating the system', *Australian Social Work*, vol 56, no 1, pp 61–70.

Bourne, R. (2003) *Invisible Lives. Undercounted, Underrepresented and Underneath: The Socio-Economic Plight of Indigenous Peoples in the Commonwealth*, London: Commonwealth Studies Unit.

Bristow, F. (ed) (2003) *Utz'Wach'il: Health and Wellbeing Among Indigenous Peoples*, London: Health Unlimited/London School of Hygiene and Tropical Medicine.

CBCI Commission for Health Care (2005) *Commitment to Compassion and Care*, New Delhi: CBCI Commission for Health Care.

Coates, K.S. (2004) *A Global History of Indigenous Peoples: Struggle and Survival*, New York: Palgrave MacMillan.

Commonwealth Department of Education, Science and Training (2002) *Achieving Equitable and Appropriate Outcomes: Indigenous Australians in Higher Education*, Canberra: DEST.

Dennill, K., King, L. and Swanepoel, T. (1999) *Aspects of Primary Health Care: Community Health Care in Southern Africa*, 2nd edn, Johannesburg: International Thomson Publishing.

Department of Health (2006) *Health Overview 2006*, Pretoria: Department of Health.

Department of Health (2008) *National HIV and Syphilis Prevalence Survey 2007*, Pretoria: Department of Health.

Eckermann, A., Dowd, T., Martin, M., Nixon, L., Gray, R., Chong, E. and Goonj, B. (1992) *Bridging Cultures in Aboriginal Health*, Armidale NSW: University Printery, University of New England.

Genat, W. (2004) 'Indigenous content in Master of Public Health programs', *Aboriginal and Islander Health Worker Journal*, vol 28, no 2, p 19.

Genat, W. (2006) *Aboriginal Healthworkers: Primary Health Care at the Margins*, Perth: UWA Press.

IGNOU (Indira Gandhi National Open University) (2007) *IGNOU Profile 2007*, New Delhi: MPDD, IGNOU.

Jones, A. (1996) *The Australian Welfare State*, Sydney: Allen and Unwin.

Keenan, J.F., Fuller, J., Cahill, L. and Kelly, K. (eds) (2001) *Catholic Ethicists on HIV/AIDS Prevention*, Quezon City, Philippines: Claretian Publications.

McCall, M. (2004) *Deaths in Custody in Australia: 2003 National Deaths in Custody Program (NDICP) Annual Report*, Canberra: Australian Institute of Criminology.

McMahon, A. (2002) 'Writing diversity: Ethnicity and race in Australian social work', *Australian Social Work*, vol 55, no 3, pp 172–83.

Ministry of Health (1997) 'White paper for the transformation of the health system in South Africa', *Government Gazette*, vol 382, no 17910, Pretoria: Government Printer.

Ministry of Welfare and Population Development (1997) 'White paper for social welfare', *Government Gazette*, vol 386, no 18166, Pretoria: Government Printer.

NACO (National AIDS Control Organisation) (1999) *Country Scenario: 1997–98*, New Delhi: Ministry of Health and Family Welfare, Government of India.

NACO (2007) 'HIV sentinel surveillance and HIV estimation in India 2007: A technical brief', www.nacoonline.org/Quick_Links/ HIV_Data/

National Health Act (2003) 'Act 61 of 2003', *Government Gazette*, vol 469, no 26595, Cape Town: Government Printer.

National Inquiry into the Separation of Aboriginal and Torres Strait Islander Children from their Families (1997) *Bringing them Home: Report of the National Inquiry into the Separation of Aboriginal and Torres Strait Islander Children from their Families*, Sydney: Human Rights and Equal Opportunity Commission.

Pervan, V., Cohen, L.H. and Jaftha, T. (eds) (1995) *Oncology for Health-Care Professionals*, Kenwyn: Juta and Co.

Phillips, G. (2004) *Committee of Deans of Australian Medical Schools' Indigenous Health Curriculum Framework*, VicHealth Koori Health Research and Community Development Unit, Melbourne: The University of Melbourne.

Quinn, M. (2000) 'Working with Australian families: Towards anti-racist and culturally affirming practices', in W. Weeks and M. Quinn (eds) *Issues facing Australian families*, Melbourne: Longman, pp 101–18.

Ravindran, R. (2004) *Living 'Life' with HIV/AIDS: Striving Towards Basic Rights*, New Delhi: Pentagon Press.

Sanson-Fisher, R.W., Campbell, E.M., Perkins, J.J., Blunden, S.V. and Davis, B.B. (2006) 'Indigenous health research: A critical review of outputs over time', *Medical Journal of Australia*, vol 184, no 10, pp 502–5.

Thomas, G. (2006) *Life Skill Education and Curriculum*, New Delhi: Shipra Publications.

Traditional Health Practitioners Act (2004) 'Act 35 of 2004', *Government Gazette*, vol 476, no 27275, Cape Town: Government Printers.

Tshabalala-Msimang, M. (2007) 'Budget speech by Minister of Health', 7 June, RSA.

UNAIDS and WHO (Joint United Nations Program on HIV/AIDS and World Health Organization) (2007) *AIDS Epidemic Update*, Geneva: UNAIDS.

VACCHO (Victorian Aboriginal Community Controlled Health Organization) (2001) *Teaching Koori Issues to Health Professionals and Health Students: A Community Report*, in collaboration with the VicHealth Koori Health Research and Community Development Unit, Melbourne: The University of Melbourne.

Van Rensburg, H.C.J. (2004) *Health and Health Care in South Africa*, Pretoria: Van Schaik Publishers.

Veeraraghavan, V. and Singh, S. (eds) (1999) *HIV and AIDS, An Interdisciplinary Approach to Prevention and Management*, New Delhi: Mosaic Books.

Wearing, M. and Berreen, R. (1994) *Welfare and Social Policy in Australia: The Distribution of Advantage*, Sydney: Harcourt Brace.

Weeks, W. (1997) *Report on National Priority (Reserve) Fund Project: Collaborative Approach to Aboriginal Studies in Social Work Education,* Melbourne: School of Social Work, University of Melbourne.

Part Four

Global health inequalities: social work policy and practice development

Addressing health inequalities: the role of service user and people's health movements

Ann Davis

All movements for change search for new knowledge that will liberate people rather than oppress them as the old knowledge does. The new knowledge helps us put value back into our experience. (Mary O'Hagan, New Zealand mental health system survivor and activist, 1993, p 17)

Service users and social work

While social work reflects a rich diversity of practice globally it shares one important characteristic – its daily encounters with some of the most impoverished casualties of unequal societies. Whatever issues service users bring to these encounters, the impact of structural inequalities on their health chances as well as health experiences are evident. As older people, parents and children living in poverty, people with HIV/AIDS, disabilities, mental health problems and learning difficulties they struggle with the scarce resources they have at their disposal to fully realise their well-being and citizenship.

The personal troubles that service users share with social workers are public issues. The emotional and physical distress and ill-health they experience reflect the political, social and economic decisions being taken in the societies in which they live; societies in which they exercise little formal power and occupy marginal or excluded positions.

Social work has always been a profession positioned between the mainstream and the margins of society. It works with the complexity and unpredictability of the human condition. At the same time it is mandated by state agencies to deliver on national social policy agendas. As Lorenz suggests the challenge for social work is how to practise 'between system and lifeworld' and not to be 'incorporated into public systems of social policy and national policies of social and cultural systems of integration' (Lorenz, 2004, p 147).

This challenge is relevant to social work practitioners in service, education and research environments. Put at its simplest: do we accept the status quo and work within the constraints and injustices of the world we find ourselves in? Or do we take seriously the global definition of social work of the International Association of Schools of Social Work (IASSW) and International Federation of Social Workers (IFSW) and strive to promote social change through our belief that the principles of human rights and social justice are fundamental to social work (IASSW/IFSW, 2004)?

Contributors to this volume have built a strong case as to why the social work profession should challenge the social order in pursuing issues of human rights and social justice in the countries in which they live and practise. This chapter gives brief consideration to the way in which this challenge can be strengthened through building alliances with service user organisations and global people's health and social movements.

Nothing about us without us: the growth of service user movements

> We felt there was a need to create a voice of our own, where we could for the first time advocate for our own rights. (Maria Rantho, co-founder of Disabled People of South Africa and first disabled Member of Parliament in the South African National Assembly, cited in Barry, 2002, p 1)

Movements of people who receive social welfare services have a long, largely hidden, history (Beresford and Holden, 2000). But from the 1960s onwards their presence has grown. Developing initially in the health and welfare regimes of North America, the UK, Australia, New Zealand and Europe they have now established a small, often fragile, but significant, local, national and global presence in spite of the considerable struggles that they have to establish and sustain themselves (Charlton, 1998).

Through their questioning of, and resistance to, the stigmatising exercise of professional, political and legal powers, service user organisations have developed new ways of engaging in political action as well as analysing the world as they know it. As such they have been identified by some as being part of 'new social movements': 'organised efforts to promote or resist change in society that rely, at least in part, on non-institutionalised forms of political action' (Marx and McAdam, 1993, p 34). Their recognition of the importance of retaining their independence from the formal structures of the political process mark them off from groups of 'welfare consumers' brought together to serve the requirements of the managerialist and marketised health and welfare systems of the late 20th and early 21st centuries (Clarke, 2004).

Service user organisations have generated a diversity of activities to pursue their concerns. These include support, information sharing and advocacy for individuals who find themselves subject to abuse and oppression within welfare systems. They also provide opportunities for a range of individuals and groups who have contact with welfare services to voice their concerns and campaign for increased choice and independence in their daily lives. A few organisations have also taken on the task of developing service user-led services by becoming direct providers of housing, employment or caring services. Through this range of activities service user organisations question the stigmatising impacts of their status as recipients of welfare and charity as well as their position as devalued and marginalised citizens or as people denied citizen status because the dominant welfare order has labelled them as 'invalid' (Barnes and Mercer, 2006).

For example, Disability Action focuses its activities on working to ensure that all people with disabilities in Northern Ireland attain their full rights as citizens, through supporting inclusion, influencing government policy and changing attitudes in partnership with disabled people. Comprising a network of 180 local organisations of disabled people it meets its aims in two main ways – campaigning for the rights of people with disabilities in order to effect changes in government policies and provision as well as delivering services and projects that meet the needs of disabled people by filling the gaps in formal service provision (www.disabilityaction.org).

The growth of organisations of people who have contact with social workers have led to critiques of traditional professional modes of working (Barnes and Mercer, 2006). As a result social workers have been invited to consider renegotiating their relationships with service users so that they give explicit consideration to forms of power sharing that have the potential to pool the energy and resources of service users and social workers. Smith summarises it as replacing 'positional' preconceptions with 'relational' strategies of power (Smith, 2008, p 139).

The contributions that service user organisations have made to the debates about the place, worth and value of social work have been viewed by some within social work as an attack on their professionalism. However, others have embraced this agenda as offering the possibility of developing new forms of ethically informed practice, education and research (Hugman, 1998; Davies and Leonard, 2005). This recognition of the potential that service user organisations and their members have to make a positive and potentially transforming contribution to social work theory, practice, research and education offers much to those practitioners concerned with addressing issues of health inequalities (Carr, 2004).

The first step in developing this potential is the recognition of the importance of social work practitioners, educators and researchers listening to, and learning from, the accounts that service users give of the ways in which they experience health inequalities in their lives. Systematic research commissioned by the UK's Disability Rights Commission (DRC) about the health inequalities experienced by people with mental health problems and learning disabilities using primary health care services in England and Wales, found that these groups were more likely than other citizens to face major physical health problems and live shorter lives. The data gathered for this report included the testimony of over 1,000 service users who described the negative responses made to them by health services (DRC, 2006).

Such testimony is all too familiar to listening social workers and they have a part to play in challenging discriminatory treatment given to service users as well as sharing the evidence they acquire of such discrimination with service user organisations. Such sharing plays a vital part in extending the range of knowledge and experiences on which these organisations can draw. In addition, the relationships which can emerge from such exchanges between social workers and service users has the potential to make a strong ongoing contribution to the impact that both parties can have in addressing health inequalities.

People who are faced with the grim realities of surviving difficulties and dangers develop knowledge and resilience which can play an invaluable part in the struggle to combat social justice and create a healthier world. Evidence suggests that what service users value most about social work is the social perspective it can bring to the recognition of their rights and needs as well as the way it works through building personal relationships (Cree and Davis, 2007; Shaping Our Lives, 2007; Doel and Best, 2008). It is this combination of perspective and practice which provides the foundation of co-working with service users around issues of inequality and injustice.

Co-working of this kind also has a lot to teach social workers as practitioners, educators and researchers about moving beyond individualising and problematising the concerns of service users to recognising common concerns about the world we share. Conceptualising service users as passive, vulnerable and helpless victims of an unjust social order constructs them as 'other', outside of the mainstream of active productive citizens. As Ruth Lister (2004, p 125) points out, 'Othering the poor' is a stance which reduces people in poverty 'to passive objects – in either the benign form of helpless victim or the malign spectre of the lazy, work-shy, welfare dependant. This passive characterization contributes to the social distancing of "them" from "us".'

A response firmly rooted in an ethical base which values those who become service users as individuals and treats them equally, opens up a wealth of possibilities of working in alliance with those who are organising around their struggle for well-being and a place in the world.

Global alliances: health and social movements

> To me disability was never a welfare issue, a charity issue.
> It was and is a social issue, a socio-economic issue, a
> development issue. This country cannot talk of development
> and progress and moving into the 21st century leaving 6%
> of its population behind. All of us together, whether we
> are disabled, parents or professionals, government officials
> or the media, if we are truly concerned about our great
> country, then we have to think a little harder, join hands
> and find ways to solve this very huge and serious problem.
> (Javed Abidi, disability rights activist and former Head of
> the National Centre for the Promotion of Employment
> for Disabled People in New Delhi, India; Abidi, 1999)

Service user organisations have grown over the last decade or so from having a local presence to having a national and global presence. The European Network of Users and Survivors of Psychiatry (ENUSP) is one example. A grassroots pan-European umbrella organisation it aims to provide ex-users and survivors of psychiatric services with 'a means to communicate, exchange opinions, views and experiences in order to support each other in the personal, political and social struggle against expulsion, injustice and stigma in our respective countries' (www.enusp. org). ENUSP also works to unify 'national organisations of (ex-)users and survivors of psychiatry across the continent to provide a direct representation of people who are or have been on the receiving end of psychiatric services'. In addition, Disabled Peoples' International (DPI), a network of national organisations or assemblies of disabled people from over 110 countries, pursues the goals of promoting the human rights of disabled persons and promoting their economic and social integration, as well as developing and supporting organisations of disabled persons (www.dpi.org).

These networks, and others, which have been created and are sustained with great effort and minimal resources, reflect the concerns that have been developed through exchanges between people across the globe who have found themselves sharing an identity generated by the categories ascribed by health and welfare services and professionals. Yet the general issues that they highlight as constraining their achievement of well-being and citizenship are common concerns across all service user organisations. They also resonate with the concerns of other global networks.

Globally, people's health and social movements, with their focus on major issues that impact on health and the forces that are creating global inequalities and oppression, have been built and sustained through complex networks of those at the receiving end alongside allies holding positions of professional and political power across the globe. One example is the People's Health Movement (PHM) which has grown from the coming together of a range of international organisations, civil society movements, non-governmental organisations (NGOs) and women's groups. This movement describes itself as 'a global coalition of grassroots and health activist organisations dedicated to addressing the burden of preventable disease globally but in particular that carried by developing countries' (www.phmovement.org). It pursues the goal of re-establishing health and equitable development as top priorities in local, national and international policy making with comprehensive primary health care as a key strategy to achieve these priorities, using its People's Charter for Health as an organising focus.

Potentially the PHM as well as the World Social Forum and the Global Forum for Health Research offer opportunities for service user and social work organisations to make contributions to the development of knowledge and action aimed at transforming health and social conditions.

Working for change together

> I have tried to get a job, but always it seems to me that there are obstacles in the way.... My social worker asked me if I was interested in assisting in some meetings as an HIV positive person. Saying yes to her was the way I became involved in 'Shaping our Lives' [a national organisation of people who use services which promotes user control]. I found this project so interesting that I thought there might be an opportunity for me to become involved working alongside social work students, helping them to get a greater appreciation of what it is like to live with a disability and the services we need. (UK member of Shaping Our Lives Group, cited in National User Network Newsletter, 2005)

The narratives of individuals who have taken their experiences of oppressive social and health regimes into activism in service user and people's health movements, often highlight transforming moments when their personal struggles and difficulties connected with like others and became a source of strength rather than vulnerability. On numerous occasions such transforming experiences make direct reference to the positive contribution of social workers who through the provision of information, resources, support or access to new opportunities played a part in their journey (Charlton, 1998). Social work practitioners, educators and researchers need to travel with this in mind. They can open doors for people ready to make a journey.

Retaining independence as a local service user organisation often means reliance on self-generated funding and the generous investment of time and skills by members. Making links with, and contributions to, global organisations and movements requires the kind of knowledge, time, resources and confidence that are usually absorbed by the struggles to sustain organisations locally and nationally. At the same time global health and social movements may find it difficult to recognise and value the input from groups who are often regarded negatively because of the stigma attached to the conditions by which they are identified, such as HIV/AIDS, mental ill-health, learning disabilities and physical impairments.

Social work too struggles to build and sustain its national and international presence and engage with the formal institutions and the emerging social movements that are working for change in key areas of the profession's concern (see Chapter 16). These struggles relate to both the relatively meagre resources that social work has at its disposal as well as the debates within the profession about the relevance of working at policy levels. In this situation of mutual difficulty it is important for those service users and workers interested in building global engagement to consider how the strategic use of the relationships and alliances that have worked locally and nationally might be of mutual benefit.

Social workers who have learnt from the strengths, creativity and survival skills of service users have much to offer to national and global initiatives on health inequalities. Experience of working in alliance with service user organisations through relationships which are based on recognition of what each brings, sharing knowledge, tackling differences through listening, learning and working through collective action to achieve agreed goals can make an important contribution to effectively addressing the health inequalities which are structured into the world we share.

References

Abidi, J. (1999) 'We (disabled people) must learn to exert ourselves', Disability Awareness in Action Newsletter, no 74, July, www.independentliving.org/docs1/abidi.html

Barnes, C. and Mercer, G. (2006) *Independent Futures: Creating User-Led Disability Services in a Disabling Society*, Bristol: The Policy Press.

Barry, S. (2002) 'Celebrating & mourning a pioneer in South Africa's disability rights movement: Maria Rantho', *Disability World*, vol 14, www.disabilityworld.org/06-08_02/news/rantho.shtml

Beresford, P. and Holden, C. (2000) 'Globalization and welfare user movements', *Disability and Society*, vol 15, no 7, pp 973–90.

Carr, S. (2004) *Has Service User Participation Made a Difference to Social Care Services?* London: Social Care Institute of Excellence.

Charlton, J. (1998) *Nothing About Us without Us*, Berkeley: University of California Press.

Clarke, J. (2004) *Changing Welfare, Changing States: New Directions in Social Policy*, London: Sage.

Cree, V. and Davis, A. (2007) *Inside Social Work*, London: Routledge.

Davies, L. and Leonard, P. (eds) (2005) *Social Work in a Corporate Era: Practices of Power and Resistance*, Aldershot: Ashgate.

Doel, M. and Best, L. (2008) *Experiencing Social Work: Learning from Service Users*, London: Sage.

DRC (Disability Rights Commission) (2006) *Equal Treatment: Closing the Gap*, London, DRC.

Hugman, R. (1998) *Social Welfare and Social Value*, Basingstoke: Macmillan.

IFSW and IASSW (International Association of Schools of Social Work) (2004) *Ethics in Social Work: Statement of Principles*, Bern: IFSW and IASSW, www.ifsw.org/p38000324.html

Lister, R. (2004) *Poverty*, Cambridge: Polity Press.

Lorenz, W. (2004) 'Research as an element in social work's ongoing search for identity', in R. Lovelock, K. Lyons and J. Powell (eds) *Reflecting on Social Work – Discipline and Profession*, Aldershot: Ashgate.

Marx, G. and McAdam, D. (1993) *Collective Behaviour and Social Movements: Process and Structure*, New York: Prentice Hall.

National User Network Newsletter (2005) Issue 8, www.shapingourlives. org.uk/downloads/newsletters/newsletter8dec.doc#bm6

O'Hagan, M. (1993) *Stopovers on my Way Home from Mars*, London: Survivors Speak Out.

Shaping Our Lives (2007) *The Roles and Tasks of Social Workers*, London: Shaping Our Lives.

Smith, R. (2008) *Social Work and Power*, Basingstoke: Palgrave.

Engagement in international practice and policy development

Imelda Dodds

Introduction

The International Federation of Social Workers (IFSW) provides a worldwide framework for formulating, supporting and disseminating professional standards on social work ethics and human rights. It can provide support for countries where social work is developing as a profession. It can help the profession to respond with policy, advocacy and programme initiatives when social workers are responding to the impact of wars, natural disasters and pandemics, and it can articulate desirable economic and social policy directions that are faithful to social work's commitment to redress social and health inequalities.

This chapter is a personal reflection on the capacity of social work to contribute to national and international practice and policy development, arising from my time as President of IFSW between 2000 and 2006. First, I briefly outline the roles which IFSW plays and the structures through which it represents social work in global institutions. Second, I indicate some of my first-hand experiences of the globalising trends and forces influencing inequalities in health. Finally, I present a specific example of IFSW contributing to action on health inequalities, action which incorporated the construction of an alliance between residents of a Kenyan slum, some of whom were also social workers, national and international social work organisations and UN-HABITAT (United Nations Human Settlements Programme).

The International Federation of Social Workers

As of 2008 the IFSW represents social workers in 85 countries across the globe. Eighty years previously in Paris, its forerunner, the International Permanent Secretariat of Social Workers, as it was called, was established, operating until the outbreak of the Second World War. It was not until 1956 that 12 national social work organisations came together in

Munich to re-establish what is now known as the IFSW. The current membership comprises an estimated 500,000 social work practitioners across five regions: Africa, Asia and Pacific, Europe, Latin America and Caribbean and North America. While changes in communication and travel between 1928 and today are profound, and understanding of global conditions is greatly improved, cooperation through close relationships is the hallmark of IFSW'S operations.

It places particular emphasis on professional standards, values and ethics, and on recognition, training and working conditions. There has always been a strong focus on supporting the establishment of national organisations for social workers. Some of these are purely professional bodies, some incorporate a trade union function, while others are collectives of distinctive national bodies that together represent social work practitioners in IFSW and internationally.

Liaison with international bodies is a central function. The Federation has maintained special consultative status to the Economic and Social Council of the United Nations since 1959. This close working relationship has continued through the establishment of representative teams in Geneva, Nairobi, New York and Vienna and through links to UNICEF, the Council of Non Government Organisations in association with the United Nations (CONGO) and membership of the International Labour Organization (ILO) special list of non-government organisations.

Central to the discharge of IFSW's commitment to social justice is its focus on human rights. A commitment to the unique worth and dignity of each person is explicit in its policy on human rights:

> The social work profession, through historical and empirical evidence, is convinced that the achievement of human rights for all people is a fundamental prerequisite for a caring world and the survival of the human race. It is only through the recognition and implementation of the basic concept of the inherent dignity and worth of each person that a secure and stable world can be achieved. (IFSW, 1996)

The IFSW promotes human rights through the operation of its Human Rights Commission. This includes raising awareness within the profession about human rights issues, for example, the infringement of the human rights of social work and welfare workers wherever they occur.

It seeks to promote health policies and practices that enhance well-being through its *International Policy on Health* (IFSW, 2008a), a policy that is linked to related statements, such as those on globalisation and the environment (IFSW, 2008b). The policy on health asserts that health and mental health issues are of basic importance to social work. The estimated 1.5 million social workers across the globe are active in very diverse fields. But an understanding of physical and mental health issues and how they impact on the individuals, groups and communities with whom we work is essential. My experience as President confirms this.

Health, poverty and globalisation

Between 2000 and 2006 I visited 24 countries from the most to the least economically developed. I found poverty in all of them, always accompanied by poor physical and mental health. Although causes and contexts varied, I saw first-hand this inextricable relationship between poverty and health, a relationship that social workers need to understand wherever they work.

Many times I witnessed the reality of the statistics that are cited throughout this book. I saw extreme poverty in Africa, Latin America and the Caribbean, South East Asia and parts of Europe. In Africa I saw the very real impact of the structural adjustment policies of the 1990s. I saw how access to basic health care was impossible for those living in extreme poverty and impossibly expensive for countless others. In developed countries like Australia, the UK and the US, I saw service systems that required people to face long waiting lists for public services and to pay costs they could ill afford. I saw indigenous communities still dealing with extreme poverty and with the health crises that come from the impacts of colonialism – displacement, cultural dislocation and geographical remoteness.

In urban and rural areas across the globe I saw the daily impact of globalisation, especially the conflicts and human rights abuses that produce mass movements of people. I met social workers working with refugees, who were fleeing from these perils. The majority are women and children, most of whom have experienced profound physical and emotional trauma in their country of departure, on the journey or in refugee camps. I learned how the intergenerational effects of being orphaned, surviving interrupted parenting and suffering trauma add to their physical and mental health needs.

Africa

In sub-Saharan Africa I met social workers working with the impacts of HIV/AIDS. In a situation where an entire generation is threatened, social workers advocate for access to affordable and effective antiretrovirals and for comprehensive education and prevention programmes. Vivid in my memory is the conversation I had with an African social work academic. Each year when she inducts her class of students she knows that up to 30% will not live to graduate.

Social workers in Africa face extensive challenges. Africa is the only continent designated for special attention in the Millennium Development Goals (MDGs). There are good reasons for this. The levels of poverty throughout Africa are staggering and the impact of health-related catastrophes is both a major contributor to and result of poverty. Natural disasters of flood and famine also regularly cause major health crises. The policies of structural adjustment, favoured by the World Bank in the 1980s and 1990s, that led to privatisation of national services have resulted in health care being out of reach of the poor (Labonte and Schrecker, 2007).

Added to this, issues of poor governance continue to undermine poverty alleviation programmes in many African countries. For example, Nigeria is an oil-rich country but according to Ewhrudjakpor (2008), 70% of the population live in poverty and only one third have access to potable water. Ewhrudjakpor cites corruption as a major contributor to failed poverty alleviation initiatives over successive governments. It is a theme repeated across the continent.

In 2005 I attended the 6th IFSW Pan African Conference, held in Nairobi, capital of Kenya. Representatives from 15 African nations were present and social workers from a further 11 countries outside Africa made the journey. It was a historic event. The Association of Schools of Social Work Africa was founded. The conference allowed conversations that had been impossible for some time because of conflict. Social workers from north and south Sudan were able to meet and reflect on the challenges of working with the impact of civil war. They met colleagues from other African nations and were free to talk about rebuilding after civil unrest. Working with the impact of HIV/AIDS was a pervasive theme. My colleagues and I from nations outside of Africa were ever conscious that ours was the role of observer and student, and that we were there for a very short period of time. In my opening address I noted that for social workers in Africa, working with the impact of poverty was a daily lived experience like none other.

Kibera

At the conclusion of the conference I was able to see the issues that confronted social workers in one of Africa's largest slums. Kibera is barely six kilometres from the central business district of Nairobi. Kibera was home to up to 1.2 million people on 250 hectares of government land. The magnitude of poverty there was extreme. Housing was at a premium: the majority of homes were built from basic rubble, sheet iron and shaky wooden frameworks. The average rented house of approximately 3m x 3m was home to 5–10 people.

Sanitation was non-existent. There was no drainage system, no reliable source of potable water and very few toilets. Such formal toilets that existed (about 10 in number) cost 2–3 Kenyan shillings to use. The most frequently used toilet was referred to as the 'flying toilet': faeces were collected in plastic bags and dumped in large piles in open space. Not surprisingly the health outcomes for the community were shocking. People were dying every day of diseases that had long since been preventable and/or treatable. Typhoid, cholera, amoebic dysentery, malaria and HIV were rife. Residents could not afford the cost of immunisation, anti-malarial tablets, mosquito nets or antiretroviral drugs. They could barely afford food. The average life expectancy was estimated at 35 and infant mortality as high as 75%.[1] The community had a great number of women and children, widowed and orphaned by AIDS. Kibera, like many slums, was also home to many displaced people, who had often left violence and conflict in their country of origin. Mental health challenges abounded.

Access to education may provide employment opportunities and the income required to provide safe, appropriate housing, food, potable water and medicine, but there was no formal educational facility available in Kibera. The small, informal faith-based schools that did operate from within the community received no stable funding and lacked the most basic of resources such as paper, pens and pencils.

While there was water and electricity going to the edge of Kibera, both were expensive and distribution was open to corruption with the illegal on-selling of utilities at inflated prices. Kerosene was a major fuel and was sold in extremely dangerous conditions that no doubt led to many deaths and serious burns injuries. Treating a major burn in such an unhygienic environment was clearly unlikely to be successful. The risk of secondary infection was high.

Change was painfully slow. But from my perspective, the remarkable thing was that it was indeed occurring. Social workers in Kenya had developed a very strong link with UN-HABITAT, which is based in Nairobi and is responsible for human settlements, particularly slums. The human service and community development focus of the social work profession has matched the knowledge and expertise of UN-HABITAT in infrastructure to great effect. At the time of my visit, UN-HABITAT had commenced working with a residents' group. The initial goals were modest but vital. First they were scoping the community to find out who was living there, what their needs were and which skills they had to assist themselves as individuals and as a community. This moved the knowledge and understanding about the community from best estimates to well-grounded evidence upon which UN-HABITAT and others could apply for development funds.

The people who are doing this work live in Kibera. They are deeply committed. Many are very well qualified, including a few trained social workers, who could not obtain work elsewhere but used their skills to benefit their community. Their immediate access to and acceptance in their own community is out of the reach of outsiders.

Once the needs of the community had been mapped, the next stage was to locate donors and introduce programmes to provide safe drinking water, sanitation, utilities, basic health care and education. There was hope that increased levels of employment through business and job creation would follow. A true partnership with residents was the only way of achieving the outcomes everyone sought. The IFSW African region through the Kenyan Association of Social Workers was working in partnership with residents of Kibera and UN-HABITAT on the Kibera programme. This was community development at the most urgent and basic level.

Though the social workers working in Kibera did not have the luxury of identifying themselves as health and mental health specialists, health issues were clearly pervasive in everything they did. In a very real sense they were dealing with the impact of global and national policies that rendered access to basic health and health care almost non-existent.

In my closing remarks to the Pan Africa Conference I noted that:

> it is crucial that development is country-owned and country-driven. Programs should be done by and with people, not for or to them. The role of donor countries, civil society and business outside of Africa must be to support this process – not attempt to impose or drive.

Kibera was and is an excellent example of this in practice.

My most recent update on Kibera reveals the all too familiar story of progress halted by political unrest, the current global crisis, the sharp rise in the cost of food, the loss of small but vital enterprises within the community and unintended consequences of the project to secure potable water and sanitation. While the 'flying toilets' have been cleared, no viable replacement has been provided. Until the events of early 2008, Kenya was more stable than many other African countries surrounding it, and received a reasonable flow of aid. Political instability as a result of national elections has presented significant challenges to social workers working with the displaced, bereaved and marginalised. The work of our colleagues in Kenya will go on for many years to come.

Conclusions

In my six years as President I was continually challenged by the reality of social work around the globe. Shock, dismay and a sense of despair were familiar emotions but they were tempered by the strength of the profession when responding to these challenges. The resilience, innovation, knowledge, skill and cooperative approach evidenced by social workers remains as inspirational to me today as it did over those years. I was privileged to observe the practice of social work knowledge and skill operating in very diverse contexts. The social policy and political edge of social work was every bit as present as the direct practice and community development. In the same way that the stories of social workers around the world affected me, I hope that this brief account of some of their work may provide insights into the importance of health and mental health at every level of our work.

Whether addressing severe poverty in Africa or HIV/AIDS, depression and violence across the globe, it is clear to me that social workers must address health issues at all levels. I am under no illusion: the task is formidable and progress cannot be achieved outside of a tightly argued, coordinated and long-term approach within social work in cooperation with civil societies, governments and business.

As well, individual social workers have a role to play in drawing attention to policy gaps, inconsistencies and harmful practices. National social work bodies have a role in mobilising the profession to advocate for change at both domestic and international levels. The role of the IFSW as the voice of social work practice at international level is crucial. It is the body which can bring together the experience of social workers around the globe to inform policy debates and to develop and promote effective strategies to address the health-related issues that confront nations and communities. It is deeply committed to doing this; but the resources it commands are modest. Greater resources would strengthen its capacity to engage its membership, both national organisations and individual social workers, in policy development, partnership building and advocacy. Policy development is only the first step in a long but critical process to bring about effective change in services and practices at domestic levels.

In social work, however local the work, we have a responsibility to think globally and participate in the processes of international development and change. The global context to the inequalities in health which social workers confront on a daily basis requires an international perspective to underpin mutual education, policy development and intervention in global and local political arenas.

Note

[1] In the absence of an established census of the area, precise figures could not be obtained. These figures were anecdotal but likely to be an accurate representation.

References

Ewhrudjakpor, C. (2008) 'Poverty and its alleviation: The Nigerian experience', *International Social Work*, vol 51, no 4, pp 519–31.

IFSW (International Federation of Social Workers) (1996) *International Policy on Human Rights*, Berne: IFSW, www,ifsw.org/en/p38000212. html

IFSW (2008) *International Policy on Health*, Berne: IFSW, www.ifsw. org/en/p38000081.html

IFSW (2008b) *International Policy on Globalisation and the Environment*, www.ifsw.org/en/p38000222.html

Labonte, R. and Schrecker, T. (2007) 'Globalization and social determinants of health: The role of the global marketplace (part 2 of 3)', *Globalization and Health*, vol 3, article no 6, www. globalizationandhealth.com/content/3/1/6

Conclusion: emerging themes for practice and policy development

Paul Bywaters, Eileen McLeod and Lindsey Napier

Introduction

Previous chapters have exemplified the contribution that social work can make to understanding and tackling global health inequalities. They have also located that practice and its policy implications in a global context, including the processes of globalisation. In doing so they have begun to map out:

- How socially constructed global health inequalities are a central issue for social work.
- The key features of social work's contribution to tackling global health inequalities.
- Implications for the further development of social work's role in tackling global health inequalities.

In conclusion, we distil the main lessons concerning these issues.

Global health inequalities: a central issue for social work

Much of the analysis of health inequalities is based on epidemiological evidence about the relationship between measures of socio-economic position and health outcomes in terms of mortality and morbidity (Graham, 2007). While many of our authors take a whole population approach to their work, most strikingly social work contributes added depth to understanding the mechanisms by which social inequalities become inequalities in health at the level of individuals or communities. As preceding chapters have shown, social workers' direct encounters with people who have been on the receiving end of health-damaging cumulative 'insults' put them in a position to listen to and reflect on that experience. From these relationships five themes have emerged which provide compelling evidence of the centrality of socially constructed health inequalities as a global social work issue.

Specific populations facing adverse global social conditions

First, our authors highlight the profound impact of adverse social conditions, often rooted in globalisation, on the health of specific populations. Across all locations they highlight how, as a result of social disadvantage, certain groups lack the basic resources for good health, such as homeless women in the US (Moxley and Washington); or experience discrimination, for example, on grounds of their sexual orientation (Fish) or their ethnicity (Quinn and Knifton, and Ho); or disablist marginalisation, in the course of living with cancer (Lethborg and Posenelli) or other life-threatening illnesses (Quin and Clarke). Making links between individuals' stories and global forces is not always easy. However, the impact of structural economic forces, privatisation and commodification, climate change and environmental destruction, and political conflict and violence are apparent. For example, the damaging effects of economic and climate change on rural populations is present in a number of chapters, especially Chapter 4. Heinonen et al also expose some of the major socio-economic factors leading to rural–urban migration in China and the health implications for remaining in the countryside, while Law reports on the health consequences for economic migrants to an urban setting – a population integral to China's global economic expansion. Blyth's account of the adverse consequences for those exposed to market forces concerning new developments in reproductive technologies exemplifies the complexity of this globalised context of practice.

Diversity, identity and inequality

Second, while these accounts are based in different national settings, they repeatedly pinpoint how multiple issues of diversity and identity, characterised by social inequality, are played out in inequalities in health. Many authors, including Nadkarni and Vikram, Ramon, and Laing, focus on the role of gender in the production of, and resistance to, inequalities in health. Women are more prominently a focus of social work intervention and action in these accounts than men. But further dimensions of social disadvantage are also apparent, concerning ethnicity, sexual orientation, age and disability, together with evidence that such issues can form the basis for collective action.

This is seen clearly, for example, in Whiteside et al's account of work with Indigenous people in Australia.

Multiple dimensions of cumulative disadvantage

Third, although from different continents the accounts consistently reveal how multiple dimensions of cumulative social disadvantage accrue in people's lives to the detriment of their health. Many of our authors point to poverty as a crucial cause of health inequalities (for example, Rose and Baldwin) but poverty is often associated with other issues such as migration (Law), homelessness (Moxley and Washington) or rural disadvantage, lack of educational opportunity and employment patterns (Heinonen et al), in each case coupled with barriers to basic health care services. Similarly, Ramon illustrates how war and political conflict affects the experience of childhood, with lasting implications in multiple ways, often taking the form of gendered violence to girls and women, which is reflected in long-term illness and disability.

Physical and mental health inequalities interconnected

Fourth, our reports of practice across varied settings internationally show that practitioners need to take into account how physical and mental health inequalities are interconnected through their common roots in social determinants. Ramon, Baldwin and Laing, among others, show how acute or chronic social inequalities have negative physical and emotional consequences across the life course. Addressing people's material and physical needs against a background of disadvantage and supporting them to take action on their own behalf, means that social workers also have to address accumulated emotional barriers which have undermined their confidence and self-esteem (Rose, and Moxley and Washington). Tackling mental health inequalities requires addressing social factors that cause and maintain vulnerability and which inhibit recovery (Quinn and Knifton).

Barriers to accessing resources and services

Finally, our accounts reveal how institutionalised barriers to equality of access to essential resources and services can compound disadvantage, to the detriment of physical health and psychological well-being. This is a persistent trend, even in countries with relatively well-developed systems of health and social care. For example, Pockett shows how the dominant discourse concerning the victims and perpetrators of violence rendered young men (especially prisoners) invisible to providers of social work services in an accident and emergency department, while Quinn and Knifton's action research highlights the impact of stigma on both decisions to access formal mental health services and opportunities to build family and community capacity. Quin and Clarke found that a widespread lack of resources to support families with a terminally-ill child was even worse when families were living in rural areas or whose child had a diagnosis which did not trigger service provision. Too often social workers were then drawn into advocating for individual families in ways which may have exacerbated a rationing lottery.

Key features of social work interventions

The practice addressing these profound and pervasive issues, described by our contributors from across a range of countries and settings, demonstrates the multiple ways and diverse settings in which social workers can work towards more equal health chances and experience. As we acknowledged in Chapter 1, predominantly we are attempting to map emerging rather than established forms of practice that enable social workers to exert leverage on health inequalities. Nevertheless, certain features can be discerned which inform the practice described.

Upstream and downstream

The first is that it is practice that pays attention to both 'upstream' and 'downstream' issues. One of the criticisms levied at social work is that its primary focus is on the individual or family and their immediate situation: that it is a rescue service when prevention would be preferable. It is true that many of these accounts focus on the casualties of health inequalities. Social work intervention is concerned with ameliorating the suffering which health inequalities represent: for people who are living in poverty or without a home, who have been subject to violence or discrimination, who have no support networks or who are dealing with their own or a family member's serious illness. These are accounts of workers helping people to access better resources, to find their way through complex systems, adjust to new situations. But they are also often accounts of practitioners looking for patterns across populations and for the underlying factors which lie behind the immediate problems, and either addressing them directly or taking them into account in framing their intervention. This population-based approach is apparent in many examples. Pockett, and Lethborg and Posenelli searched out patterns of inequality in service delivery using techniques (data-mining and screening, respectively) which shed light on who was and was not receiving a service among the whole population of potential recipients. Ng and Pong's account of strengthening social capital in Hong Kong and Thomas's account of mass education on HIV/AIDS are both top-down interventions, but many other examples (including Law, Heinonen et al, Ho, Quinn and Knifton, Whiteside et al) are accounts of addressing an issue on a community- or population-wide basis, from the bottom up.

Rights, social justice and mutuality

Second, the work is commonly based on concepts of equal rights and social justice, for example, gender equality (Liang, and Nadkarni and Vikram) and equal protection of lesbian, gay and bisexual (LGB) people (Fish). These are not only recognised as being of universal validity, but, as these authors show, can only be realised on a national basis to the extent that they are established internationally (see also Blyth). In keeping with a perspective that is seeking to establish more egalitarian social relations, the accounts also stress the importance of practitioners fostering mutuality and solidarity with service users: working with people rather than 'doing to them'. This is apparent across examples drawn from a wide range of settings and countries including work with Indigenous Australians (Whiteside et al), rural and urban Chinese communities (Heinonen et al, and Ng and Pong), women's movement activists in India (Nadkarni and Vikram) and minority ethnic groups in Scotland (Quinn and Knifton). Where advocacy is a central plank of intervention, moving to self-advocacy is a core objective (Moxley and Washington).

Diverse methods, diverse skills

Third, practice accounts are characterised by the diversity of methods adopted, with groupwork and community work commonplace, while, of course, such approaches involve the building of multiple individual relationships as well. These case examples are also often characterised by outreach work by practitioners who have identified a critical issue and use research and/or education as a means of entry to the target population and to secure programme funding. As Ng and Pong, argue, this diverse range of approaches requires a wider range of skills than social workers often employ, including skills in raising awareness of key social problems and possible collective solutions. It means organising initiatives across generations or diverse social groups and promoting social entrepreneurship; as well as applying the skills in research, education, group and community engagement already discussed. As Ng and Pong further argue, our examples suggest that social workers may need to be 'located' differently, for example, making themselves known proactively in communities and to policy makers or being based in commercial workplaces, rather than being primarily reactive and office-based.

Multi-level, multi-sectoral interventions

Fourth, the examples highlight how, across different countries, social workers work with and through complex intersecting social spheres, managing cognitive, interpersonal, organisational and political dimensions to their practice. For example, to shift service provision for cancer patients, Lethborg and Posenelli had to negotiate their way through a range of actors with the capacity to prevent change including other social workers, medical staff and hospital managers. This required both a strategic approach to creating change and skills to manage the interpersonal impacts. Similarly, Quinn and Knifton's work required them to engage with diverse minority ethnic communities who feared the stigma of mental illness, and with policy makers, to extend the programme from the local to the national arena. This sophisticated approach often requires working across sectors, for example, public and commercial (see Law's work), or professions. It also involves working to promote complex models of practice for health in which physical and emotional dimensions are seen as integrated rather than separate, in which the social and the biological are seen as closely connected and in which both individuals and populations are a focus of attention. These are assumptions which move beyond current conventional professional practice in health care and health or social care policy making.

Further development of social work addressing global health inequalities

We have presented the case for global health inequalities, and social work's contribution to tackling them, being put on the social work map. Nevertheless, we are aware that despite the evidence in this book of practice on these issues being carried out around the world, it is at a very early stage of development. Evidence of social work's impact on health outcomes at other than a small-scale, individual or local level is sparse. Social work's contribution to tackling health inequalities is only beginning to gain recognition among other disciplines and professions engaged with these issues (see Dowler and Spencer, 2007). However, our accounts also contain, in a prefigurative form, social work educational, research and policy initiatives essential to the further development of social work, and to its recognition as being integral to tackling health inequalities globally among policy makers, other professions and members of social movements.

Educational development

Developing the capacity for social workers to address global health inequalities requires taking account, through education, of globalisation as a key context for practice. The international perspective we have adopted has enabled us to feature social work educational initiatives which hold lessons for social work education more generally, including established curricula. For example, Law's imaginative use of student placements in China, where social work education is at a relatively early stage of development, demonstrates the benefits of community work strategies, which have virtually disappeared from the mainstream social work curriculum in some countries, for example, the UK. Volumes such as ours begin to map out how not only current but future practitioners need to become better informed about:

- Transnational issues, such as the impact on health of reproductive rights.
- Convergent global issues, such as the near universal marginalisation of lesbian, gay and bisexual people's rights, to the detriment of their health, and the struggle for the history and current circumstances of indigenous peoples and health-related questions to be properly represented in social work training.
- Divergent global issues, such as the need to move beyond the Eurocentric/anglophone perspective which tends to dominate social work texts, if due recognition is going to be given to the nature and extent of health-damaging social conditions. It is clear, for example, from Carbonatto's account of South African social work education, that practitioners need to learn about the relationships between the local context of practice and globalised structures and influences.

Research: evidence into practice

The social work reported here from across different national settings frequently incorporates research projects as the medium for intervention with communities. This reflects the recognition that research findings may bring leverage with policy makers (for example, Ho, Quinn and Knifton, and Whiteside et al). Research linked to education-related programmes is another key mechanism employed to influence groups, communities or wider populations including social workers (see Chapter 14). Building practice based on mutuality, as previously highlighted, can also underpin social work approaches to developing research evidence about social work action on health inequalities. Accounts in earlier chapters, where research is a key medium of intervention, have often emphasised partnership and mutual involvement in terms of setting research aims, negotiating access, implementation, analysis and reporting. This is seen, for example, in Quinn and Knifton's work. The articulation of common agendas and language for understanding health inequalities exhibited in this book, provides the basis for future international research development within social work. However, clearly, social workers addressing health inequalities through research also need to build interdisciplinary collaborations, as Whiteside et al have successfully done, not only to learn from others, but to extend the repertoire of research skills available, and to maximise the impact of findings.

Policy formation and dissemination

To influence policy making on health inequalities globally, and in a globalised world, social work not only needs to develop an informed global imagination through practice, education and research, it needs to develop active representative structures to promote and implement it. At present for a profession of over half a million people worldwide, the impact of social work on international policy development is extremely weak. Dodds makes it clear that, despite good intentions and some significant interventions, such as the developing partnership between the International Federation of Social Workers (IFSW) and UN-HABITAT (United Nations Human Settlements Programme) (see www.ifsw.org/home), social work's capacity to act internationally is overdue for development. Social work's identity as an integral element in combating health inequalities has yet to gain recognition through the policies and practices of major international bodies seeking to address unequal health chances and experience. This is reflected in its complete absence from major international publications on these issues such as the final report of the Commission on the Social Determinants of Health (CSDH, 2008) or Global Health Watch 2 (Hansson et al, 2008). There are several accounts in earlier chapters of practice which has successfully made the transition from grassroots knowledge and action to policy making influencing local, regional or national populations. This is well exemplified by Lethborg and Posenelli, and Whitehouse et al.

Translating this capacity into an international context requires the use of three key vehicles for policy formulation. First, there is the strategic engagement with existing international social work organisations to raise the profile of global health inequalities as a target for social work. Some initial steps have been taken on this. For example, the IFSW commissioned the Social Work and Health Inequalities Network (SWHIN) (see www.warwick.ac.uk/go/swhin) to lead work on a new international policy on health (IFSW, 2008), a policy which now foregrounds global health inequalities for the first time. Such a document facilitates wider attention being given to the issue, for example, leading to presentations at national association conferences in Brazil, Israel, the UK and Australia.

Second, there is the creation of new free-standing organisations, specifically caucusing to target health inequalities as a key issue for international social work engagement. SWHIN was formed in 2004 and has over 150 members worldwide. Through its email list, website and video-conferencing, as well as conference presentations and seminars, SWHIN disseminates news on policy and practice developments and research findings and encourages exchanges of work in progress of international relevance, such as Law's pioneering work on the health issues of internal migrants in China.

Third, social work as a discipline and profession cannot go forward on global health issues in isolation. It needs to form alliances with other groups with common agendas. As illustrated by our contributors, often the transition from practice to policy making, and from the local to the larger scale, is underpinned by the development of key alliances with groups or structures with the capacity to roll out pilot initiatives, best seen in Heinonen's partnership with the All China Women's Federation. Internationally, as Davis argues, there is substantial potential for social workers to build strategic relationships with service user and popular social movements, such as the Peoples' Health Movement or Jan Swathya Abbiyan (see Chapter 2) where a common policy agenda can be established.

Our authors have demonstrated that in diverse settings around the world, social workers are recognising and responding to the challenge of daily encounters with people's experience of health inequalities. In doing so they are struggling with multidimensional intersecting inequalities of power, as they champion people who are dying, who need care and rehabilitation, who are campaigning for their rights to health and who are trying to promote the health of those close to them against inhuman social conditions. Social work practice as reported here, including education, research and policy making, requires the continuing collective application of creativity, analysis and skill not only to make but to develop its contribution to tackling health inequalities as a global problem.

References

CSDH (Commission on the Social Determinants of Health) (2008) *Closing the Gap in a Generation: Health Equity through Action on the Social Determinants of Health*, Final Report of the Commission on Social Determinants of Health, Geneva: World Health Organization.

Dowler, E. and Spencer, N. (eds) (2007) *Challenging Health Inequalities*, Bristol: The Policy Press.

Graham, H. (2007) *Unequal Lives*, Maidenhead: Open University Press.

Hansson, E., Lloyd, B., McCoy, D., Ntuli, A., Padareth, A. and Sanders, D. (eds) (2008) *Global Health Watch 2. An Alternative World Health Report*, London/New York: Zed Books.

IFSW (International Federation of Social Workers) (2008) *International Policy on Health*, Berne: IFSW, www.ifsw.org/en/p38000081.html

Index

Note: Government departments, national bodies and legislation are listed by country

A

Abidi, J. 269
abortion
  safe 30
  sex-selective 28, 30
  United States 30
Abramovitz, M. 211
Abrams, F. 79, 80
Acheson, D. 7
Adamson, G. et al 77
advocacy
  families caring for children with life-limiting conditions 211–16
  human rights approach for social workers 32-3, 101
  Leaving Homelessness Intervention Research Project (LHIRP) 153–4
  New York migrant workers 65
  social support 142, 156
Africa
  infant mortality and life expectancy 8–9, 279
  Kibera slums, Nairobi 279–81
  poverty 278–81
  see *also* South Africa
African American women
  heart disease and diabetes 122
  homelessness 150–6
African cultures
  health and illness 255–6
African Medical and Research Foundation 121
Alma Ata Declaration (International Conference on Primary Health Care) 15, 23–4
Alston, M. and Kent, J. 54, 55, 56, 58
Altman, J. and Hinkson, M. 122, 123
Andersen, A. et al 77
Anderson, G.F. et al 27
Anderson, I. and Whyte, J.D. 245
Anderson, I. et al 245
Anderson, J. 44
Anson, O. and Sun, S. 173
Aspinall, P.J. and Mitton, L. 146
Astbury, J. and Cabral, M. 107, 111
asylum seekers
  sexual orientation 148
  social work with 66–7
Aubert, R. et al 44
Australia
  AASW (Australian Association of Social Workers) 247
  Aboriginal and Torres Strait Islander Social Justice Commissioner 7
  ABS (Australian Bureau of Statistics) 64, 121, 220, 245
  AIHW (Australian Institute of Health and Welfare) 64, 123, 244
  climate change 53–6, 57–8
  Australian Farm Institute 51
  Family Wellbeing empowerment programme (FWB) case study 166–71
  HREOC (Human Rights and Equal Opportunity Commission) 123
  National Inquiry into the Separation of Aboriginal and Torres Strait Islander Children from their Families 245
  NBCC (National Breast Cancer Centre) 198, 202
  NCCH (National Centre for Classification in Health) 219
  NCCI (National Cancer Control Initiative) 198, 202
  NHMRC (National Health and Medical Research Council) 166–7
  social work education 246–9
Australian Aborigines
  disadvantages and inequalities 244–6
  Family Wellbeing empowerment programme (FWB) case study 166–71
  impact of physical, psychological and social oppression 64
  inequalities of occurrence of heart disease and diabetes 122–3
  relationship with social workers 64, 166–7, 244, 247

B

Badawi, M. and Biamonti, M. 211, 215
Baldwin, N. 285
Bandura, A. 40
Banister, J. 28
Barbados Fertility Centre 78–9
Barker, A. 57
Barnes, C. and Mercer, G. 267
Barnes, C. et al 124
Barnett, A. and Smith, H. 79, 80
Barry, S. 266
Bartley, M. 99
Barton, M. et al 198
Bate, S. 239
Bauert, P. et al 244
Bennett, B. and Zubrzycki, J. 247
Beresford, P. 123
Beresford, P. and Holden, C. 266
Bergart, A. 81
Bernard van Leer Foundation 29, 30
Bhutta, Z. et al 94
black communities
  mental health inequalities in Scotland 193–7
Black, R. et al 92
Blackwell, D. et al 38